MORE PRAISE FOR

Why Cities Lose

"This astute and illuminating book will change how you think about electoral fairness and political representation in America. *Why Cities Lose* meticulously demonstrates how winner-take-all congressional districts systematically underrepresent urban voters in legislatures and destructively polarize politics along urban-rural lines—not just in the United States, but also in Canada and the United Kingdom. The result is distorted representation in all winner-take-all democracies, even those with independent redistricting processes. At a time when politics in America feels so unfair, this book clarifies how much our skewed electoral system is to blame. For anyone who wants to fix America's broken politics, this is absolutely essential reading."

—**Lee Drutman,** author of *The Business of America is Lobbying*

WHY
CITIES
LOSE

WHY CITIES LOSE

THE DEEP ROOTS OF THE
URBAN-RURAL POLITICAL DIVIDE

JONATHAN RODDEN

BASIC BOOKS

New York

Basic Books
Hachette Book Group
1290 Avenue of the Americas, New York, NY 10104
www.basicbooks.com

Printed in the United States of America

First Edition: June 2019

Published by Basic Books, an imprint of Perseus Books, LLC, a subsidiary of Hachette Book Group, Inc. The Basic Books name and logo is a trademark of the Hachette Book Group.

The Hachette Speakers Bureau provides a wide range of authors for speaking events. To find out more, go to www.hachettespeakersbureau.com or call (866) 376-6591.

The publisher is not responsible for websites (or their content) that are not owned by the publisher.

Print book interior design by Amy Quinn.

Library of Congress Cataloging-in-Publication Data

Names: Rodden, Jonathan, author.
Title: Why cities lose: the deep roots of the urban-rural political divide / Jonathan Rodden.
Description: First edition. | New York: Basic Books, 2019. | Includes bibliographical references and index.
Identifiers: LCCN 2018057050| ISBN 9781541644274 (hardcover: alk. paper) | ISBN 9781541644250 (ebook)
Subjects: LCSH: Electoral geography—United States. | Cities and towns—Political aspects—United States. | Democratic Party (U.S.) | Voting research—United States. | Right and left (Political science)—United States. | Representative government and representation—United States.
Classification: LCC JK1976 .R65 2019 | DDC 324.0973—dc23
LC record available at https://lccn.loc.gov/2018057050

ISBNs: 978-1-5416-4427-4 (hardcover), 978-1-5416-4425-0 (ebook)

LSC-C

10 9 8 7 6 5 4 3 2 1

To my parents

Contents

Introduction

I N MOST DEMOCRACIES, the path to victory is simple: win more votes than your competitors. For the Democratic Party in the United States, however, this is often not good enough. For example, in the 2012 election, Democratic candidates for the House of Representatives received 1.4 million more votes nationwide than Republican candidates, but the Democrats ended up with only 45 percent of the seats in the House. In 1996, the Democrats also won the popular vote—that is, the total votes cast across all of the individual races—without winning control of Congress. Democrats must win big in the overall popular vote, as they did in the "blue wave" elections of 2018 and 2006, in order to win a majority of seats in the House.

The Democrats' problem with votes and seats is even more pronounced in state legislatures. Consider the state of Michigan, where it has become commonplace for the Democrats to win the statewide popular vote without winning a majority of seats in either chamber of the Michigan legislature. In 2012, for instance, the Democrats received around 54 percent of the total votes cast in elections for both state legislative chambers in Michigan, but they came away with only 46 percent of the seats in the Michigan House of Representatives, and 42 percent of the seats in the state senate. This has been happening over the last decade in the other states of the industrialized Midwest as well, including Minnesota, Missouri, Ohio, Wisconsin, and Pennsylvania. Most recently, it happened in Virginia in 2017, and once again in Michigan, Ohio, Wisconsin, and Pennsylvania in 2018.[1] Remarkably, as of 2019, the Republican Party has controlled the Pennsylvania Senate for almost forty consecutive years, even while losing the statewide popular vote around half of the time. The Republicans have controlled the Ohio Senate for thirty-five years, during which time Democrats won half of the state's US Senate elections and around one-third of the gubernatorial elections.

The popular vote is also largely irrelevant, of course, in determining the composition of the US Senate. Democrats have won more votes than Republicans in elections for eleven of the fifteen Senates since 1990, but they have only held a majority of seats on six occasions.[2] Yet underrepresentation of Democrats in the US Senate is no mystery. It happens because, as a legacy of the bargain made at the Constitutional Convention in the eighteenth century, large Democratic states like California and New York have the same Senate representation as small Republican states such as Wyoming and the Dakotas.

But in Congress and state legislatures, districts are drawn to be as equal as possible in population. For example, Democratic California and Republican Wyoming both get two senators, but California sends fifty-three representatives to Congress while Wyoming sends only one. And within states, legislative districts are required by law to be very similar in population. It is puzzling, then, that Democrats have been able to dominate the national popular vote in presidential and Senate elections since 1990—not to mention party registration and party affiliation as expressed in opinion surveys—while only winning control of Congress for five of the last fifteen sessions. And it is puzzling that there are so many "purple" and even "blue" states like Pennsylvania where citizens routinely elect Democratic senators, governors, and attorneys general, but where Democrats have had little chance of winning a majority of the congressional delegation or state legislature.

For many frustrated Democrats, the explanation is simple: partisan gerrymandering. Republicans gained control of many state legislatures in time for the most recent round of redistricting in the early 2010s, then drew odd-shaped boundaries that packed as many Democrats as possible into a handful of districts that they easily won, leaving the remaining districts with Republican majorities. Armed with sophisticated geospatial software and a large budget, Republican operatives carefully drew maps that distributed

Republicans as efficiently as possible across districts so as to win the maximum number of seats.[3]

There is much truth to this widely accepted account, but it provides an oversimplified and ultimately misleading answer to a complex question. *Why Cities Lose* demonstrates that the Democrats' problem with votes and seats goes much deeper, and is far more intricate, than the impact of a handful of political operatives in a room with a computer. Without a doubt, gerrymandering makes things *worse* for the Democrats, but their underlying problem can be summed up with the old real estate maxim: location, location, location.

In most of Europe, legislators are chosen from large districts with multiple winners, and parties are represented in proportion to their share of the vote. In such a system, the geographic location of a party's support is not of primary importance. In the United States, legislators are elected from smaller districts where there is a single winner. In such a system—known as "majoritarian" democracy—the geography of a party's support is extremely important. In many US states, Democrats are now concentrated in cities in such a way that even when districts are drawn without regard for partisanship, their seat share will fall well short of their vote share. It matters a great deal how the districts are drawn, and by whom, but because of where Democrats live, the very existence of winner-take-all geographic districts has facilitated the systemic underrepresentation of Democrats.

To understand the roots of this phenomenon, it is important to grasp the deeper problem that gave rise to it: our highly polarized partisan geography. To see why the contemporary Democratic Party so often loses with a system of winner-take-all districts, we must first comprehend how Democrats and cities came to be synonymous. *Why Cities Lose* explains the rise of contemporary urban-rural polarization—a trend that is worrisome for the stability and health of American democracy regardless of one's partisan or ideological perspective—and then reveals how this development has affected political representation.

The rise of urban-rural polarization over the last century is striking. Figure 1 is a plot based on county-level data from one hundred years of US presidential elections, excluding the states of the Deep South. The horizontal

axis represents the population density of each county: higher numbers indicate that a county is more urban. The vertical axis represents the share of the
presidential vote received by the Democratic candidate. The relatively flat
dotted line indicates that in 1916, Woodrow Wilson's support was no higher
in urban counties than in rural counties. After the New Deal and World
War II, the dashed line indicates that John F. Kennedy's vote share in 1960
was strongly correlated with population density. He lost in most rural counties and won solid majorities in most urban counties. And the solid line indicates that by 2016, the urban concentration of Hillary Rodham Clinton's
support was astounding. She lost by large margins in rural counties and won
overwhelming majorities in urban counties.

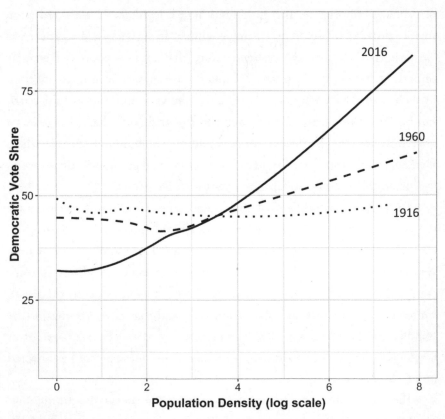

Figure 1: County-Level Population Density and Democratic Presidential Voting over the
Last Century

By the early part of the twenty-first century, the Democrats had become an almost exclusively urban political party. From coast to coast, their support is now concentrated in the downtown cores and inner suburbs of cities. Democrats have come to dominate not only large cities like Philadelphia and Pittsburgh, but also medium-sized cities like Reading, Pennsylvania. They have come to dominate not only knowledge-economy hubs like Seattle and San Francisco that are gaining population, but also poor postindustrial cities like Detroit and Akron that are losing population.

Because of this geographic divide, American elections have come to be seen as high-stakes sectional battles pitting the interests and identities of cities and inner suburbs against those of exurbs and the rural periphery. This urban-rural polarization is a serious problem in its own right, but in many US states, it has also created a geographic distribution of partisans that allows Republicans to win seat shares well in excess of their share of the vote. In turn, this asymmetry between votes and seats only further fans the flames of urban-rural sectionalism.

Among wealthy democracies, overt partisan gerrymandering is a uniquely American phenomenon, but urban-rural political conflict is not. While most industrialized democracies abandoned the practice in the early twentieth century, the United States is one of several former British colonies—including Canada and Australia—along with Great Britain itself, that still rely on a centuries-old English approach to representative democracy: forming a national legislature by selecting representatives from a series of geographic winner-take-all districts. Stark urban-rural polarization, along with an underrepresentation of urban parties, has emerged in those countries as well. In Britain and Australia, the support base of labor parties has been overwhelmingly urban since their formation in the industrial era. The same has been true of the New Democratic Party (NDP) in Canada for several decades. As in the United States, Canadian and British elections have become hostile, polarized battles pitting voters in cosmopolitan and postindustrial city centers against exurban and rural traditionalists.

The implications for partisan representation are strikingly similar. If we add up the popular vote for every British parliamentary election held between 1950 and 2017, the Conservative Party has received around 41 percent of the votes cast, and Labour is only slightly behind with 40 percent. Yet the Conservatives have been in power for 63 percent of that period. In recent elections, the Conservatives repeatedly have been able to form governments with only around 37 percent of the vote in part because of the highly effective geographic distribution of their support. The Australian Labor Party (ALP) and its competitors on the right have split the popular vote almost exactly down the middle since 1950, yet during that period, the right has been in power for 68 percent of the time. In Canada, in 2018, populist Doug Ford was elected premier of Ontario, with his Conservative Party receiving 60 percent of the seats in the provincial parliament, based on only 40 percent of the votes. If we look at national and provincial or state elections since World War II in Britain, New Zealand, Australia, and Canada, we find that the party winning the most seats—and forming a government—lost the popular vote on thirty-six occasions. The beneficiary was the party of the right on twenty-eight of those occasions.

The striking underrepresentation of these urban parties abroad can be explained by a problem of political geography that is very similar to the one plaguing the Democrats in the United States. Left party candidates run up excessive margins of victory in their core urban bastions, but they find it difficult to craft a platform that will allow them to win in the crucial suburban constituencies. As with the Democrats in the United States—who seem perpetually at war with themselves over the soul of the party—this creates enormous tension within the parties of the left in Commonwealth countries. Above all, the urban ideologues do battle with the suburban pragmatists. And in recent years, in both the United States and the Commonwealth countries, there is an emerging fault line between successful global cities and declining postindustrial ones. However, these left-leaning parties of the Commonwealth face an additional problem that Democrats in the American two-party system do not: this tension often fuels temporary and even long-term splits between multiple parties of the left.

In short, political geography has not only disadvantaged mainstream parties of the left, including the Democrats, but it has also made them into unhappy families. One side of the family pushes the cosmopolitan agenda of the global cities and their suburbs, and the other side pushes the "old left" agenda of the struggling manufacturing towns. Moreover, urban stalwarts from safe seats butt heads with suburban pragmatists. If urban progressives are able to wrestle control of the party, they are likely to end up with a platform that allows them to win impressive victories in cities while falling short in the pivotal districts required to form legislative majorities. And if the suburban moderates gain control, the urban ideologues might revolt and form their own party.

The experience of Britain and its former colonies, where electoral districts are drawn by independent commissions, belies the notion that the Democrats' representation problem is merely a matter of gerrymandering. In fact, throughout the postwar period, underrepresentation of the urban left in national legislatures and governments has been a basic feature of all industrialized countries that use winner-take-all districts. And these countries have produced significantly more conservative policies in the long run than the countries that long ago adopted more proportional forms of representation.

Why, then, has the underrepresentation of the Democrats in Congress only become apparent in the United States in the last three decades? This book will show that when we look at *presidential* elections, Democrats have been more geographically concentrated than Republicans since the New Deal. Initially, this pattern was also visible in congressional elections, but it vanished from the 1960s to the 1980s because of the highly localized nature of American electoral competition. For several decades, self-styled Democratic candidates were able to distance themselves from their party's presidential candidates and win in Republican-leaning districts.

The seeds of the Democrats' current problem were sown in the late nineteenth and early twentieth centuries, in the era of iron, steel, and steam power. As modern cities were taking shape, masses of peasants, immigrants, and freed slaves migrated from the countryside and from abroad to take industrial jobs, and labor unions began to mobilize urban workers, at first for socialist parties, and eventually for the Democrats. In the most industrialized states, a correlation between population density and Democratic voting first emerged during the New Deal era. By the 1940s, Democratic presidential votes in the North were concentrated in cities. And to a surprising extent, votes for Democrats today are still concentrated in the triple-deckers, apartment buildings, and workers' cottages built in close proximity to the factories, smelters, warehouses, ports, rail hubs, and canals of the late nineteenth century. In much of the United States, a map of the nineteenth-century railroad network is a map of Democratic voting today.

But the transformation of the Democrats into a truly urban party was delayed by their long-lasting coalition with rural Southern segregationists, which began to fray during the civil rights era and was only fully severed in the 1990s. And even outside the South, for a period lasting from the 1960s to the 1990s, Democratic candidates for Congress and state legislatures were able to successfully eschew the party's national reputation as an advocate for urban labor and socially progressive ideas. They won not only in cities, but in quite a few exurban and rural districts that consistently voted for Republicans in presidential elections. Democratic candidates—often given colorful monikers including "boll weevils" and "blue dogs"—crafted their own idiosyncratic local brands and fought to bring earmarked expenditure projects to their constituents.

Those days are over. Largely in response to their northern urban base, the Democrats have taken progressive positions as a party first on race in the 1960s, and then on social issues like abortion, gender, and sexuality in the 1980s, and more recently, immigration. Candidates who did not embrace those views were pushed aside, and voters who did not embrace them found their way to the Republican Party. Voters' preferences on these issues are highly correlated with population density. As voters sorted into the parties on these issues, the correlation between population density and Democratic voting grew, and idiosyncratic nonurban Democratic legislators dwindled to the point of near-extinction.

In addition to social issues, the story of growing urban-rural polarization in the United States depends crucially on two striking trends in economic geography. First, manufacturing activity departed long ago from the rail and water-borne transit nodes in city centers and moved to exurban and rural places along interstates, especially in the South. Democrats have maintained their strength in the places where manufacturing is a distant memory. But as part of this transition, Republican candidates have been replacing Democrats as the advocates of the embattled traditional manufacturing sector.

Second, economic dynamism and jobs have become increasingly concentrated in a relatively small number of cities. Educated workers have clustered in global cities like San Francisco, Seattle, and Boston, where incomes—and the cost of living—have soared, while much of the rest of the country has been left behind. Democratic state and local officials had been ensconced in these cities since the old manufacturing days, and it was local Democrats who, in close collaboration with universities and entrepreneurs, became advocates for the nascent globalized knowledge-economy sector.

Largely because of their preexisting urban base, the Democrats have become the party not only of poor postindustrial service workers and racial minorities, but also of social progressives, and now, incongruously, they are the party of science, technology, and the globalized knowledge economy. Responding to their exurban and rural base, the Republicans have become a party that emphasizes not only low taxes and less economic regulation but also gun rights and traditional social values along with the interests of traditional manufacturing, natural resource extraction, and agriculture. Remarkably, in the era of Donald Trump, in response to a segment of their exurban and rural manufacturing base, the Republican Party has embraced trade protection.

These odd bundles of policies came together because of economic and political geography. The Democrats, quite simply, have evolved into a diverse collection of urban interest groups, and the Republicans into an assemblage of exurban and rural interests. Soon it might be useful to dispense altogether with the terms "left" and "right," which have lost much of the meaning they had in the early twentieth-century context of class conflict. In the United States, the party of the left is now strongly allied with well-compensated urban professionals and venture capitalists who benefit from global free trade, and the party of the right rails against trade and global capitalism. It might be more accurate to refer to the main dimension of political conflict in the United States as "urban" versus "rural."

This transformation in the structure of democratic politics is not unique to the United States. Many other advanced industrial countries also experienced turbulent social changes related to gender and sexuality in the 1960s and 1970s, and in response, parties staked out opposing positions on a variety of noneconomic issues. The concentration of social progressives in city centers is ubiquitous, and in many countries, parties of urban labor eventually adopted socially progressive positions.

Likewise, many other countries are also seeing knowledge-economy jobs cluster in affluent global cities. In countries like Britain and Australia, urban labor parties have similarly become the parties of educated, high-income, cosmopolitan knowledge-economy workers. Like the Democrats, these parties have become diverse and deeply conflicted coalitions between cosmopolitan urban elites and the denizens of the old working-class neighborhoods. And as in the United States, the backlash against the negative side effects of globalization, including wage stagnation and the loss of manufacturing, has been exploited primarily by the exurban and rural parties of the right. Something similar has happened in countries ranging from Austria and Hungary to Italy and France.

But while urban-rural polarization is on the rise around the industrialized world, it may be especially consequential in the United States. A key argument of this book is that *cities lose* only when this type of geographic polarization is combined with an old-fashioned system of winner-take-all electoral districts like the one in the United States and in the British Commonwealth. Moreover, this geographic conflict is sharpened in the United States by a uniquely rigid two-party system. In countries with proportional electoral systems and multiple political parties, the introduction of issues like abortion and immigration, and the nationalist anti-elite backlash to globalization, do not encourage political elites to organize so clearly into only two mutually hostile, geographically defined camps. And in those countries, political geography does not undermine the representation of urban voters. In the United States, elections have unfortunately come to be viewed as winner-take-all battles between different sectors of the economy and dissimilar ways of life.

WHY CITIES LOSE proceeds in three steps. First, it explains the origins of urban-rural polarization in the United States and beyond, drawing on insights from urban economics and political science and data from a wide variety of sources. It brings the story to life through the example of the state of Pennsylvania, and in particular, the city of Reading—a classic case of industrial rise and decline giving birth to the geographic concentration of Democrats. The first section of the book establishes a strikingly similar pattern of political geography not only in and around American cities, but also around Canadian, British, and Australian cities. It also explores subtle differences in this pattern of political geography, distinguishing between postindustrial cities, knowledge-economy cities, and sprawling new auto-oriented cities.

Second, the book explains how these patterns of political geography have come to undermine representation of the Democrats, as well as of labor parties in Commonwealth countries. Once again, to get a clear sense of the argument, it is useful to dwell in some detail on the state of Pennsylvania, where a high-stakes battle about political geography, gerrymandering, and representation recently took place in state court. The Pennsylvania case study sets the stage for the analysis of other states and ultimately other countries. An important conclusion is that while gerrymandering has allowed Republicans to build upon their geographic advantage, in some states, artful gerrymandering might also be the only way for Democrats to overcome that advantage. While many Democrats like the idea of a party-blind redistricting process that produces geometrically compact districts, such a process would actually be quite beneficial to the Republicans in a number of competitive states. Another lesson is that since progressives are concentrated in cities, the Democrats' geography problem goes well beyond the mechanics of votes and seats. In many states, the pivotal *voter* in a statewide election is more progressive than the pivotal *district* in the congressional delegation or the state legislature. As a result, if the Democrats set their sights on winning statewide races and presidential elections, they are tempted to adopt platforms that will mobilize urban turnout that helps them win the popular vote, even though these same platforms weigh heavily on their candidates in crucial suburban districts. In today's era of highly polarized and nationalized politics, it is difficult for the Democrats to craft the type of moderate policy reputation that allows them to win Congress and state legislatures absent an idiosyncratic electoral wave in their favor. Labor parties in Commonwealth countries have faced a similar problem for almost a century.

Finally, *Why Cities Lose* explores prospects for the future. The problem of urban-rural polarization is especially troublesome for Democrats because of its implications for representation in Congress and state legislatures, but it has high costs for everyone. When Republicans win control of the presidency and Congress, the interests of American cities—other than perhaps anticommunist Cubans in Miami's Little Havana—are not represented. And when Democrats win control, most of rural America—outside of Native American reservations—feels frozen out. Ideally, a democratically elected national government would have incentives to consider policies that are in the national interest, rather than to fight for one geographically defined bundle of interest groups at the expense of another.

There are several avenues for the potential reduction of urban-rural polarization. The United States could follow the lead of European countries and, more recently, New Zealand, and replace the system of geographic winner-take-all districts with a more proportional electoral system. Perhaps the most attractive feature of the multiparty systems associated with proportional representation is that they combat the tendency to force all political competition into one overarching urban-rural conflict. Alternatively, even without serious reforms, a combination of demographic trends and political incentives might ultimately lead to a self-correction that lowers the temperature of urban-rural polarization. It is tempting for some Democratic candidates to double down on their progressive urban core voters in pursuit of the presidency and statewide offices. Nevertheless, to win and retain power in Congress and state legislatures, there is countervailing pressure for Democrats to return to their historical pattern of heterodox, locally tailored platforms outside of city centers.

The Republicans may also be forced to change their strategy. Educated suburban areas have moved sharply toward the Democrats in recent years. Moreover, as urban African Americans move to the suburbs and educated young people migrate in search of opportunities, the newest and fastest-growing suburban and even exurban areas—many of them in the Sun Belt—are becoming more politically competitive and trending Democratic.

In the medium term, if neither reform nor demographic change is sufficient to diminish urban-rural polarization, the United States must find ways to function as a divided society. Neither party will find it easy to shake off the influence, or reputation, of its geographic base. During periods of Republican control, many voters in cities and knowledge-economy suburbs will continue to view the federal government as a hostile power aiming to undermine their interests; voters in many exurbs and rural areas will feel the same under Democratic administrations. Perhaps it is fortunate, then, that the United States has a tradition of federalism that empowers state and local governments to cater to local majorities. Urban Democrats have discovered a new fondness for states' rights and municipal autonomy during the recent period of unified Republican federal control. And Republicans will surely rediscover their traditional affection for federalism and local control when the Democrats return to power. If dysfunction and geographic sectionalism continue to prevail at the federal level, voters and interest groups on both sides will look increasingly to state and local governments for action.

CHAPTER 1

Geography and the Dilemma of the Left

THE STORY OF why cities lose in democracies with winner-take-all districts does not begin with the advent of sophisticated gerrymandering or the outbreak of contemporary culture wars. Rather, it begins with the birth of leftist mobilization in urban working-class neighborhoods during the era of rapid industrialization, known as the "second industrial revolution," which took place from around 1870 to the outbreak of World War I.

A good place to begin the American version of the story is at 8 p.m. on July 23, 1877, near the intersection of Seventh and Penn Streets in downtown Reading, Pennsylvania. According to historical accounts, many downtown residents were out enjoying the cool evening air, and a group of curious onlookers, including women and children, were examining a rail car that had been taken over earlier in the day by striking railroad workers.[1] A group of 350 state militiamen, marching on the tracks from the rail depot to the tap of a few drums, opened fire on the crowd without warning, killing several men including police officers. A mob broke into the Reading Armory and a local gun store. A bloody battle ensued, and ten Reading citizens, none of whom were rioters or strikers, were left dead. Reading descended into chaos. Railroad tracks and an important bridge were destroyed, and an uneasy calm was not restored until the arrival of federal troops.

The Reading Railroad strike was just one part of a national strike called by the Brotherhood of Railway Engineers and Firemen in response to massive pay cuts amidst a deep recession. Similar violent incidents were occurring around the United States throughout the summer of 1877. The strikes had started in Baltimore and spread to New York, but the strikes in Pennsylvania were among the largest and most violent, and from there, they quickly spread to many of the industrial towns of Ohio, Indiana, Illinois, and Missouri as well. Unrest occurred not only in Pennsylvania's large cities like Pittsburgh and Philadelphia, but also in smaller industrial outposts like Johnstown, Bethlehem, Harrisburg, and Hazelton. Unrest emerged in Toledo and Zanesville, Ohio; Terre Haute and Fort Wayne, Indiana; Effingham and Mattoon, Illinois; and Sedalia and St. Joseph, Missouri.

A thirteen-year–old boy named James Maurer was present among the crowd in downtown Reading that day, and later described "the hysterical sobs and shrieks of mothers and fathers, and the groans of the wounded and dying."[2] For Maurer, this "tragic act in the real drama of class struggle"[3] was a call to action. In the ensuing years, he joined up with a group of young radicals associated with the Knights of Labor and the Socialist Labor Party, and eventually, the Socialist Party of America. Maurer went on to serve as a Socialist representative in the Pennsylvania State Legislature from 1910 to 1918 and became the leader of the Reading Socialists—a group that dominated Reading politics for decades. The Reading Socialists worked with labor unions, published a newspaper, and owned a large building and even a park where they hosted picnics for workers. They elected several popular mayors and controlled the city council for much of the 1920s and 1930s, and routinely sent legislators to the capital of Harrisburg to fight for policies like workers' compensation and pensions. Twice, Maurer was the Socialist candidate for vice president of the United States.

Something very similar was happening in other countries that were experiencing rapid industrialization during the same time frame. As peasants were moving to cities to take jobs as wage laborers in Britain, Europe, and then Australasia and North America in the late nineteenth century, they were mobilized through cooperative efforts of labor unions and, soon thereafter, workers' parties. Strikes, labor unrest, and heavy-handed responses by firms, armed gangs, and governments led labor leaders to form political parties and begin running for office in the late nineteenth century. The Belgian Labor Party was founded in 1885, the Swedish Social Democratic Party in 1889, and the Australian Labor Party in 1890; the British Labor Party started contesting seats a few years later. Each of these parties was formed in the midst of urban strikes, labor unrest, and anti-labor violence.

Though much has changed since the labor unrest and mobilization that took place from the late nineteenth century through the Great Depression, Europeans, North Americans, and Australians still inhabit the basic landscape of cities and party and electoral systems that took shape during that period. In the late nineteenth century, legislatures in Europe, North America, and Australasia were formed exclusively via winner-take-all districts. Not long after workers' parties started running for office, they realized they suffered from a basic problem: manufacturing and mining activity, and hence the voters most likely to respond to their appeals, were highly concentrated in urban legislative districts. This created a dilemma for workers' parties. If they maintained the purity of the socialist rhetoric favored by their radicalized urban supporters, they would not be able to form the alliances with voters in more centrist districts that were necessary to achieve electoral victory. However, to make those alliances was to invite challenges from insurgent radicals and communists. By focusing on the needs of the geographically concentrated working class, workers' parties were able to win decisive victories in industrial cities, but they found it difficult to transform votes into commensurate seats.

It is important to understand the rise of urban workers' parties and the dynamics of their geographic dilemma in the early twentieth century for three reasons. First, this era foreshadows the dilemma faced by the Democrats and other urban parties today. The occupational basis and ideological content of urban parties has changed dramatically, but the basic political geography—and the dilemma faced by urban parties—is the same.

Second, in the early twentieth century, European countries enacted reforms that resolved this burgeoning dilemma: they abolished single-member district representation schemes and replaced them with systems of proportional representation. Political geography and the emergence of workers' parties led broad coalitions of elites to embrace electoral reform in Europe—and hence preserve nascent multiparty systems—but not in Britain, North America, and Australasia.

Third, even though they were absorbed into the Democratic Party during the New Deal and have become a footnote in the history of the United States, James Maurer and the Reading Socialists allow a useful glimpse of a road not taken—an understanding of the ways in which the United States is unique among industrialized countries. The period of labor conflict, violence, and union mobilization was just as intense in the United States as in Europe—and perhaps even bloodier—but it never led to the emergence of a political party based purely on the interests of urban labor. Rather, urban labor became one of several factions within an existing political party that continued to be many things to many people. Without a nationwide threat from an urban workers' party beyond Reading and a few other hotspots, the United States developed neither the partisan division on the left that has characterized Canada and the United Kingdom, nor the broad constituency for electoral reform that emerged in Europe. It emerged from the era of labor conflict with one of the purest two-party systems in the world, thus setting the stage for the arrival of extreme urban-rural polarization in later decades.

THE INDUSTRIAL REVOLUTION left behind a geographic political legacy that we continue to grapple with today. The present-day geographic clustering of Democrats flows from the concentration of early manufacturing activity. But why was industrial activity in the early twentieth century so geographically concentrated? An obvious reason was the cost of moving inputs and finished goods between suppliers, producers, and customers. Another important factor had to do with the benefits of having a large group of specialized workers and relevant employers in close proximity to one another—an advantage known as "labor market pooling."[4] In the era of heavy industry, high transportation costs often led to the development of industrial activities in close proximity to natural resources, coal in particular.

Pennsylvania was no exception, and heavy industry developed in industrial cities arrayed on railroad lines near the bituminous coalfields of western Pennsylvania and the anthracite coalfields of eastern Pennsylvania. Reading is located in close proximity to the latter. After getting a start as a canal-based transportation hub for coal and finished goods on their way to Philadelphia, Reading developed into a successful base of innovation in railroad technology, anchored by the Philadelphia and Reading Railroad. For a brief period in the late nineteenth and early twentieth centuries, migrants came in droves to Reading to work in railroad, automobile, piano, and hardware manufacturing.

The era of steam and rail did not last long in Reading, and by the 1920s it was a labor-market pooling center for textiles, specializing in garments and especially hosiery. In addition to the large industrial cities that grew up during the nineteenth century, the northeastern manufacturing core of the United States is dotted with small rail-based manufacturing centers that

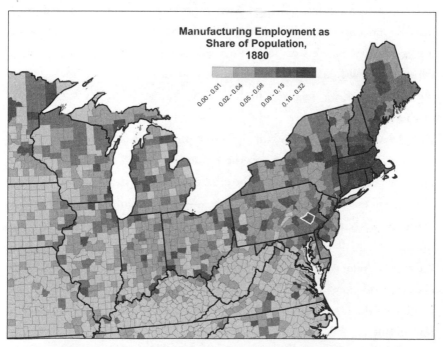

Figure 1.1: The County-Level Geographic Concentration of Manufacturing in 1880

once housed some kind of dynamic local manufacturing cluster during the era of rapid industrialization.

Something similar happened in all of the countries of North America, Europe, and Australasia that industrialized during that period. Port cities and hubs of transportation and commerce like Philadelphia, Chicago, Toronto, Manchester, Sydney, and Melbourne grew quickly, along with smaller, often more specialized cities that sprouted up on water and rail-based transportation routes connecting the larger cities. Small cities grew, and entirely new cities sprouted up around natural resource extraction points, such as in the German Ruhr area.

The map in Figure 1.1 focuses on what economic geographers refer to as the US manufacturing core: the region where the vast majority of manufacturing activity took place in the late nineteenth century.[5] Based on the 1880 census, the darker the shading, the higher the proportion of the county population that had a job in manufacturing. Not only was manufacturing activity regionally concentrated in the Northeast and upper Midwest, but within most of the early-industrializing US states, manufacturing activity was quite heavily concentrated in a rather small number of counties. For instance, Berks County, where Reading is located, is indicated on the map with a white border. It is one of twelve counties in Pennsylvania where manufacturing employment was relatively high by 1880 standards, surpassing 8 percent of the total population. In only two Pennsylvania counties—Philadelphia and Delaware—did manufacturing employment surpass 20 percent.

But there were exceptions to the pattern of within-state concentration. For instance, in New England—the cradle of the industrial revolution in the United States—manufacturing activity was quite evenly distributed across counties. Early textile factories were not concentrated in Boston, but in a number of smaller mill towns like Chicopee, Lawrence, and Lowell, and industry developed in a string of small and medium-sized cities like Manchester, Bridgeport, New Haven, Worcester, and Springfield. With the exception of the far North, New England's industrial towns are quite close to one another.

The county-level data used to produce Figure 1.1 do not come close to conveying the extent of geographic concentration of manufacturing in the

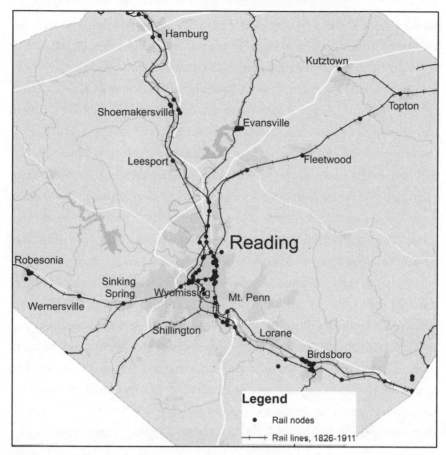

Figure 1.2: Nineteenth-Century Rail Nodes and Rail Lines, Berks County, Pennsylvania

late nineteenth century. Factories and the housing constructed for workers were also highly concentrated *within* the manufacturing counties. Virtually all factories in the early twentieth century required rail access. The interstate highway system had not yet been built, and trucking had not yet started to replace rail transport. Thus, early twentieth-century railroad maps provide an excellent proxy for factory location.[6]

Figure 1.2 zooms in on Reading and surrounding parts of Berks County, revealing that rail nodes—places where goods could be loaded and unloaded in the vicinity of nineteenth-century factories—were highly concentrated in the center of Reading, as well as in the complex of mills built in Wyomissing, just west of downtown, and in Birdsboro to the south, which was known for its large foundries and machine shops. There were some additional small factories along the Philadelphia and Reading Railroad, but the rest of Berks County was largely agricultural, and in the late nineteenth century, the majority of its population lived in the countryside.

There is nothing atypical about Reading, or for that matter, about Pennsylvania or North America. In Europe and Britain as well, manufacturing in the nineteenth century was highly clustered in space, usually near transportation nodes and natural resource points. This was an era in which workers had neither the time nor the resources for lengthy intra-urban commuting. Dense working-class housing was constructed in close proximity to the factories. For example, the urban core of Reading still consists of small brick houses that were built for the largely German working class migrating from the surrounding farms and from abroad in the nineteenth century.

In such environments, events like the Reading Railroad Massacre changed the politics of the late nineteenth century. In cities like Reading, labor unions gained adherents and organizational strength throughout Europe, Britain, North America, and Australasia in the 1800s. And it was in such environments that socialist and labor parties gained a foothold and eventually transformed political competition, sowing the seeds of the urban-rural polarization that dominates politics today.

FROM PENNSYLVANIA TO Britain to Belgium, once workers' parties entered the fray, they faced a basic problem with the system of winner-take-all districts. Since industrial workers were concentrated in urban working-class neighborhoods clustered around rail nodes, warehouses, and factories, even if these parties performed very well and earned the support of vast majorities of workers, their votes would inevitably be concentrated in well under half of the winner-take-all legislative districts.

James Maurer and the Reading Socialists understood this problem very well. Their intense mobilization efforts in downtown Reading were successful. They were able to win majorities in the urban city council wards dominated by manual laborers—which was enough to win some city council majorities—but it was much harder for them to prevail in wards with a larger mix of white-collar workers and business owners. Their support in rural Berks County was minimal. Thus, it was not possible for them to win any countywide offices, and their urban pocket of support was far too small to overcome the numbers of rural voters in state senate and congressional races.

However, the Reading Socialists found their sweet spot in the lower chamber of the state legislature: the Pennsylvania House of Representatives. Among US states, Pennsylvania has some of the smallest districts for its lower state legislative chamber. At that time, Reading's city boundary was coterminous with the boundary of the state legislative district. This created the opportunity for the Socialists to turn their highly concentrated support base into a seat in the state legislature.

This is a general phenomenon. When a small new party attempts to enter the electoral fray in a system where there are already two major parties, it is most likely to win some seats if its supporters are geographically concentrated in a handful of districts.[7] This is what happened for the Reading Socialists, and for socialist and labor parties in some of the most industrialized districts in Europe in the early twentieth century. However, if such a party wishes to expand to the point where it might win a majority of seats, the geographic concentration that helped it gain its initial foothold ultimately becomes a serious impediment.

This was true for workers' parties in two ways. First, they ended up "wasting" too many votes in their core districts; that is, winning by very large margins in some districts when those votes would have been more helpful elsewhere. This is often described as an "inefficient" geographic distribution of support. Second, if districts were drawn at the proper scale to allow for some seats in working-class districts, the party developed a coterie of incumbents who won their seats with a class-based appeal. In many cases, the party's most successful urban incumbents then came to have considerable influence over the party's platform and its reputation. Moderation in the pursuit of victory outside the proletarian districts did not come naturally to such individuals. Moreover, when those leaders organized strikes that turned violent, and earned their legislative seats in partnership with organized labor, using the language of class conflict—perhaps even participating in the Socialist International and traveling to the Soviet Union—the task of broadening the party's class appeal became very difficult. Concerted efforts to form alliances with skilled workers, small business owners, or farmers often lacked credibility.[8]

From Reading to London and Liège, voters outside the urban core came to view these parties of the urban left with suspicion—as something vaguely foreign and menacing. Parties of the urban left were also riven by a perpetual battle for the party's soul, pitting the urban firebrands and true believers against those who wished to soften the party's reputation in order to win the crucial districts outside the urban core.

The stakes in battles like these are high in systems with winner-take-all districts. If the urban firebrands gain the upper hand for a long period, the party might condemn itself to perpetual electoral defeat—winning urban and mining districts but little else—perhaps even creating the opportunity for an alternative center-left party to supplant it in the moderate districts. However, if the moderates sacrifice too much in the pursuit of victory, the party might suffer from a debilitating fracture.

While the story of the Socialists' failure in the United States is multifaceted, this kind of internal conflict played a role. In fact, James Maurer and many of the Reading Socialists were noteworthy for their moderation, and much of their success in local politics was based on issues like property tax valuations, infrastructure, and competent city management.[9] However, a group of radicals attempted to pull the party to the left in the 1930s, and the Socialists—including the Reading contingent—fell into rancorous disarray, just as one of the old "bourgeois" parties—the Democrats—made a concerted effort to ally with labor leaders and take up the mantle of the railroad and hosiery workers in places like Reading.

In Europe, as workers' parties tried to gain initial traction in urban districts, they faced another vexing problem: there was already a party occupying the left side of the political spectrum when they arrived on the scene. For instance, the Liberal Party of Belgium already had a foothold among urban skilled artisans and workers. The same was true of Radikale Venstre ("the radical left," known in English as the "Social Liberals") in Denmark, an urban breakaway from a more rural liberal party, Venstre ("the left"), both of which competed against an aristocratic conservative party called Højre ("the right"). In Britain's two-party system at the turn of the century, the Liberal Party was the main competitor to the left of the Conservatives, having earned significant support among workers newly able to vote, by introducing reforms like health and unemployment insurance as well as pensions for elderly workers.

Unlike in North America and Australasia, at the turn of the century low-income industrial workers in many European countries did not yet have full and equal franchise. The old elites attempted to protect themselves from the demands of urban workers by instituting property and income requirements for voting, and in some cases by giving more votes to wealthier citizens, or by vesting power in unrepresentative upper legislative chambers that were dominated by the elites. An important part of the rallying cry of socialists and workers' parties in Europe was the extension of the franchise and the abolition of these practices. In some countries these reforms were sudden—following from periods of instability, strikes, and violent urban street protests—but in some cases the change was gradual, as workers slowly gained the franchise by surpassing income and property requirements during periods of wage growth.

As European socialist and workers' parties agitated for full and equal franchise, they debated what would happen if they ever got it. Around 1850, some optimists, including Karl Marx and Friedrich Engels, believed themselves to be at the vanguard of a movement of the "immense majority," leaders of a proletariat that included "all but a handful of exploiters."[10] In their view, socialist candidates would quickly be able to win in districts throughout the country with free and fair elections. Old "bourgeois" parties like the liberals would be swept aside and supplanted.

However, it was wrong to conclude that all manual laborers would side immediately with the workers' parties. In many cases, the preexisting party of the left—like the UK Liberals and Danish Radical Left—had been making overtures to skilled laborers before the arrival of the workers' parties. In fact, these liberal parties often strategically opened the door to partial expansion of the franchise when this helped give them the upper hand vis-à-vis their conservative opponents. Liberals warned workers that even if they preferred the workers' or socialist parties, sincere votes for the socialist candidates in urban districts would divide the left and allow conservatives to win. They convinced many workers that it was better to vote strategically for the largest party of the left—the liberals—even if this was their second preference, rather than run the risk that a conservative candidate would win the district. Thus, initially, labor unions often endorsed liberal candidates rather than the insurgent socialists.

From the very beginning, workers' parties faced a vexing coordination problem with liberals in districts with working-class populations. The uncomfortable solution was to form temporary cartels with the liberals in which each party would agree to strategically withdraw its candidates in selected districts to avoid handing the district to the minority conservatives. These deals were difficult to strike, and often undone by cheating. It was through such active coordination between the old and new left party that the latter was able to enter parliament for the first time in many European countries, including Belgium, Sweden, Denmark, the Netherlands, and the United Kingdom, and in New Zealand.[11]

When these new parties began contesting elections, they initially competed for very few seats, the vast majority of which were in densely populated urban industrial areas, though some were in districts with mines, ports, and commercial fishing operations.[12] In the early twentieth century, while the workers' parties were gaining strength and diversifying their support base, they still only threatened the old parties in a limited number of districts. This was true even in Germany and Denmark, which already had equal, universal male franchise in the early twentieth century.

The difficulty of the plurality electoral system became readily apparent for the socialist and labor parties. As they tried to expand beyond their initial districts and take over the left side of the political spectrum, they found that their seat share fell far below their vote share in almost every European country. Their support was too deeply concentrated in a handful of districts, and in many cases they were hamstrung by the need to coordinate with "bourgeois liberals," whom many socialist leaders detested.

Consider the Social Democrats in Germany. In every election from 1890 to 1907, they won more votes than any other party, but they never won the most seats. Their main competitor on the right sometimes received twice as many seats despite receiving a million fewer votes. In the parliamentary elections of early twentieth-century Denmark, the Social Democrats routinely won the most votes while winning far fewer seats than their competitors. In 1915, the Liberal and Labor Parties in Norway won almost identical vote shares, but the Liberals received almost four times as many seats as Labor. In 1918, the Norwegian Labor Party had more votes than any other party, but the Conservative Party and Liberal Party *each* had twice as many seats.

Similar dramatic underrepresentation of the urban left was a source of consternation, anger, and in many cases street violence throughout Europe in the early twentieth century.[13] Several countries were on the cusp of civil war. The urban-rural polarization of the United States today is mild compared with the social polarization between the underrepresented urban working class and the vastly overrepresented conservative allies of European aristocracy at the outbreak of World War I.

RECOGNIZING THEIR ELECTORAL geography problem, leaders of European socialist and labor parties found a solution in the writings of British reform advocates like Thomas Hare, Henry Droop, and above all, John Stuart Mill. They came to see proportional representation (PR) as their salvation. Specific proposals varied from one country to another, but the basic idea of proportional representation was simple: small, single-member districts drawn around a single city or neighborhood would be replaced by much larger districts that encompassed an entire region, with each district electing several representatives. Each party's candidates would be placed on a ranked list, and its parliamentary representation would be drawn from that list in proportion to its vote share. With this system, 35 percent of the vote would correspond to roughly 35 percent of the seats. And under this system, supporters of workers' parties and liberal parties in urban areas would no longer need to worry that a sincere vote for their preferred party would split the left vote and hand the district to the conservatives. Wilhelm Liebknecht, leader of the German Social Democratic Party, made the case very clearly: "Under the present electoral system the greater part of our votes is lost—whereas under proportional representation our strength in parliament would be doubled or tripled."[14]

After some debate, the adoption of large, multimember districts with PR became part of the official platform of socialist and labor parties throughout Europe in the early twentieth century. In street protests and legislative maneuvers, workers' parties called not only for full franchise and the end of plural voting, but also for proportional representation. Remarkably, in only a couple of decades, they achieved both.

The adoption of PR was in some cases, as in Germany, Switzerland, and Austria, driven primarily by the agitation of the workers' parties. However, in most cases, electoral reform cannot be seen as a concession to the muscle of these parties and their supporters, either on the street or in the legislature. Rather, the workers' parties found willing reform partners among some legislators within the existing parties, especially the liberal parties, who saw the expansion of the franchise and the entry of socialist and labor candidates in their districts as existential threats to their political careers. In many countries, liberals from urban districts had advocated for limited franchise expansion, but they quickly came to understand that they had unleashed a process they could no longer control, and full franchise would soon lead many of them to lose their urban seats to socialist or labor candidates. If they tried to shade their platform to the left to forestall the rise of these parties, they would only give ground to the conservatives. Fearing that they would soon be squeezed out of existence, urban liberals became some of the strongest advocates of proportional representation in Belgium, the Netherlands, Italy, and Norway, among other countries. At a crucial moment, by bargaining for electoral reform, these parties saved themselves from likely obliteration.

Analysis of parliamentary votes on these electoral reforms reveals that while socialists and workers' parties voted uniformly in favor of reform, among the old non-socialist parties, support was concentrated among those whose seats were most threatened by socialists.[15] In some cases, that included conservatives as well. In Belgium, rural Catholic members of the legislature presided over safe seats, and they fought to keep the old plurality electoral system. However, urban representatives from the Catholic Party were beginning to fall below the winning threshold as the workers' party gained strength, and they came to advocate for PR as a way of saving themselves. In Scandinavia, a large number of incumbent conservatives were from urban districts where the electoral incursion of the socialists put them at risk. Threatened with extinction, urban conservatives in Sweden, Denmark, and Norway also came to appreciate the merits of proportional representation, and they joined reform coalitions that voted for PR in parliament.

The rise of proportional representation in Europe was in many ways a direct result of the geographic dilemma of the urban left. As urban workers gained the franchise and leaned toward socialist and far-left parties, electoral competition in cities was thrown into disarray. The workers' parties were badly underrepresented in legislatures and plagued by coordination problems with existing parties. For their part, risk-averse urban representatives of the old parties realized they might be destined for the dustbin of history as politics transformed into a polarized electoral battle between parties of urban workers and their opponents.

For both the insurgent workers' parties and the urban incumbents from the old parties, proportional representation was a way out. After the introduction of PR, social democratic and workers' parties saw an immediate and sometimes dramatic increase in their legislative representation. After the transition to proportional representation in 1915, the Danish Social Democrats immediately received a seat share roughly equal to their vote share for the first time in their history. By 1924, they were at the head of a coalition government. In Norway, the Labor Party had received only 14 percent of the seats with 32 percent of the vote in 1918. After the transition to PR in 1919, it received a seat share much closer to its vote share, and by 1927 it was the largest party in parliament. After the adoption of proportional representation and the abolition of plural voting in 1919, the Belgian Workers' Party won 38 percent of the seats in the legislature and joined a coalition government, and by 1925, it was the largest party in the Belgian Federal Parliament.[16] The German Social Democrats had received 11 percent of the seats with 29 percent of the vote in 1907, and 28 percent of the seats with 35 percent of the votes in 1912. After the introduction of proportional representation in 1919, they received 38 percent of the vote and became the largest party in parliament with 39 percent of the seats. These parties went on to thrive and form governments for much of the postwar period, and along with workers', socialist, and social democratic parties in other continental European countries, they helped build and maintain the Northern European welfare state.

Another lasting legacy of electoral reform in early twentieth-century Europe was the survival of urban liberal parties, which still play an important role in European politics today. Already in the nineteenth century, these parties had gained a base among urban artisans, business owners, professionals, and intellectuals who were opposed to the dominance of the monarchy, aristocracy, and church, but also alarmed by the rhetoric of the workers' parties. The survival of liberal parties meant that educated, middle-class urban voters were not forced to choose between the rural aristocracy and the workers' parties. Liberal parties like the Danish Social Liberal Party, the Swedish Liberals, and the German Free Democrats still play this role today, sometimes coalescing with the urban workers' parties and sometimes with more rural parties of the right. Moreover, in addition to these liberal parties, proportional representation also preserved urban parties of the right in many countries. In this way, proportional representation eased the pressure that was pushing industrializing European countries toward polarized two-party systems, pitting urban against rural interests.

IN CONTINENTAL EUROPE, uncertainty and fear associated with the rise of workers' parties in the cities ran so high that established parties took a gamble on reform. In Britain and its former colonies, however, the elites remained confident enough in their party's success that the existing system survived. Australia in particular followed a different historical path. The Australian Labor Party (ALP) was not an insurgent that threatened existing parties. On the contrary, the ALP is Australia's oldest political party. It had already been organized in some of the Australian colonies before the formation of the Federation of Australia in 1901, and it quickly came to dominate the left side of the spectrum thereafter. It did not have to fight a battle for entry against another left-wing party with strong links to workers' and labor unions in urban districts. The early non-socialist parties—the Free Traders and Protectionists—were more like collections of local notables than coherent political parties, and soon after the formation of the federation, the two non-socialist parties merged. Thus, the pressures that led to electoral reform in Europe never emerged in Australia.

In the United Kingdom and New Zealand, however, labor parties entered the fray at the turn of the century in a context rather similar to that of most European countries: longstanding two-party competition between rural conservatives and urban liberals. Similarly, Labour in the United Kingdom started running candidates in industrial and mining districts, but struggled to successfully coordinate with the urban Liberals, and hence could not transform its growing support into legislative seats. Like its European comrades, Labour strongly advocated for proportional representation.

Faced with an expanding electorate in industrialized areas and the rise of the Labour Party, some Liberals began to see the benefits of electoral reform. But most of the party's legislative incumbents believed they could continue with the status quo and remain the dominant party in cities. Their strategy was to marginalize Labour, urging leftist voters that a vote for Labour was a wasted vote that would only hand urban districts to the hated Tories (Conservatives). When absolutely necessary, they pursued the sporadic coordinated withdrawal of candidates from urban districts in tense collaboration with Labour. The Liberals were confident in their ability to keep Labour at bay, and they were successful, until a sudden and devastating incursion of Labour candidates into their districts in 1918.

With the benefit of hindsight, it is clear that the British Liberals were in a position quite similar to that of their copartisans in Belgium and the Netherlands. As trade unionists defected to the Labour Party in urban districts, the UK Liberals were increasingly placed in the same impossible position as the Belgian Liberals—squeezed between the preexisting conservative party and the new challenger on the left. Proportional representation was their best hope. Yet parliamentary voting records reveal that opinion among British Liberals was still divided as late as 1918, with a majority still hoping to reclaim their rightful place as the dominant urban party.[17] Only a few years later, the Liberals were well on their way to being supplanted by Labour as the party of the left. Most Liberals soon realized they should have fought tooth and nail for proportional representation while they had the chance. They quickly adopted PR as a platform, but it was too late. Before long they had become a minor party, replaced by Labour as the mainstream urban party.

For their part, once they had achieved dominance on the left, Labour leaders set aside their initial support for proportional representation. Seeing the opportunity to squeeze out the Liberals, they rallied around the retention of the plurality electoral system. As with elites in parties throughout Europe, the strongest voices in favor of single-member districts were of the safe urban incumbents with little to gain from reform. To this day, the left side of the political spectrum in Britain remains divided, with the descendants of the once-dominant Liberals (now called the Liberal Democrats) still underrepresented in Parliament and still pushing in vain for electoral reform.

The New Zealand Liberals suffered a remarkably similar fate. After a golden era of dominance in the late nineteenth century, they were squeezed out by Labour once it began fielding candidates in urban districts. By the onset of the Great Depression, Labour had become the dominant party of the urban left. Although proportional representation was one of the founding principles of the Labour Party, it was soon forgotten. As in Britain, once they tasted success and managed to vanquish the Liberals, Labour incumbents in New Zealand quickly learned to embrace the single-member district system under which they had achieved victory.

Unlike in Australia, New Zealand, and Britain, a workers' party did not make serious headway in Canada until the Great Depression. As a result, serious pressure for electoral reform did not emerge at all in early twentieth-century Canada. Labor unrest came to many Canadian cities in the 1910s and 1920s, along with socialist candidates. As with Reading and Milwaukee, small socialist hotspots emerged, but the socialists never congealed into a successful national movement. Winnipeg, which experienced a major strike and labor unrest in 1919, experienced a brief surge in support for socialist candidates, along with the industrial districts of Alberta and southern Ontario.

As with Maurer and the Reading Socialists, however, Canada's socialists were only able to win city and local legislative elections in working-class

neighborhoods. These parties typically advocated for proportional representation, but they never gained the strength to achieve it, and the Liberal Party
never felt sufficiently squeezed to push for it.

Things got more interesting during the Great Depression, when a group
of embattled wheat farmers in Canada's west formed the Cooperative Commonwealth Federation (CCF). Starting as a prairie populist movement, the
CCF focused on agricultural prices and the interests of farmers vis-à-vis
banks and railroads, but it eventually forged links with urban labor groups.
The CCF went through a gradual transformation into a party of urban labor, and merged with other labor groups to form the New Democratic Party
(NDP) in the 1960s. Today, most of the NDP's support comes from urban
constituencies with a history of early twentieth-century industrialization.

When Canada finally got a unified workers' party, the result was rather
different than in the other countries with winner-take-all districts. Neither
the Liberals nor the NDP has been squeezed out of existence, and neither
has led a successful push for electoral reform. As in other places, the entry of
a labor party into urban districts led to a coordination problem. Appealing
to the same logic as liberal parties in early twentieth-century Europe, the
Canadian Liberals have for decades warned urban voters that support for the
NDP will split the left vote and allow the minority Conservatives to win urban seats. And indeed, this frequently takes place. Yet the Liberals have been
able to maintain a tenuous upper hand for decades, relegating the NDP to
only a handful of victories—mainly in core urban districts—while focusing
on winning in the suburbs and achieving dominance in a large number of
districts in Quebec. The Canadian Liberals have faced the same challenge as
UK and New Zealand Liberals did around World War I: an insurgent party
on their left flank. They chose roughly the same strategy as their Commonwealth counterparts. Rather than advocating for proportional representation, they held fast and attempted to occupy a broad swath of the center-left,
appealing to urban workers to vote strategically for the Liberals rather than
waste votes on a third party.

The Liberals were not overtaken and replaced by the insurgent labor-
oriented party, as happened in the United Kingdom and New Zealand, but
neither did they vanquish the left-wing insurgents, as the US Democrats

had eventually dispatched the Socialists. Rather, the Canadian Left has settled into a unique and uneasy long-term divide. Like other insurgent leftist
parties in plurality systems, the NDP has lost out in the transformation
of votes to seats over the years and, thus, has long been a staunch advocate of proportional representation. The Liberals have flirted with electoral
reform on occasion—especially when it appears the NDP might finally
overtake them—but like other mainstream parties with a taste of electoral
victory, they have always found a reason to preserve the plurality system.
That system has worked for the Liberals in Canada because of a geographic
electoral quirk that was unavailable to Liberals in New Zealand or in the
United Kingdom: the longstanding dominance of the Liberal Party in the
province of Quebec.[18]

Each of these countries has its unique features, but the factors that led to
the retention of single-member districts are easily summarized. In Australia,
New Zealand, and Britain, workers' parties took over the urban districts
quickly, and their leaders immediately lost interest in electoral reform that
might offer a lifeline to alternative urban parties. In Canada, the insurgent
workers' party pushed for electoral reform—and continues to do so today—
but it never found allies among the traditional political parties. Many of the
same dynamics explain the stability of the plurality electoral system in the
United States.

LET US NOW return to the Reading Socialists and the road not taken in the
United States. With some comparative perspective, it should now be clear
why proportional representation never emerged as a serious nationwide proposal by a major American party. Although nineteenth-century labor unrest
and unionization took place in American cities, as in European ones, neither
of the major parties faced a serious challenge from Socialists outside of local,
ethnically homogeneous pockets like Reading and Milwaukee. Since a serious threat never materialized, advocates of proportional representation have
been largely limited to very small parties, like Greens and Libertarians, who
are unable to achieve representation due to the logic of strategic voting in
winner-take-all elections.

The failure of the United States to develop a workers' or socialist party is a topic that has received a great deal of attention.[19] Some of the cited explanations include the ethnic, racial, and religious fractionalization of the working class, high wages relative to Europe, effective use of coercion against strikers, a vast geography that included a frontier, and federalism. Some of the most popular explanations are cultural: Engels lamented the presence of a "bourgeois" political culture among the American working class, which he attributed in part to the lack of a feudal history that would facilitate class-based political mobilization.

Yet it is easy to forget that the strikes and violence of the late nineteenth century were as intense and bloody in the United States as the ones that gave rise to workers' parties in Europe. And it is simply not the case that the urban strikes and labor union mobilization of the late 1800s and early 1900s had no implications for future party conflict in the United States. The crucial difference is that instead of giving rise to a separate workers' party, this entire movement was eventually incorporated into the existing Democratic Party, which became the party of the urban left.

The United States followed a very different path to the emergence of a cohesive urban, left-wing party than any of the other former British colonies. Instead of supporting a new socialist party, urban labor unions eventually joined forces with an existing party—one that had historically favored rural interests, supporters of "free silver," and slaveholders, in addition to other groups. This uniquely American path is impossible to understand without first reckoning with an institutional feature of American democracy that sets it apart from the political systems of all of the countries of Europe and the Commonwealth discussed thus far: presidential rather than parliamentary democracy.

In all of the plurality, single-member district electoral systems of early twentieth-century Europe, as well as those of the contemporary United Kingdom and the Commonwealth, cabinet ministers and the chief executive are chosen after legislative elections, and they serve at the pleasure of the legislature. The prime minister and cabinet are drawn from the legislature, and they cannot stay in power if the legislature decides to remove them via a no-confidence vote. In the United States, on the other hand, the chief executive is elected through a completely separate procedure, and cannot be removed by the legislature in the absence of such "crimes and misdemeanors" that would trigger the impeachment process. The same is true of state governors vis-à-vis state legislatures.

For good reason, a great deal of attention and resources are focused on presidential elections in the United States. In contrast, constituency-level organizational efforts are more important in parliamentary systems like Canada's, which created the right conditions for the successful entry of third parties such as the Cooperative Commonwealth Federation in the 1930s.[20] In the United States, in contrast, it is typically difficult for third parties to enter the fray in gubernatorial or presidential elections, and the two-party competition of presidential elections is reproduced at the district level.

Perhaps the most important link between the American system of presidential democracy and the lack of third parties lies in the ability of congressional candidates to successfully differentiate themselves from the national party. The American party labels can have remarkably different meanings in different parts of the country, giving candidates flexibility to tailor their own platform to the needs of their district. Compare this with Canada, where if the voters in a particular district are dissatisfied with the platform of one of the major parties, a candidate from that party cannot credibly promise to buck the party leadership or reform it from within once in Ottawa. In a parliamentary system, voters and candidates alike know that leaders of the majority party can use a powerful tool called the no-confidence procedure to induce the cooperation of their members. The logic is simple: if renegade members of parliament (MPs) threaten not to vote for the party's agenda, the prime minister can threaten to call for a no-confidence vote, at which point the renegade MPs would bring down the government and force new elections by sticking to their oppositional stance. The party leadership reckons this would be as unpalatable to the renegade backbenchers as to everyone else in the party. As a result, party discipline around a coherent platform is much more pronounced in parliamentary systems than in presidential ones.[21]

In contrast, in the United States it is quite common for both Democrats and Republicans to run, and win, on a platform that is openly hostile to the leaders of their party. They can credibly claim that if elected, they will go to Washington, or the state capital, and provide constant challenges to the party leadership, holding out on key issues and bargaining for a position preferred by the district's constituents. When there are geographically concentrated interests or ideological views that might facilitate the entry of a third party in certain districts in Canada or the United Kingdom, the result in the United States is the emergence of a different flavor of Democrat or Republican. Recent examples include "Tea Party" Republicans and "Democratic Socialists." For this reason, the two US parties—especially the Democrats—are famously heterogeneous. As Will Rogers joked, "I am not a member of any organized political party . . . I am a Democrat."

This important fact raises the question—Why is there no socialism in the United States?—in a different light. Some urban incumbents in the Democratic Party routinely espouse platforms that are at odds with the national party platform, and not notably different from the platforms of many European Social Democratic or workers' parties. It is simply not the case that after the Socialists failed in the early twentieth century, the United States never developed a party of urban labor. Rather, the Democrats under Franklin Delano Roosevelt (FDR) became such a party, at least in parts of the United States, while continuing on as something quite different elsewhere.

American-style presidential democracy led to a unique American solution to the dilemma of the urban left. Instead of birthing a new party in the era of rapid industrialization and labor mobilization, one of the major parties forged links with labor unions and took up the cause of urban workers, even while simultaneously representing the interest of a variety of other actors—Southern segregationists chief among them.

BEFORE MOVING ON to explore the evolution of urban-rural polarization in the United States after the New Deal, let us briefly summarize some lessons and preview their implications for current-day politics. In most advanced industrial democracies, contemporary party systems and patterns of political geography have their origins in events like the Reading Railroad Massacre and the working-class mobilization of the late nineteenth and early twentieth centuries. In Europe, Britain, Australasia, and eventually Canada, that historical moment gave rise to new urban workers' parties that challenged or replaced existing urban parties, whereas in the United States, it eventually led to the partial transformation of the Democrats into an advocacy group for urban workers.

When workers' parties first entered the fray in industrialized societies, they faced a set of interrelated problems due to their geographic concentration. They had trouble coordinating with existing parties of the urban left. They found it difficult to select a platform that could lead to parliamentary majorities. And they lost badly in the transformation of votes to seats. Parties of urban workers throughout Europe came to understand that a system of winner-take-all districts was bad for them.

In Europe, these problems were nipped in the bud by the adoption of proportional representation in the early twentieth century, which led to the representation of both workers' parties and preexisting liberal parties throughout the twentieth century. In Britain and its former colonies, the old plurality systems survived, in large part because of the self-interest of elites from both conservative and workers' parties. In the Commonwealth countries that retained the old pre-industrial system of winner-take-all districts, this geographic dilemma continued throughout the postwar period.

In the United States, the full urbanization of the Democratic Party happened much later than with workers' parties in other industrialized countries. But the seeds were sown in the late nineteenth century. When we talk about the urban-rural divide in America, the most palpable causes are those most recent in memory: the realignment of the South, the rise of social and cultural partisan battles, and the emergence of the knowledge economy. But these factors only served to expand and sharpen a geographic divide that emerged in the era of iron, coal, and steam. The geographic dilemma facing the Democrats today is a variant of the dilemma faced by workers' parties throughout Europe, Britain, and Australasia in the early twentieth century.

CHAPTER 2

The Long Shadow of the Industrial Revolution

F AST-FORWARD NINETY YEARS from the night of the Reading Railroad Massacre to a conversation in the 1960s at a working-class bar in the fictionalized version of downtown Reading, portrayed in the second of John Updike's "Rabbit" novels. Earl Angstrom is a proud union member who recently arranged a job for his son, Harry ("Rabbit"), at a unionized print shop. Over a Schlitz beer after work, Earl describes to Harry his deep appreciation for the Democrats, the New Deal, and the Great Society, effusing about Lyndon B. Johnson (LBJ): "Believe me he did a lot of good for the little man." Speaking of Medicare, he says: "It's like a ton of anxiety rolled off my chest. There's no medical expense can break us now."

By the time Earl was sharing that beer with his son, he was approaching retirement, and the golden era of manufacturing in Reading was long over. The mills were closed and the entire hosiery industry had moved to the South. The long decline of Reading and other northern postindustrial cities and towns had already begun, and the Reading Socialists were a distant memory. Yet somehow the urban workers of Earl's generation had become loyal members of a party that, in the heyday of the Socialists, had been the party of rural farmers. Well into the 1920s, in fact, support for Democrats in the Northeast still came predominantly from rural areas, and Republicans controlled many of the cities. Today, however, Democratic candidates are dominant at all levels of government in Reading and many cities like it.

The Democrats became an urban party because of a dramatic transformation that took place during Earl Angstrom's formative years. Franklin D. Roosevelt assembled a coalition based on the policy agenda of the New Deal in the 1930s, and the Democrats managed to implement at the national level some of the policies advocated by the Reading Socialists early in the nineteenth century. In contrast to most of the surrounding conservative suburbs and countryside, the urban working class in manufacturing cities like Reading had become solidly Democratic during this period. These cities remained Democratic as they slowly deindustrialized, and they remain so today. The contemporary urban-rural partisan cleavage, already foreshadowed during the era of the Reading Socialists, took its initial shape during the Great Depression.

The previous chapter explored the earliest stages of urban labor's engagement in electoral politics. In this chapter, we'll come to understand the form this engagement eventually took in the United States—that is, the incorporation of the forces of urban labor into the Democratic Party in Pennsylvania and other industrialized states—and we'll begin to understand the long legacy of this transformation for (1) urban-rural polarization, and (2) the underrepresentation of Democrats.

The political geography of early industrialization is not ancient history. Even today, it is not contemporary manufacturing, but early twentieth-century manufacturing that predicts Democratic voting. Democrats are clustered in cities of all sizes that are arranged along lakeshores, canals, and rail lines, where manufacturing activity was most intense in the 1920s. The geography of manufacturing has changed quite dramatically since then, moving from the dense cities of the Northeast to sparse exurbs and rural areas, especially in the South. Today, the Democrats win majorities in dense places along the railroad tracks, like Reading, that lost their industries decades ago in the era of organized labor. The Republicans, in contrast, have been winning majorities in the sparsely populated regions along interstates where manufacturing still takes place, and where deindustrialization is a contemporary fear rather than a historical memory.

This pattern of political geography explains much of today's urban-rural polarization, as well as the contemporary underrepresentation of Democrats in Congress and state legislatures. As industrial cities became overwhelmingly Democratic, the Democratic Party became increasingly concentrated in space relative to the Republicans. The excessive clustering of Democrats in cities today is thus rooted in the early twentieth century.

While focusing on the early days of manufacturing, this chapter will also show that urban-rural partisan polarization has grown most dramatically since 1980—well after the decline of urban manufacturing and private sector unions and the departure of Earl Angstrom's generation from the workforce. Urban-rural polarization has also now expanded to places that never experienced much labor activism or working-class mobilization. Thus, the early industrial era is only the first chapter of the story of American geographic polarization. But the social, cultural, and economic battle lines that have sharpened since the 1980s were initially structured by the human geography of the industrial era. The locations of warehouses and low-income apartment buildings, the strength of public sector unions, and the partisanship of city governments all cast a long shadow that is still with us.

PRIOR TO THE Great Depression, US political parties took opposing stances on a variety of issues including slavery, race, reconstruction, monetary policy, tariffs, banks, prohibition, and immigration. These cleavages created stable regional voting patterns—with Republicans dominating in the North and Democrats in the South—but there was no systematic relationship between urbanization and party support.

Recall that because the United States does not have a parliamentary system of government, the parties' candidates have few incentives to adopt clear nationwide platforms and support them once in office. American political parties can be very different things to different people in different places. In many states, in the late 1800s and early 1900s, the Democrats performed better in rural areas than in cities. However, an exception took hold in part of the Northeast. Starting with Tammany Hall—the system of politics that controlled New York's city and state politics for decades—the Democrats began to cultivate a support base among urban immigrant workers, especially from Ireland.

Similarly, colorful Democrats like James Curley came to dominate Boston politics in the early twentieth century. These local bosses began to cut deals with national Democratic presidential candidates, and the allegiances of local politics started to bleed into presidential politics. Even though states like New York and Massachusetts were solidly Republican overall in presidential voting in the late nineteenth century, Democratic candidates started to win majorities in the densely populated, industrialized counties of New York and Massachusetts in the early part of the twentieth century. While they remained a more rural party in much of the country, a clear positive correlation between population density and the Democrats' presidential vote share emerged across the counties of New York and Massachusetts.

The Democratic political machines were rooted in ethnic politics rather than class struggle, but to fend off challenges from candidates favored by organized labor, Democrats like New York governor Al Smith increasingly embraced a pro-labor agenda. What started as an idiosyncratic local connection between urbanization and Democratic voting in New York quickly spread to the rest of the industrialized states in 1928 when the Democrats chose Al Smith, the Irish-Catholic, anti-prohibition New Yorker, as their presidential nominee. As governor of New York, Smith had fought for pensions, workers' compensation, workplace safety, and other policies that benefited urban workers, bringing them into the fold of the Democratic Party. It was not quite the agenda of the Socialists, but it was the beginning of the Democrats' transformation into a party of the urban working class.

Pennsylvania is a good example of the rapid realignment of industrialized states in 1928. To demonstrate this, Figure 2.1 brings together county-level data from one hundred years of presidential elections in the state of Pennsylvania. In each small scatter plot, the horizontal axis represents the county's population density.[1] Relatively urban, and hence densely populated, counties like Philadelphia and Allegheny (home to Pittsburgh) appear on the right in each graph, while relatively sparse rural counties, like those in the mountainous and agricultural parts of the state, are on the left. The vertical axis in each graph represents the Democratic vote share in presidential elections.

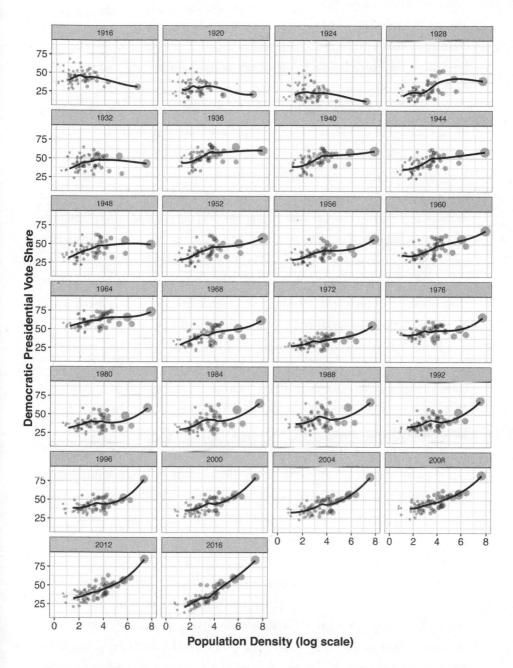

Figure 2.1: Population Density and Democratic Voting across Pennsylvania Counties, 1916–2016

The size of the data markers corresponds to the overall population of the county, so that a larger bubble means a county has more people. The bold line traces out the relationship between population density and voting. A downward-sloping line indicates that when counties are more dense and urban, they are less Democratic (that is, more Republican). An upward-sloping line indicates the opposite: denser counties are more Democratic.

In the first three panels, we can see that in the early part of the century, Democrats in Pennsylvania received more support in rural areas than in urban areas. But suddenly in 1928, with the nomination of Al Smith, the most densely populated counties like Allegheny and Philadelphia—represented by the two large gray bubbles on the right side of the graph—became much more Democratic, along with several other industrialized counties like those containing Scranton and Wilkes-Barre. With this sudden positive correlation between population density and Democratic voting, Pennsylvania, along with other industrialized states, came to look like New York.

Smith was no socialist, and much of his appeal in big cities appears to have been due to the politics of ethnicity and Catholicism. Smith only received 26 percent of the vote in heavily German (and heavily industrialized) Berks County, for instance. The Democratic Party's full embrace of urban labor did not occur until after FDR's election in 1932. By 1936, after the heart of the New Deal agenda had been implemented, the urban, industrialized parts of Pennsylvania, including Berks County, had become solidly Democratic. As we see in Figure 2.1, they have remained so ever since. For the first time, urban workers who had been mobilized by labor leaders since the nineteenth century were aligned with a major party that could compete at every level from the presidency to local government.

To get a sense of the strength of the relationship between population density and Democratic voting across counties, it is useful to calculate the slope of the lines in Figure 2.1 using linear regressions.[2] In 1916, when Woodrow Wilson was the Democratic presidential candidate, going from a very rural county like Montour to a relatively urban one like Lackawanna (home to Scranton), a doubling of population density was associated with a 7 percent *decrease* in Democratic voting. By 1940, a doubling of population density was associated with a 5 percent *increase* in Democratic voting.

The story is much the same in all of the other early-industrializing states. We can visualize this by calculating those slopes—capturing the relationship between population density and Democratic voting—for all counties of the manufacturing core rather than in Pennsylvania alone. These slopes are plotted over time with the solid line in Figure 2.2. Larger positive numbers correspond to a stronger direct relationship between population density and Democratic voting. For instance, a value of 0.1 on the vertical axis means that a 100 percent increase—or doubling—of county-level population density is associated with a 10 percent increase in the Democratic vote share.

A strong positive relationship between density and Democratic voting emerged in the manufacturing states in 1928, and it remained rather stable from the New Deal until around 1980, when it began a period of steady increase that has lasted until the present day. In the 1930s and 1940s, the county-level electoral map of states like Ohio and Michigan came to look similar to today's electoral maps. Franklin D. Roosevelt received strong majorities in counties with manufacturing agglomerations, like Cleveland and

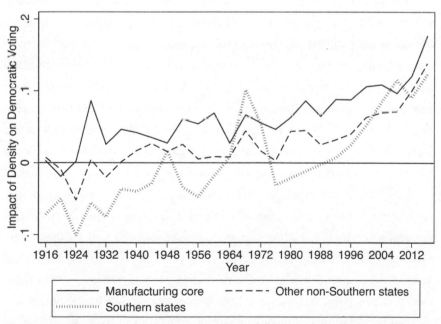

Figure 2.2: The Relationship between Population Density and Democratic Voting over Time, by Region

Youngstown, and Detroit and Flint, while his Republican challengers won majorities in the surrounding rural counties.[3]

It is noteworthy that an equally strong relationship between population density and Democratic voting did not emerge outside the manufacturing core during the New Deal era. With a dashed line, Figure 2.2 also displays the strength of the relationship between population density and Democratic voting in the non-southern states outside the original manufacturing core— the Great Plains, Mountain West, Southwest, and West Coast. A positive relationship between population density and Democratic voting did emerge during the New Deal in the North outside the manufacturing core, but it was weaker. This is because Democratic majorities began to emerge in the manufacturing cities of the West, and in the cities on the western fringes of the eastern manufacturing core, including Minneapolis/St. Paul, Kansas City, Omaha, Wichita, and Des Moines. But at the same time, population density and Democratic voting were still uncorrelated in much of the nonindustrialized parts of the Great Plains, Mountain West, and the West during the New Deal.

By no means did the New Deal make the Democrats into an urban party everywhere. The flexibility of party labels in a decentralized presidential system allowed the Democrats to continue as a completely different type of party outside the manufacturing core. In the South, the relationship between population density and Democratic voting remained consistently negative throughout the same period. This can be seen with the thick dotted line in Figure 2.2. When Roosevelt took office in 1933, almost half of the Democrats in Congress were rural Southern segregationists.[4] Faced with the dilemma identified in the previous chapter—a geographically concentrated working class with little chance of controlling half the seats in the legislature on its own—Roosevelt was forced to make a Faustian bargain with Southern segregationists, providing support for segregationist policies favored by Southern Democrats in exchange for their votes in favor of the New Deal agenda. As described further in the next chapter, the emergence of a correlation between population density and Democratic voting in the South was delayed for decades because of this arrangement.

In sum, in the 1930s, the base of the Democratic Party in the United States finally came to resemble that of workers' parties in Europe. But initially, this only happened in the places with factories, foundries, mills, warehouses, and labor unions that had mobilized the urban working class in the previous fifty years.[5] The Democrats became an urban party in the manufacturing states in the 1930s. This phenomenon did not expand to the rest of the country until the 1980s.

INDUSTRIAL CONFLICT, WORKING-CLASS mobilization, and the rise of unionized urban Democrats during the New Deal seem like ancient history, as do urban, white, working-class Democrats like Earl Angstrom. Yet the geographic pattern of partisanship established during this period has cast a long shadow over contemporary political geography. To comprehend the persistence of this shadow, we must come to understand the legacy of the buildings and urban form that emerged during the nineteenth century.

The era of heavy industry in the Northeast and Midwest did not last long. Soon after the workers unionized, the mills and factories near the city centers closed, their owners heading south in search of cheaper labor. In Reading, for instance, the entire hosiery industry departed for the South during a brief period of labor unrest in the late 1940s and early 1950s.

In addition to the rise of labor unions, the construction of the interstate highway system also changed the calculus of location choice for capital owners. No longer tethered to the nineteenth-century rail grid, capital owners moved to distant exurbs and rural areas, and above all, they moved to the South.[6] American manufacturing today is no longer situated along nineteenth-century railroads and canals in urban centers in proximity to working-class housing. Today, it is situated along interstate highways in sparsely populated areas where land and utilities are cheap, tax abatements are easier to wrangle, where nonunionized workers commute by automobile, and finished goods are shipped by trucks. In the early twentieth century, population density and manufacturing went hand in hand. In the county-level data from censuses around the turn of the century, population density and manufacturing employment were highly correlated. Today, the correlation has reversed.

Outside the Sun Belt, the location of most of today's American cities can be traced directly to manufacturing and the rail and water-borne transportation network of the late nineteenth century. The bricks, mortar, and concrete of cities live on long after the manufacturing has gone. Residential buildings for workers were constructed in and around city centers in the late nineteenth and early twentieth centuries to keep up with exploding demand. But when demand dries up, the buildings do not suddenly disappear. Sometimes they end up vacant, as in large swaths of Detroit, but often they do not. When a city's manufacturing base shrinks and economic activity dies down, population loss is not as immediate or dramatic as one might expect, in large part because of the durability of urban housing.[7] Economic malaise does not mean that everyone picks up and leaves when an area goes into decline. While those with the best labor market prospects might flee a declining city, a substantial population of low-skilled workers stays behind, not only because of family ties, but also because the housing is affordable relative to areas with more jobs. The affordable working-class housing from the early nineteenth century can even attract new, poor migrants from other cities, regions, or countries. For instance, the affordable working-class housing of downtown Reading has attracted Hispanic immigrants, especially those escaping the economic crisis in Puerto Rico.

As John Updike put it, "Cities aren't like people; they live on and on, even though their reason for being where they are has gone downriver and out to sea."[8] The same applies to the parties of the left that emerged to represent their residents in an earlier era. They live on, even after their reason for "being where they are" has disappeared. The party that emerged as the champion of urban workers during the New Deal morphed into the party of postindustrial cities and towns.

The geographic and political legacy of nineteenth-century industrialization is not ancient history. It is crucial to understanding the geographic distribution of Democrats and Republicans today. Whether we examine state-level, county-level, or even precinct-level data, the relationship between historical manufacturing and contemporary Democratic voting is striking.

1920

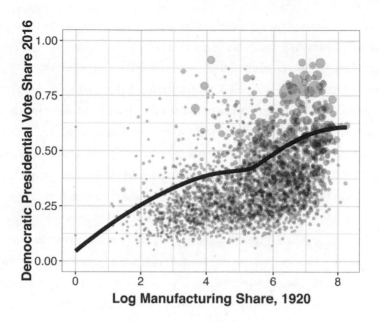

2010

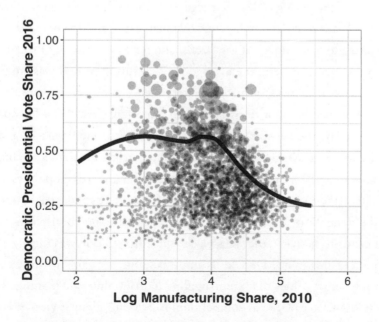

Figure 2.3: Hillary Clinton's 2016 Vote Share and County-Level Manufacturing Employment, 1920 Census versus 2010 Census

Support for Democrats is still overwhelmingly clustered in the dense parts of the manufacturing core that turned to FDR during the New Deal. But places where manufacturing thrives *today* are solidly Republican.

Figure 2.3 plots Hillary Clinton's share of the two-party vote in the 2016 presidential election on the vertical axis, against the share of the population employed in manufacturing on the horizontal axis. The top graph looks at manufacturing levels in the 1920 census—right around the apex of the golden age of American manufacturing—and the bottom graph looks at manufacturing levels today. Again, the size of the data markers corresponds to the size of the county. The overall relationship is captured by the solid line. The top graph, using the 1920 census data, reveals that to a striking extent, today's Democratic voting is correlated with manufacturing employment almost one hundred years ago.

The bottom graph, using data from the 2010 census, reveals a stunning transformation. While *historical* manufacturing is correlated with modern Democratic voting, *contemporary* manufacturing is correlated with modern Republican voting. This correlation between contemporary manufacturing and Republican voting did not emerge in 2016. In fact, the county-level association between contemporaneous manufacturing and Democratic voting had started to break down in the 1960s, and it was gone by the Reagan era.

In the New Deal era, the average manufacturing worker was employed in a very large firm in a large urban center, where labor relations were strained and support for the right to strike was an important part of the Democrats' appeal. Today, the average manufacturing worker is employed in a vastly smaller firm well outside the city center, where strikes are a foreign concept, and labor unions are only for schoolteachers and municipal employees.

Today, the Democrats are the party of urban, postindustrial America, and the Republicans receive more votes in exurban and rural places where manufacturing activity still takes place. The 2016 election was merely a continuation of this trend. Donald Trump made further gains in the exurban and rural communities that are struggling to maintain some manufacturing activity in the face of global competition. But taking a longer view, it is clear that the Democrats are still quite dominant in postindustrial areas where manufacturing activity came and went in earlier decades.

The county-level data only begin to convey the influence of the industrial revolution on today's political geography. The previous chapter explained that even in the days of the Reading Socialists, there was a stark urban-rural divide within Berks County itself—the left was dominant in the urban core but struggled to gain votes elsewhere—and that divide remains. Since the New Deal, Democrats have been dominant in Reading. In fact, their dominance has only grown. Yet one would not get that impression by looking at election results from Berks County, which has trended as a whole toward Republicans since the 1950s.

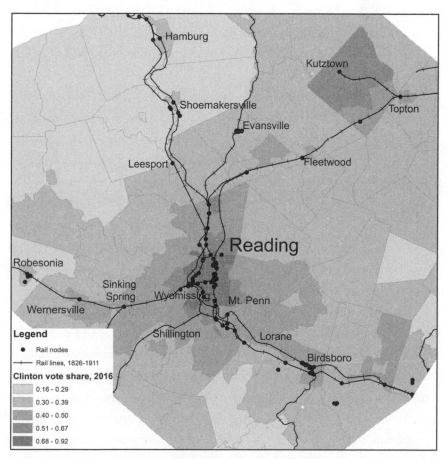

Figure 2.4: Historical Railroad Infrastructure and Hillary Clinton's 2016 Precinct-Level Vote Share, Berks County, Pennsylvania

Like many postindustrial cities, Reading has lost a great deal of its population. In 1930, Reading's population peaked at 111,000, which was around half of the total population of Berks County. However, Reading's population today is only 88,000, while the population of Berks County has grown to over 411,000, so that Reading now only accounts for 21 percent of its population. Urban leftists were outnumbered by rural conservatives in the days of James Maurer, but they are much more so today.

To visualize this, look at Figure 2.4, which presents a map of Hillary Clinton's 2016 vote share in the precincts of Berks County. While she only received 45 percent of the vote in Berks County, Clinton won an overwhelming victory in Reading—receiving around 80 percent of the vote in most of the city. However, the urban-rural divide in Berks County is quite striking. Donald Trump won small majorities in most of Reading's suburbs, and Clinton received less than 25 percent of the vote in the most sparsely populated parts of Berks County.

Reading is not an isolated example. Political pundits often use county-level data to conjecture that postindustrial towns in the manufacturing core have become Republican. The reality is more complex. Even in 2016, the majority of voters in old industrial towns like Scranton, Lancaster, and York still voted for the Democratic presidential candidate, Hillary Clinton. The same is true of places like Muncie and Terre Haute, Indiana, and Canton and Ashtabula, Ohio. However, as these towns lose population and exhibit lower levels of turnout, they are increasingly swallowed up by their very conservative exurban and rural peripheries, where turnout is quite high, which turns the county red as a whole.

The result of all this is a pattern of correlation between population density and Democratic voting that, like a fractal in the natural sciences or mathematics, repeats itself at every scale. In fact, as we move from states to counties to individual neighborhoods, the relationship only grows stronger. For instance, when we look at precinct-level data from recent elections, we see that there is a very strong correlation between population density and Democratic voting *within* most of Pennsylvania's counties. In 2008, this relationship was statistically significant in every single one of Pennsylvania's forty-two largest counties. In 2016, even though Hillary Clinton lost support in some smaller Pennsylvania towns, the precinct-level relationship between population density and Democratic voting held up in around two-thirds of these counties, and it was especially strong in those counties, like Berks and Lancaster, that had been most industrialized in the early twentieth century.

Something similar can be seen in counties around the country. In the United States as a whole, the precinct-level relationship between population density and Democratic voting today is strong everywhere, but it is especially pronounced in counties where manufacturing was most prevalent in the early twentieth century.[9] The Democrats are now an urban party throughout the United States, but this phenomenon is most pronounced in the old manufacturing core.

The electoral map of Berks County in Figure 2.4 communicates the extent to which Democratic voting still corresponds to the nineteenth-century geography of manufacturing. Democratic votes are clustered not only in the row houses and apartment buildings constructed for industrial workers around the turn of the century in downtown Reading, but also around the nineteenth-century rail hubs that mark the locations of the long-shuttered factories, mills, and workshops that once hugged the Philadelphia and Reading Railroad. The corners of Berks County that were most untouched by the industrial revolution are those that are most Republican today.

Similar precinct-level data for the rest of the United States tells a similar story. Figure 2.5 zooms out from Reading to the entire eastern side of Pennsylvania, where a number of medium-sized nineteenth-century industrial agglomerations are arranged in a ring around Philadelphia. Figure 2.6 pans to the west, including Pittsburgh, Cleveland, and their surroundings. Both maps also include the nineteenth-century rail infrastructure. In these maps, precinct boundaries have been smoothed out in order to illuminate areas of Democratic clustering along nineteenth-century rail lines.

Urban neighborhoods near the railroad tracks in each nineteenth-century industrial center vote overwhelmingly for Democratic presidential candidates today. Much of the industrialization in eastern Pennsylvania had origins in proximity to coal mines, and indeed, some of the areas of Democratic voting indicated in Figure 2.5 correspond almost exactly with maps

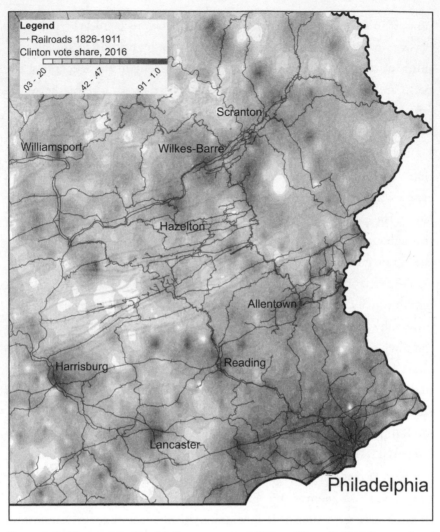

Figure 2.5: Historical Railroad Infrastructure and Hillary Clinton's 2016 Precinct-Level Vote Share, Eastern Pennsylvania

of anthracite and bituminous coalfields. The heavily industrialized corridor between Scranton and Wilkes-Barre is especially noteworthy.

Similar observations can be made throughout the United States. Democratic voting has persisted in former mining areas like the coal mines of southern Illinois, the lead mining region of western Wisconsin, the so-called lead belt of southeast Missouri, and the copper mining communities of northern Michigan. In each of these cases, the mining activity has almost

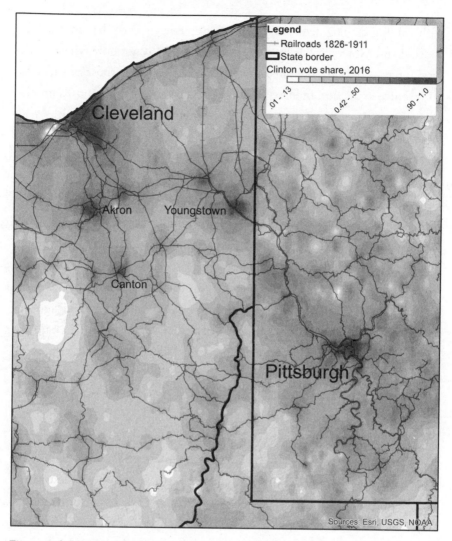

Figure 2.6: Historical Railroad Infrastructure and Hillary Clinton's 2016 Precinct-Level Vote Share, Western Pennsylvania and Eastern Ohio

or completely ceased—in some cases decades ago—yet Democratic voting in the early twenty-first century is substantially higher than in other neighboring towns and rural areas that did not develop an industrial working class, labor unions, and solidarity associated with strikes in the late nineteenth and early twentieth centuries.

Similar to the patterns we see in manufacturing, mining employment in the distant past correlates with contemporary Democratic voting rather than with mining employment today. As the Republican Party has increasingly courted rural voters, it has become closely associated not only with the sectoral interests of traditional manufacturing, but also with those of the natural resource extraction industry. In places like West Virginia and Kentucky, for instance, Republican candidates have courted mining communities with the promise of a return to coal.

Democrats are clustered not only in large nineteenth-century industrial cities and the smaller isolated agglomerations found at ports and rail junctions, but in some cases, in ribbon-like patterns along transportation corridors, where industrial activity and working-class neighborhoods gradually filled much of the space between major cities in the early twentieth century. The most obvious example is the so-called Acela corridor stretching from Washington, DC, to Boston, but veins of Democratic voting can also be seen along the rail corridors connecting cities like Detroit, Chicago, Indianapolis, Cincinnati, and their minor satellite agglomerations along the Illinois and Michigan Canal, and along rivers like the Ohio, Monongahela, Allegheny, and Mississippi. For instance, note the concentration of Democrats in the industrialized corridors along the three rivers snaking away from Pittsburgh to the north, south, and east.

Wherever several rail lines joined together during the nineteenth century, an industrial outpost was born. Each of these industrial towns joined the New Deal coalition in the 1930s, and each was still voting predominantly for Democrats in the early twenty-first century. In fact, nineteenth-century rail nodes are an excellent guide to the location of contemporary Democrats. Drawing on data from thousands of precincts, I have calculated the distance from the center of each precinct to the nearest rail node. Using data from Ohio and Pennsylvania, Figure 2.7 displays the relationship between Hillary Clinton's precinct-level vote share in 2016 and the distance to the nearest historical rail node. The graph shows that Clinton won solid majorities in precincts in very close proximity to rail nodes. In both states, at least half the population lives less than three kilometers from a nineteenth-century rail node. In both states, once a precinct is more than 2.5 kilometers from a rail node, the Democratic vote share dips below 50 percent. And once we are more than six kilometers from a rail node, it drops below 40 percent. In rural

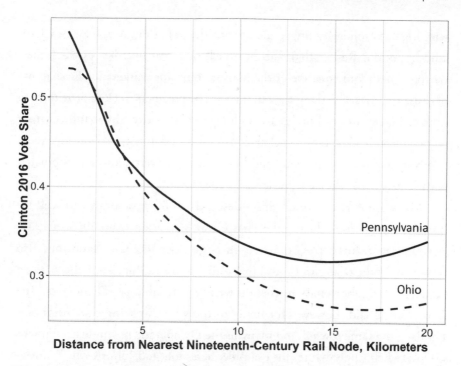

Figure 2.7: Distance to Historical Rail Nodes and Hillary Clinton's 2016 Precinct-Level Vote Share, Pennsylvania and Ohio

areas that are quite far from any early industrial outposts, it falls below 30 percent. These graphs look very similar in all of the other industrialized states.

Proximity to a rail node is correlated with a variety of other contemporary demographic factors that also predict Democratic voting—above all, population density itself. The built environment surrounding historical rail nodes often consists of working-class housing from the nineteenth and early twentieth centuries. Much of this housing was built during an era when workers in factories and warehouses did not own cars and lived within walking distance of work. These neighborhoods are still characterized by older, denser housing stock including apartment buildings, row houses, multifamily structures, and small, tightly packed single-family houses.

WHY SHOULD THE location of shuttered nineteenth-century factories and abandoned rail depots matter for twenty-first-century voting behavior? Does working-class solidarity linger, along with the pollution, in the air of Cleveland or Akron? Rather than the air, much of the answer lies in the bricks, mortar, wood, and concrete of the housing built for workers in the shadows of those factories and along the rail tracks. The precincts in close proximity to nineteenth-century rail nodes are no longer characterized by manufacturing employment. Today, they are characterized by a relatively old housing stock, relatively low median income, and high rates of poverty, and are populated with renters with relatively low levels of education.[10]

Many are African Americans—descendants of those drawn to seek industrial employment during the First Great Migration from 1916 to 1940. African Americans settled not only in large cities like Cleveland, but also in smaller industrial cities like Lima and Canton, Ohio. And the African American neighborhoods in these towns vote reliably for Democrats. The same can be said, however, for many of the white working-class neighborhoods in the same towns. And many of the Democratic postindustrial towns are overwhelmingly white, for example, Scranton and Johnstown, Pennsylvania, and Terre Haute and Muncie, Indiana. The precinct-level relationship between density and Democratic voting has still been very strong in recent elections in a number of counties that are almost completely white. This was especially true in the 2008 presidential election.

While much has changed, the Democrats are still the party of the New Deal and the Great Society, and their economic platform features greater levels of risk-sharing and redistribution, and more investment in public housing, health, and antipoverty programs. It is not surprising that the Democrats maintain support in relatively poor, postindustrial communities left behind by the exodus of manufacturing that took place in the middle of the twentieth century.

Indeed, whether conducting analysis at the level of counties or precincts, some of the relationship between population density and Democratic voting can be accounted for by factors like income, home ownership, and race. However, in multiple regressions that control for these factors, the impact of historical manufacturing, while diminished somewhat, does not disappear.[11] In other words, something more contributes to the nexus of historical manufacturing and left voting than just the presence of old housing, poor people, renters, minorities, and service sector workers.

This leaves open the possibility that Democratic voting in at least some of these communities is maintained in part through something that social scientists refer to as "neighborhood" or "contextual" effects. Perhaps the social milieu of daily life—the conversations and interactions with localized circles of contacts including family, coworkers, and friends—shapes and reinforces partisanship.[12]

Some political scientists believe that this type of dynamic can even link generations within the same community. They argue that partisanship, like religion, is passed from one generation to the next.[13] Let us return for a moment to the fictional conversation between Earl and Harry Angstrom discussed at the beginning of the chapter. Earl was a case study of what has come to be known as the "Michigan Model" of vote choice—named after a group of survey researchers at the University of Michigan in the 1950s who contributed to a classic book called *The American Voter*. Earl had built up a strong and stable psychological attachment to a political party, influenced in large part by conversations at the print shop and at working-class bars in his urban Reading social milieu. He interpreted world events through that partisan lens. For instance, speaking to Harry about the moon landing, he reasoned, "The pretty boys in the sky right now, Nixon'll hog the credit but it was the Democrats put 'em there, it's been the same story since I can remember, ever since Wilson—the Republicans don't do a thing for the little man." It is through such conversations between father and son that, according to the Michigan Model, partisan attachments are passed along from one generation to another. And indeed, at least initially, Harry adopts his father's socially conservative, patriotic, working-class identification with the party of the "little man."

It may seem far-fetched to imagine that the persistence of Democratic voting in postindustrial neighborhoods flows largely through party identification that is simply passed along from parents to children. In Reading, most of the German working class left the urban core decades ago, and were replaced by new Spanish-speaking migrants, so this explanation of partisan stability seems less plausible. However, many postindustrial towns have experienced far less upheaval than Reading. Some cities have avoided dramatic job and population loss, and they have maintained more stable populations. Muncie, Indiana, for instance, is roughly the same size today as in 1960. In towns with sufficient intergenerational residential stability, it is quite plausible that long-term partisan stability is explained in part by the passing of partisanship—just like religion—from one generation to the next.

Moreover, voting behavior can also be transmitted across generations via institutions that outlive individuals. Labor unions are undoubtedly a crucial part of this story. American labor unions were decimated by the departure of northern factories for the nonunion South. For instance, the unionization rate in Reading was down to 23 percent in the early 1980s, and by 2016, it was less than 9 percent.[14] This pattern is typical for a postindustrial town in the old manufacturing core.

However, the overall unionization rate misses something important about the enduring legacy of unions. In places where labor unions were strong among industrial workers in the New Deal, a class of professional union organizers emerged. Naturally, as private sector unions struggled, they turned their efforts to the public sector. Absent the competitive pressures of the private sector, they have had much more success sustaining themselves among employees of municipal and state governments, public hospitals, and school districts. In Reading, for example, 62 percent of public sector workers were unionized in 1983, and today the figure is up to 65 percent. Note that according to the Greater Reading Chamber of Commerce, three of the top six employers in Reading include the county government, the state government, and the school district—all unionized.

Very high rates of public sector unionization are a fascinating legacy of early industrialization. Communities with a history of early industrialization and labor organization in the nineteenth and early twentieth centuries do not have distinctive private sector unionization rates, but their rates of public sector unionization are quite striking. These rates exceed 50 percent not only in large postindustrial cities like Cleveland, Detroit, and Pittsburgh, but also in smaller postindustrial outposts like Akron, Canton, Battle Creek, East Stroudsburg, Erie, Johnstown, Williamsport, and the like. In all of these postindustrial cities and towns, the manufacturing and private sector unions are gone, but the public sector unions live on. As a result, the legacy of Democratic voting lives on as well.

The importance of early industrialization in driving contemporary public sector unionization can be seen clearly both across and within states. In contrast to high public sector unionization rates in the cities and towns of the original eastern and western manufacturing cores, rates are very low in the cities and towns of the South, Southwest, and Mountain West, where industrialization had not yet occurred during the era of labor mobilization, and strong unions were not around to push for state laws that made it possible for public sector unions to thrive. Variation within states is equally striking. While public sector unionization rates are close to zero in much of Alabama, there is a history of labor unrest and union activity in the city of Birmingham, dating to the days of coal mining and heavy industrialization in the nineteenth century. Birmingham's public sector unionization rate in 2016 was around 32 percent, which is extraordinarily high for the South.

Public sector union members throughout the United States vote overwhelmingly for Democrats. This is likely an important part of the explanation for the persistence of Democratic voting in postindustrial towns. Even small increases in population density associated with driving from a rural area to a small town in much of the United States—especially if it is a county seat such as Bloomsburg or Stroudsburg, Pennsylvania—are associated with significant increases in the Democratic vote share. In many cases these towns are populated with a substantial number of unionized municipal employees, nurses, and schoolteachers. In an environment where private sector employment opportunities are often scarce, the public sector can account for a surprisingly large part of the local workforce. That jump in Democratic voting associated with increased population density is especially large in counties with a history of early industrialization and the strong public sector unions that go along with it.

In addition to labor unions, another institution that might generate partisan stability over time is the city government itself. In many of the cities and towns that industrialized in the late nineteenth and early twentieth centuries and embraced the Democrats during the New Deal, the Democrats gained control over and became entrenched in the city government. In many of the cities of the eastern and western manufacturing cores, Democrats have dominated city councils and school boards for decades, such that the only competitive local elections are the Democratic primaries. In alliance with public sector unions, Democrats in many postindustrial cities and towns have had a substantial influence on the distribution of public sector jobs and contracts. Thus, the Democratic Party became the natural home for individuals with ambitions for local elected office, appointed positions, or stable public contracts.

THE LOCATION OF today's Democratic voters in the dense industrial neighborhoods of the past is fascinating, but it is much more than a historical curiosity. The problem of representation for the Democrats stems not from the location of their supporters in cities—or along railroad tracks—but from the fact that their voters are more geographically concentrated across electoral districts than Republicans. As discussed, this phenomenon has its roots not in the recent era of computer-assisted gerrymandering, but in the era of rapid urbanization and industrialization in the early twentieth century.

During the era of rapid urbanization in the early twentieth century, the US population as a whole became far more geographically concentrated in a relatively small number of urban counties. And as we have just seen, a strong relationship between urbanization and partisanship emerged during the New Deal in the industrialized states. When the Democrats became a party of urban workers, their geography quickly came to resemble that of workers' parties in early twentieth-century Europe, the United Kingdom, and Australia, in that their support was more geographically concentrated than that of their opponents. Initially this happened only in the industrialized states, but it eventually spread to the rest of the country.

To demonstrate this, I borrow an index that was originally developed to measure the geographic concentration of economic production.[15] Zero indicates that a party's presidential voters are evenly distributed across all counties, and at the other extreme, one means that all of the party's voters are concentrated in the smallest county.[16]

Let us begin once again with Pennsylvania. Figure 2.8 displays the county-level geographic concentration index for Democrats with a dashed line, and for Republicans with a solid line. It shows that Republican votes were more geographically concentrated than those of Democrats until 1928. Since then, Democratic presidential votes have been far more

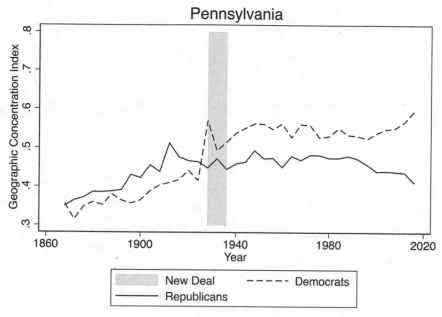

Figure 2.8: The County-Level Geographic Concentration of Democratic and Republican Presidential Votes, Pennsylvania

geographically concentrated than Republican votes. Moreover, the gap has only grown over time.

Figure 2.9 extends this analysis to the entire country, displaying separate graphs for each region.[17] It gives us a wealth of information about the evolution of US political geography. First, the upward trends for both Democrats and Republicans reflect that, as the overall population increases, rural areas lose population and urban areas grow, so that Americans across the country become increasingly concentrated in urban counties. However, there are stark regional differences in the timing of this process. In the early-industrializing areas—the northeastern manufacturing core and the West Coast—there was a sharp increase in population concentration from the industrial revolution until around World War II. Since then, population concentration has leveled off, as the cities of the Northeast started to lose population and spill over into neighboring counties; and the population in the West, while growing, also became more geographically dispersed. In other parts of the country, population growth and city growth came much later—especially in the Sun Belt—and the process of population

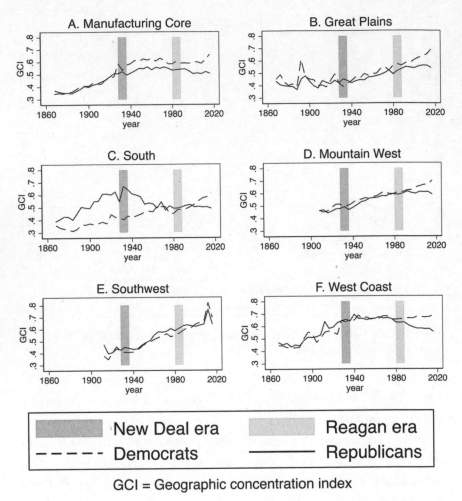

Figure 2.9: The County-Level Geographic Concentration of Democratic and Republican Presidential Votes, by Region

concentration experienced in the nineteenth and early twentieth centuries in manufacturing states is still happening.

The most striking story told by Figure 2.9 pertains to partisanship. In the northeastern manufacturing core, the geographic concentration of Democrats and Republicans increased in tandem from the time of the industrial revolution until the New Deal. Then quite suddenly, a gap opened up in 1928 when the Democrats began to mobilize urban workers. Democrats were increasingly concentrated in urban counties, while the geographic concentration of Republicans leveled off and then declined starting in the

Reagan era. A similar gap opened up in the Great Plains states at around the time of the New Deal—when Democrats started to cluster in places like Omaha and Kansas City—and it has persisted ever since, growing substantially wider since the Reagan era.

In the Mountain West and the West Coast, the partisan gap in geographic concentration did not emerge until around the time of the Reagan administration, when the trend toward the geographic concentration of Democrats continued apace, but Republican voting was increasingly geographically dispersed.

In the Southwest, the postwar population growth has been highly concentrated (mostly in Maricopa County, Arizona, and Clark County, Nevada), but in the sprawling new automobile-era cities of the Southwest, there is no nineteenth-century manufacturing core—no concentration of dense working-class housing built for earlier generations of factory workers. Accordingly, the relative concentration of Democrats is less pronounced than elsewhere.

Finally, the South displays an idiosyncratic pattern that was quite different from the rest of the country—until recently. Republicans were far more concentrated than the rural Southern Democrats until the New Deal, after which the geographic concentration of Republicans began its gradual, long-term decline. Democrats, on the other hand, have gradually become more geographically concentrated since the Civil War—a trend that was interrupted briefly for two elections when Jimmy Carter was the Democratic presidential nominee, but has gathered steam since the Reagan administration. The two lines on the graph crossed shortly after the Reagan era, signifying the completion of the process of Southern realignment, and now the relative geographic concentration of Democrats in the South is on par with the rest of the country.

All of this suggests a profound "nationalization" of American political geography. Although the process started in the manufacturing core, the Democrats have come to be more geographically concentrated across counties than Republicans almost everywhere but the Southwest.[18] The most important thing to notice in Figure 2.9 is the emergence of a gap between the solid and dashed lines in each region. The size of that gap—the relative concentration of Democrats—has converged across regions, such that it is now the same almost everywhere. This trend is illuminated in Figure 2.10, which plots the size of that gap over time, so that a positive number indicates that Democrats are more concentrated than Republicans. It shows that while the old manufacturing states led the way in the relative geographic concentration of Democrats, this phenomenon has experienced a remarkable convergence across regions since the Reagan era, and is now stronger than ever.

Keep in mind that the graphs in this chapter have been based on *counties*, the boundaries of which cannot be manipulated by politicians. Later, we will explore what happens when winner-take-all congressional and state legislative districts are drawn. This broad national trend toward the geographic concentration of Democrats is important for understanding the contemporary underrepresentation of Democrats in Congress and state legislatures.

In spite of this pronounced national trend, there is still considerable variation from one state to another. For instance, Democrats today are far more concentrated in Missouri than they are in Connecticut, and as a result,

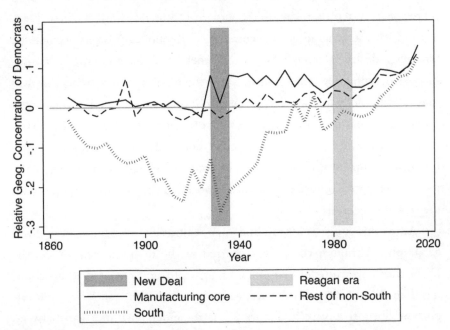

Figure 2.10: The Relative County-Level Concentration of Democrats, by Region

we will see in later chapters that the Democrats' representation problem is more pronounced in Missouri. Part of the explanation for contemporary cross-state variation in the representation of Democrats and Republicans lies in the era of heavy industry. First, Connecticut is more Democratic than Missouri today in large part because Connecticut was more industrialized in the early twentieth century. Second, Democrats today are more geographically concentrated—and hence more underrepresented—in Missouri than in Connecticut because early manufacturing was more concentrated in Missouri.

Recall from the previous chapter that nineteenth-century manufacturing was far more concentrated in some states than others. Mills and factories were not particularly concentrated in New England or South Carolina, in contrast to states like Missouri, where most of the early twentieth-century manufacturing activity took place in St. Louis and Kansas City, or states like Illinois (Cook County) and Maryland (Baltimore). In states where manufacturing employment was dispersed in the 1920s, Democrats are relatively less concentrated today. And in states where manufacturing was highly concentrated in the past, Democrats are highly concentrated today.

To see this, using the same index introduced above for voting, let us calculate the county-level geographic concentration of manufacturing employment in the 1920 census. This manufacturing concentration index appears on the horizontal axis of Figure 2.11, and the relative county-level concentration of Democrats in the 2016 presidential election appears on the vertical axis. In the lower left corner of the graph, the states where manufacturing employment was dispersed in the 1920s are the states where Democrats are relatively less concentrated today. This includes Republican states that had little early industrialization—like Arizona and South Carolina—and Democratic states—chiefly in New England—that were among the first to industrialize.

In the upper right corner of the graph, states where the industrial working class was highly concentrated in the early twentieth century are the same states where Democrats are highly concentrated today. In later chapters, we will see that these are the states where Democrats now struggle to transform votes into seats.

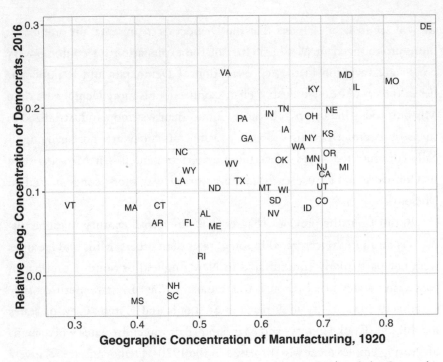

Figure 2.11: The Geographic Concentration of Democrats in 2016 and the Geographic Concentration of Manufacturing in 1920

LET US BRIEFLY review the lessons of this chapter. In the United States, Democrats are highly concentrated in cities—small and large—where an industrial working class emerged in the late nineteenth century. The correlation between population density and Democratic voting—and the relative geographic concentration of Democrats—emerged rather suddenly when the Democratic Party developed an economic platform geared toward attracting the votes of urban workers at around the time of the Great Depression. The urban-rural orientation of party competition that occurred much earlier in Europe, Britain, and Australia finally came to the United States. The economic, class-based political cleavage that emerged in the nineteenth century and crystallized during the New Deal is the origin of the urban-rural divide that characterizes politics in the United States today. The geography of early twentieth-century industrialization is instrumental in determining where Democrats cluster and win elections today.

But the long shadow of the industrial revolution is only the beginning of the story of urban-rural polarization. Today's intense urban-rural divide is based on much more than a class cleavage that has lingered since the New Deal. First of all, many of the dense places that vote for Democrats today are not poor. Many of their voters are in high tax brackets, relatively few make use of means-tested antipoverty programs, and public sector union members represent only a small portion of their voters. In fact, some of the most economically productive counties in the United States—San Francisco, California, and King County, Washington, for example—are among the most Democratic. There are similar pockets of well-healed, urban Labor voters in Britain and the Commonwealth countries. Moreover, some of today's very Democratic cities—like Santa Barbara, Palo Alto, or Ann Arbor—had rather little experience with early industrialization. The lingering legacy of the industrial revolution is a better explanation for Democratic voting in Scranton than in Santa Fe.

Second, in many of the time-series graphs shown above, it is clear that although the relative urban concentration of Democrats started with the New Deal, this phenomenon began a second period of explosive growth around 1980. A steadily increasing correlation between population density and Democratic voting was experienced in every region of the country—indeed in almost every individual state—since the Reagan administration. It is difficult to explain this sharp contemporary increase in the urban-rural voting divide with exclusive reference to the New Deal class cleavage.

An important part of the story remains to be told in the next chapter. The geographic cleavage that emerged in the 1930s was transformed and revitalized in recent decades when a new set of interests and issues were built onto the edifice of the New Deal partisan alignment.

CHAPTER 3

From Workers' Parties to Urban Parties

THE URBAN-RURAL ORIENTATION of political conflict in the United States today was seeded by turn-of-the-century industrialization and rooted in the political mobilization of urban workers within the Democratic Party. But to understand the full bloom of American urban-rural polarization in recent decades, we must understand the subsequent transformation of party competition, which now features a battle between different sectors of the economy and opposing cultural identities. These interests and identities are highly correlated with urban residence, and by politicizing them over the last four decades, the two American political parties have generated far more geographic polarization than occurred in the New Deal era. Moreover, as part of this process, urban-rural polarization has spread from the manufacturing core to almost every corner of the country.

Both American parties are internally heterogeneous, and struggle with constant in-fighting between different factions with different interests and regional bases of support. The previous chapter described how an urban faction within the Democratic Party was able to wrestle control of the presidential nomination in 1928. The Democrats' initial foothold in cities had more to do with ethnic patronage than class politics, but it soon became clear that of the two major parties, the Democrats were more likely to be receptive to the interests of urban labor than the Republicans. This episode showed how an initial geographic foothold for a political party can become self-perpetuating, even if the initial reason for the foothold fades away. When new urban interest groups arise and press their demands, incumbent politicians in the urban political party face strong incentives to respond. The same is true for rural interest groups and parties of the right.

This chapter explains how that same logic led the Democrats and Republicans to transform in two respects since the 1970s. First, the Democrats gradually became the champions of burgeoning urban interests in the globalized knowledge economy, and Republicans took up the causes of exurban and rural manufacturing, agriculture, and natural resource extraction. Second, the Democrats were led by a segment of their urban base to take up progressive positions on racial and social issues, while Republicans took up the conservative positions of their rural base. After the national parties became associated with clear positions on these issues, a new set of educated urban and suburban dwellers became Democrats, and a new set of exurban and rural traditionalists became Republicans. The long-term result was a ratchet effect, whereby urban-rural polarization built upon itself. Along the way, the meaning of "left" and "right" have changed to the point that by the time of the 2016 election, they are practically synonymous with "urban" and "nonurban."

MUCH OF THE action in this transformation took place in the period from the late 1970s to the present—the era of globalization, the rise of the knowledge economy, and the women's movement. But before delving into the political geography of that era in further detail, it is useful to situate these emergent economic and cultural differences between town and countryside in a broader historical perspective. Today's urban-rural battles are only the latest variations on a much older theme.[1] As Marx and Engels put it, "The antagonism between town and country begins with the transition from barbarism to civilization, from tribe to state, from locality to nation, and runs through the whole history of civilization to the present day."[2]

Prior to industrialization, there was a rivalry between the economic interests of towns—represented by burgeoning commercial elites like

Alexander Hamilton—and those of landed rural elites such as Thomas Jefferson, who wrote, "I think our governments will remain virtuous for many centuries; as long as they are chiefly agricultural. . . . When they get piled upon one another in large cities, as in Europe, they will become corrupt as in Europe." In the United States, the antipathy between urban and rural elites was heightened by the fact that part of the latter group depended on slave labor. The US Constitution was born of a fragile compromise between these factions. The framers of the US Constitution believed they had created a system that would be immune to partisan polarization. But within a few years, enmity had emerged between the urban, cosmopolitan Federalists and the rural Democratic-Republicans.

Even after the industrial revolution and the rise of working-class mobilization, the material and cultural bases for these deep conflicts have not gone away. On the contrary, they have transformed and intensified. The story of this chapter is that twentieth-century versions of these classic conflicts have been layered on top of the party systems that emerged from the industrial revolution. In majoritarian democracies like the United States, this means that the urban-rural polarization of voting behavior and political rhetoric—rather than fading with the decline of manufacturing and the traditional left-right cleavage—has been reinvigorated in recent decades. New manifestations of these old economic and cultural battles have become intertwined with one another in the late twentieth century and have perhaps reached their apotheosis in the age of Trump and Brexit.

At the heart of the antagonism between Hamilton and Jefferson was a battle about economic production and trade. In order to build a nascent manufacturing sector that could compete with more established manufacturers abroad, urban elites like Hamilton pushed for tariffs and other forms of protection from import competition, while rural elites like Jefferson pushed for free trade. In addition to slavery, the political battle between urban industrialists and rural free traders was often one of the most significant political divisions before the rise of class cleavage.[3]

The initial growth of cities came primarily from the simple fact that proximity was advantageous for some types of economic production. Many cities sprouted up and grew in the nineteenth century because they provided advantages in transportation and labor markets that facilitated manufacturing, which generated higher wages than agriculture. Naturally, the urban manufacturing sector developed a different set of policy preferences than the agricultural sector.

The economic advantages of colocation, and hence the economic and political interests of cities, have changed dramatically in the twentieth century throughout the industrialized world. While the advantages of urban colocation in manufacturing have fallen away and the geography of manufacturing has become far more dispersed, very powerful forces of agglomeration have taken hold in the so-called knowledge economy. The rise of new computer technology, software, and the growing importance of knowledge and innovation for economic prosperity has become known as the "third industrial revolution." Some of the cities left behind by manufacturers in the first half of the twentieth century have subsequently been reborn as hubs of innovation, and educated individuals now seek higher wages by clustering in cities that generate benefits from the externalities associated with the production of innovative technology. Residents of these knowledge-economy cities have developed distinctive preferences related to investments in education, scientific research, and global trade. The old battle between Hamilton and Jefferson has been rekindled but turned on its head: citizens of major urban centers now benefit tremendously from global trade, while many of the free trade skeptics reside in the parts of the periphery that have been most adversely affected by globalization and the third industrial revolution.

There is no philosophical or ideological reason why the party of the industrial working class—the party of Earl Angstrom and the "little man"—should become the party of Silicon Valley, science, and global free trade. If anything, one might argue that the classical liberal values associated with free trade, the free movement of people, and limited regulation cluster together in an ideologically coherent way. Based purely on political philosophy, perhaps it would have been more sensible for the party of the right to embrace global free trade, liberal immigration policies, comparative advantage, creative destruction, research universities, and innovation.

It was not political philosophy, but political geography, that led the Democrats in the United States, and labor parties elsewhere, to embrace the knowledge economy. Like the rise of the manufacturing economy before, the rise of the knowledge economy has been highly concentrated in cities. In cities like Boston, Toronto, London, and Sydney, which have managed to remake themselves as knowledge-economy centers, the nineteenth-century warehouses have been repurposed as high-end office space for technology firms, and the brick row houses and workers' cottages constructed for the industrial working class are now subjects of fierce bidding wars by well-compensated technology workers, specialized professionals, and venture capitalists.

As described in the previous chapter, from city hall to state legislatures to Congress, one legacy from the era of manufacturing and labor unions in these cities has been the dominant presence of Democrats in positions of political power. The same was true with labor parties in Australia and Britain. Parties of the left had become urban parties, and they gradually adapted to represent a new set of urban clients. As manufacturing workers were replaced by educated technology workers in the urban row houses of global cities like London, Sydney, New York, and San Francisco, the vote shares of the Democratic and Labor Parties only increased.

The period since the 1960s has seen dramatic changes not only in economic production, but also in social values. The upheavals of the industrial revolution also greatly enhanced a preexisting difference between the cultural and social outlooks of urban and rural dwellers. In the terms of classic sociologists, the new industrial cities of the late nineteenth century replaced traditional rural *Gemeinschaft* relations based on church and kinship with an impersonal, cosmopolitan *Gesellschaft*.[4] Extended ties to the family and church were torn asunder as people moved to cities, and workers were suddenly surrounded by an incredible diversity of religions, languages, and ways of life. Family structures too were altered by female participation in the labor force.

The urbanization spurred by the industrial revolution ushered in a growing challenge to traditional social hierarchies and the authority of religious leaders. Throughout the industrialized world, these challenges gathered strength in the turbulent 1960s and 1970s. The locus of these challenges was often in city centers and on college campuses. Likewise, the defenders of religion, traditionalism, and nationalism were located largely in exurbs and rural areas. In the United States, all of this was compounded by the spatial concentration of African Americans in city centers, and the ongoing suburbanization of whites. Battles over the women's movement, sexuality, and the role of religion quickly made their way into the arena of partisan electoral competition. Secularism, feminism, cultural pluralism, and antiwar rejections of nationalism were often bundled together with a host of other values including environmentalism.[5]

In European countries with proportional electoral systems, this led to the rise of new parties and repositioning among old parties. In the United States, with its winner-take-all districts and high barriers to entry for new political parties, this explosive new cleavage was folded into the existing party system. This led to a deepening of urban-rural political polarization.

As with globalization and the rise of the knowledge economy, there is no philosophical or ideological reason why the party of economic redistribution and risk-sharing should also be the party of reproductive choice and gay marriage. And there is no good reason why a platform of low taxes and limited economic regulation should be bundled together with heavier government regulation of matters related to sexuality.

Again, these odd bundles of policy platforms have their origins in political geography. Progressive social values took root in urban centers, where the Democrats had already become dominant. For American progressive activists seeking to shape the policy agenda, urban Democrats were the obvious choice. And since the only competitive elections in US cities are often the Democratic primaries, Democrats who ignored these activists increasingly did so at their own peril. Likewise, rural and exurban Republicans became the natural allies of religious traditionalists.

By the late 1980s, it had become clear that the Democrats were the party not only of the New Deal and civil rights, but also of abortion rights and a newly salient secular social agenda. As a result, many socially conservative exurban and rural voters—even those who grew up with a fondness for the New Deal and Great Society—started to vote for Republican candidates. And urban social progressives—even some who prefer lower taxes and smaller government—migrated to the Democratic Party. The net result was a striking increase in urban-rural polarization.

WITH THIS BIG picture in mind, let us now take a closer look at how the parties, pushed by their respective geographic bases, began to take distinctive economic and social positions in recent decades, and how this in turn affected the geography of voting.

Technological change, the decline of manufacturing, and the rise of the knowledge economy had a large impact on Pennsylvania, and on the fictional Angstrom family. Earl's steady union job as a linotype operator involved an old-fashioned, labor-intensive technology. Because of a switch to more efficient, modern print technology from Philadelphia, Harry Angstrom never got the union job his father tried to arrange for him. He was cast adrift and ended up selling used cars. Manufacturing jobs in Reading and similar cities disappeared, and working-class housing in the city center that had once been occupied by unionized manufacturing workers like Earl was taken over by poor renters working in the service sector, many of them African Americans and Hispanics. Just like the old occupants, however, these new occupants are Democrats.

Only a few miles away, Philadelphia has moved in a different direction. While many of its old working-class neighborhoods have suffered the same decline as downtown Reading, its urban core has been reinvented as a hub of innovation and high-paying knowledge-economy jobs. Young people have been attracted to the city center for its culture and nightlife, and property values are increasing. Some of the working-class housing of the nineteenth century, and sometimes even the factories and warehouses, have become desirable and expensive residential properties and offices. The new postindustrial occupants vote just as overwhelmingly for the party of the left as do the poor, minority service workers living nearby.

A recent study by Enrico Moretti summarizes research in economics, sociology, and urban studies that heralds the rise of a new class of globally connected knowledge-economy cities that have created immense wealth in the postindustrial era. Moretti divides American cities into three types. First, there are "brain hubs" like San Francisco and Boston, with a strong innovation sector and a well-educated labor force, where initial advantages in education and investment continue to grow over time. At the other extreme are cities like Reading, which have not made the postmanufacturing transition, and continue to lose jobs and residents. In the middle are cities that still hold out hope of becoming full-fledged knowledge-economy hubs.[6]

In many of these "brain hub" cities, large global firms have established their headquarters, and they outsource a series of highly specialized services, such as accounting, legal work, public relations, programming, and telecommunications.[7] Just as manufacturing activity led to so-called agglomeration economies in the past, these contemporary activities benefit from colocation in large cities. A growing body of research suggests that the knowledge economy—economic production based on innovation and creativity rather than physical goods—has an inherent tendency toward geographic agglomeration well beyond that of traditional manufacturing and services. As information technology has lowered the costs of communication, the importance of geographic proximity in the knowledge economy has only grown, as have the returns to successful new ideas, which can now spread quickly around the world. As with specialized manufacturing workers in an earlier era, it is advantageous to have a variety of skilled technology workers and employers in the same urban area. This is attractive to workers, who can change jobs easily, and for prospective employers, who can draw from a deep well of talent. This proximity also facilitates spin-offs and new ventures. Moreover, cities facilitate interactions that generate innovation. The interaction of many skilled people in cities makes it easier for each individual to improve her skills and innovation potential, and these interactions speed up the formation of new ideas and discoveries. This colocation has led to increasing returns for idea-producing cities like Boston and New York.[8]

Moretti argues that starting in the 1980s, American cities have become "increasingly defined by their residents' level of education."[9] While manufacturing activity has become increasingly geographically dispersed in exurbs and rural areas, where costs are often lower than in cities, the knowledge economy—along with new college graduates, specialized high-end service jobs, and ultimately wealth and prosperity—have become increasingly concentrated in high-education urban centers.

We can get a sense of the geographic concentration of the knowledge economy by looking at county-level indicators for educational attainment, patents, and employment in knowledge-intensive professions. In the 1970s, county-level rates of college graduation were only weakly correlated with population density. The share of college graduates in the population has grown everywhere over the subsequent forty years, but the growth has been far stronger in metropolitan counties. The gap between rural and metropolitan counties was around 10 percentage points in 1970, but by 2010, it had grown to over 20 percentage points. Far more than in the past, college graduates are now clustered in city centers, suburbs, and college towns.

A better way to appreciate the geographic concentration of innovation and the knowledge economy is to examine the geography of patents for inventions. In the period between 2000 and 2015, around three-quarters of all such patents issued in the United States originated in the forty most innovative metro areas. Over half of all patents originated in just fifteen metro areas. In fact, almost 30 percent of all patents came from five metro areas, and 15 percent of all patents originated in the San Francisco Bay Area alone.

We can also look at county-level data from the Bureau of Labor Statistics on employment in the knowledge economy, including in high-tech manufacturing and services, information technology, and knowledge-based professional services.[10] Although there are over three thousand counties in the United States, the top forty account for 41 percent of such knowledge-economy jobs, while accounting for less than 30 percent of the population.

The forces of agglomeration associated with the knowledge economy are creating strong incentives for high-skilled individuals to move to a relatively small set of successful cities. This "brain drain" leaves lower-skilled individuals behind in the rest of the country outside those knowledge-economy hubs, stuck with largely stagnant wages and living standards.

The trend toward geographic concentration in the knowledge economy has been well-documented by economists, but the implications for electoral politics have received little attention. To a remarkable extent, the Democratic Party has become dominant in these emergent innovation agglomerations, and as a result, its geographic concentration has increased since the rise of the knowledge economy.

Figure 3.1 captures this phenomenon in three different ways. The top graph considers the county-level relationship between education and partisanship.[11] The dotted line indicates that in 1976, counties with relatively

College Education and Democratic Voting

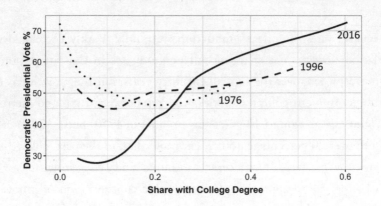

Patents and Democratic Voting

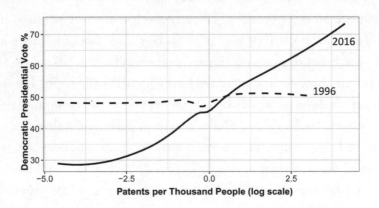

Knowledge Economy Employment and Democratic Voting

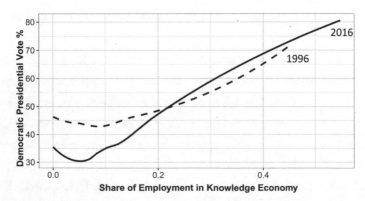

Figure 3.1: The Relationship between Knowledge-Economy Indicators and Democratic Vote Share in Presidential Elections, US Counties

large shares of college graduates were slightly more likely to vote for the *Republican* presidential candidate, Gerald Ford, than counties with few college graduates. The dashed line reveals that by 1996 the relationship had reversed, and counties with larger shares of college graduates were slightly more likely to vote for the *Democratic* candidate, Bill Clinton. And the solid line indicates that by 2016 the relationship between county-level education and Democratic presidential voting had become even stronger. In counties where 20 percent of the population had a college degree, Hillary Clinton's vote share in 2016 was around 42 percent, while in counties where half the population had a degree, it jumped to around 68 percent.

The next graph examines county-level innovation by counting up patents per one thousand people. Relying on patent data averaged over the 1990s, the dashed line reveals that there was not yet a discernable relationship between innovation and Democratic voting during the Clinton era. However, the relationship emerged rapidly in the 2000s, and there is now a striking relationship between patent activity and Democratic voting. In counties where patents are rarely or never filed, Hillary Clinton's vote share was around 30 percent, while it surpassed 70 percent in the counties that produce the most patents.

Finally, the story is similar when we look at employment in knowledge-economy jobs as a share of total employment. As with college education, on this indicator the correlation with Democratic voting had already emerged in the Clinton era, and it has subsequently strengthened. Hillary Clinton performed very poorly in the large number of counties with very little knowledge-economy employment, but she received large majorities in a relatively small number of large, knowledge-intensive counties.

What explains the striking affinity between education, innovation, and Democratic voting in metropolitan areas that have been lucky enough to become magnets for technology investment? First of all, most of these new brain hubs, including New York, San Francisco, Chicago, Boston, and Seattle, emerged in cities with a strong manufacturing history, and hence a Democratic Party that was already dominant by the 1980s. Many knowledge-economy firms developed distinctive policy preferences in an environment where the mayor and city council, as well as state and federal legislative representatives—and often governors—were Democrats. It was natural that they would turn to Democrats as potential policy advocates.

Moreover, the affinity between the Democratic Party and science-based researchers can perhaps be traced all the way back to FDR, who substantially increased funding for scientific research at major universities. Many of the university-based technological innovations that lit the fuse for localized explosions of knowledge-economy employment were associated with government-funded projects, often involving the military. Foreshadowing the campaign strategies of Bill Clinton, Barack Obama, and Hillary Clinton, George McGovern had already started to target engineers and scientists as potential allies in 1972. An important moment in the burgeoning courtship between the Democratic Party and the knowledge-economy sector was the governorship of Michael Dukakis in Massachusetts in the 1980s, which focused on brokering deals between Boston-based universities, high-tech companies, and venture capitalists as part of the so-called Massachusetts miracle.[12]

Not all of the knowledge-economy clusters emerged in cities like Boston, which had been dominated by nineteenth-century manufacturing. Some took off in communities—like Palo Alto, San Diego, and Austin—with far less manufacturing and labor history, and hence a less dominant Democratic Party. Yet in these communities as well, the Democratic vote share eventually conformed to the trend established in cities like Boston, continuing to rise along with knowledge-economy employment since the 1980s.

As the knowledge-economy sector came together, its leaders developed a distinctive bundle of policy preferences, and one by one, metropolitan Democratic incumbents in local, state, and federal government started to push the items on this agenda. They worked with technology firms on issues related to immigration and on visas for technology workers; they pushed to strengthen patent protections for pharmaceutical, financial, and information technology companies; and to gain copyright protections for entertainment studios, and intellectual property protections for internet and software firms. They became advocates for increased federal education funding, especially through universities, and pushed for investments in science and technology. In the Clinton era, some in the Democratic Party even embraced financial market deregulation and reduced capital gains taxes.

Finally, at least at the level of the presidency and among metropolitan incumbents, Democrats embraced free trade deals, like the Trans-Pacific Partnership (TPP), that seemed explicitly geared to help technology firms in the urban knowledge hubs, perhaps at the expense of increasingly low-skill manufacturing outside urban centers. The national reputations of the parties were not very distinctive on issues of free trade and globalization in the 1990s and early 2000s. In fact, Republicans in Congress were more supportive of the North American Free Trade Agreement (NAFTA) than Democrats, and the same was true of the ill-fated TPP agreement. But by 2016, the full embrace by Barack Obama—and then Hillary Clinton—of Silicon Valley, free trade, globalization, and the knowledge economy had become part of the Democratic Party's national brand. Campaign finance data indicate that donations from knowledge-intensive industries and occupations, including internet and computing services, pharmaceuticals, media, and academia flow disproportionately to Democrats, while donations from traditional industries like construction, mining, agriculture, and banking flow to Republicans.[13]

Even in recent years, in the absence of strong stances by its presidential candidates, the Republican Party had not developed a coherent alternative position to the Democrats on issues related to free trade and globalization. That changed dramatically with the nomination of Donald Trump in 2016, which suddenly connected the Republican label to a package of policies that are explicitly opposed to globalization, expansion of international trade, and increasing investments in education and scientific research. The growing political cleavage based on economic sectors—pitting the urban (and suburban) knowledge economy against the exurban and rural manufacturing and natural resource sectors—crystallized with the Trump nomination. As a result, the already strong aggregate relationship between education, knowledge-economy employment, and Democratic voting grew even stronger in 2016. While Republicans gained support in exurban and rural areas struggling to maintain manufacturing employment, the Democrats gained support in higher-density areas with significant knowledge-economy employment.

All of this goes a long way toward explaining the evolution of the relationship between population density and Democratic voting described in the previous chapter. Since the 1980s, the economic geography of the

United States has changed in a profound way, and a growing industry and education divide has contributed to the increasing geographic concentration of Democrats. Democrats are clustered not only in impoverished postmanufacturing city centers like Reading, but increasingly in growing, affluent city centers like Seattle and San Francisco, as well as in smaller knowledge-economy hubs like Durham and Ann Arbor.

Something similar is happening in countries around the world. Highly educated professionals are clustering in dynamic knowledge-based cities, and the periphery is left with lower-skilled workers who are increasingly feeling left behind by the global economy. Speaking at the World Economic Forum in Davos, Switzerland, in January 2018, Prime Minister Paolo Gentiloni of Italy warned of the danger of a "split between a cosmopolitan digital elite and an army of precarious and underpaid local workers."[14] In majoritarian countries like the United States, Canada, Australia, and Britain, that split has mapped onto the party system from the industrial era in a rather surprising way: the mainstream parties of the left—because of their urban roots—have become the parties of the cosmopolitan digital elite.

THIS IS A fascinating transformation, but there is much more to the political inclinations of the young city dwellers flocking to San Francisco, Boston, and Seattle than policy preferences about intellectual property, free trade agreements, and H1B visas. This population also has distinctive "cosmopolitan" preferences on issues like abortion, gay marriage, race, and social diversity. By no means is this a new or uniquely American story. Cities have always attracted diverse populations. Over the course of the twentieth century, urban populations became far more secular than denizens of the surrounding rural areas. Urban churches have closed their doors while rural and exurban congregations thrive. Universities, rental housing, amenities, and employment opportunities attract an influx of young people to successful cities, which have become increasingly important as centers not only of economic production and employment, but also of consumption.[15] Individuals with a desire for diversity and openness to new experiences are drawn to the bright lights and bustle of city centers.

Many others—including John Updike's socially conservative Rabbit Angstrom—find the secularism and racial and ethnic diversity of the city unsettling and the anonymity demoralizing. Many find cities to be chaotic, dirty, and unappealing, preferring instead the open spaces, solitude, homogeneity, and traditionalism of exurbs, small towns, and rural areas. The initial decision to leave the farm during the industrial revolution was often a conscious choice that reflected some basic aspects of the individual's tolerance for risk and openness to new experiences. Likewise, the density of one's living environment today is often a choice—especially among higher-income individuals—reflecting basic values and preferences.

Few would argue with the observation that for a variety of reasons, urban residents tend to have different social values and preferences than rural dwellers. These attitudinal differences between urban cosmopolitans and rural traditionalists have gradually come to be connected to party competition in Western democracies over the course of the twentieth century. In Europe, hostility to the church and an aggressive secular agenda were built into the platforms of socialist parties from their inception, and religiosity has long been a correlate of votes for conservative parties. After World War II, parties took positions on such issues as the role of women, abortion rights, and homosexuality. Voters' opinions on these issues are in large part driven by church attendance and religiosity, which are in turn negatively correlated with population density.

As with science and technology policy, the American parties' platforms on these issues were inchoate at the beginning of the turbulent 1960s. By the end of the Reagan era, however, the Republican Party had adopted much of the policy agenda of Evangelical leaders like Jerry Falwell Jr., and the party label was clearly linked with Evangelical Christianity and the anti-abortion movement. The Democratic Party label had become linked with the women's movement and a bundle of secular issue positions related to abortion, homosexuality, and prayer in schools.

This alignment of party platforms in the 1970s and 1980s is fundamentally a story about political geography. Like many stories in American politics, it begins with race: it is difficult to understand the evolution of the parties' platforms on religion and social issues without first understanding the evolution of their platforms related to race and civil rights. From 1916 to World War II, the First Great Migration brought large numbers of African Americans to the cities of the manufacturing core. As low-wage manufacturing workers, their interests were often aligned with the New Deal, and even while the Democrats maintained themselves as the party of racial oppression in the South, African Americans started to become valuable allies of the Democrats in the manufacturing cities of the North.

By the late 1930s, urban Democrats had started to respond to pressure from their constituents, including the Congress of Industrial Organizations (CIO), to support civil rights.[16] This bottom-up urban pressure to transform the Democratic Party on issues of race played out over a long period of time, and of course faced stiff resistance from rural Southern Democrats. The National Democratic Party did not come to embrace civil rights until the 1960s. This set the long process of southern partisan realignment into motion, and as we saw in the previous chapter, there was an accompanying regional convergence in urban-rural polarization.

The early stages of the racial realignment also laid the foundation for the politicization of religion in the subsequent decades. Some Evangelical leaders who began to organize around the issue of abortion after the 1973 *Roe v. Wade* decision had already mobilized against government interference in racially segregated Christian schools in the South. Despite the fact that Democrat Jimmy Carter was an Evangelical, by the early 1980s it was clear that largely exurban and rural white Evangelicals would advance their cause via the Republican Party rather than through the Democrats, who, along with the evolution of a liberal platform on racial integration, had already begun the process of accommodating urban social progressives. While the parties' platforms and reputations on social issues had previously been unclear, they took shape in the 1970s.

When this happened, conservative Christianity and accompanying conservative social views were already highly correlated with population density. That is, urban areas were substantially more progressive than rural areas even before the parties took distinctive positions on these issues. To see this, it is useful to examine survey data. In joint work with Aina Gallego, I have selected a series of questions about abortion, homosexuality, and other social issues from the General Social Survey (GSS), which were asked at various times from the 1970s to the present. We used these questions to generate a scale measuring how liberal or conservative each respondent is on this set of social issues. We have done the same thing for classic economic issues related to the role of government in the economy. These scales can be interpreted from left to right, in that people who provide consistently progressive responses receive a low score on our scale, and those with the most conservative responses receive a high score. The scales have a mean of zero and standard deviation of one.

The GSS contains some useful information about the residential context of each respondent. Figure 3.2 plots the averages of the scales for all respondents falling into each of several spatial categories, tracking changes over time. First, it is clear that the geographic differences in economic preferences that generated the divergence between urban and rural voting behavior in the era of urban manufacturing and the New Deal are still alive, and well. There is a huge gap between the economic preferences of those

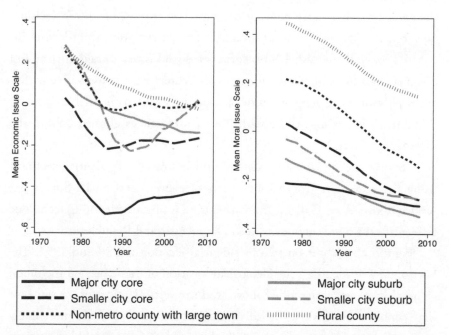

Figure 3.2: The Evolution of American Economic and Moral Issue Preferences over Time, by Geographic Location, General Social Survey

residing in the core of large cities and those residing in their suburbs. Voters in the core of smaller cities are also more liberal than those living in their suburbs. And the most economically conservative voters are those living in rural areas.[17]

The right-hand panel in Figure 3.2 shows that residents of cities—large and small—as well as of their suburbs, are substantially more liberal on moral issues than are residents of nonmetropolitan areas. In fact, there has been an interesting convergence over time, such that residents of smaller cities as well as of suburbs have come to resemble residents of large central cities on this dimension. While growing tolerance on issues like homosexuality and women's rights can be seen among survey respondents in each geographic area, nonmetropolitan counties and especially rural areas are still substantially more conservative than cities and their suburbs.

Interestingly, Figure 3.2 demonstrates that during the era of growing polarization in American politics over the last forty years, the basic policy orientations of individual voters in urban, suburban, and rural America have not grown further apart, even on issues related to moral values. If anything, their positions may have converged a bit. After the *Roe v. Wade* decision, however, the parties' *platforms* diverged. The parties went from having incoherent or indistinguishable platforms on social issues to taking clear and divergent positions on these salient issues. Voters with conservative preferences on moral and religious issues increasingly sorted themselves into the Republican Party, and those with liberal preferences aligned behind the Democratic Party.[18]

To visualize the changing ideological basis of US presidential elections, using the same data from various years of the General Social Survey described above, Aina Gallego and I have used a machine learning technique to identify the dividing line between Democratic and Republican voters.[19]

Figure 3.3 focuses on two presidential elections: 1980 and 1992. The horizontal axis identifies the ideological location of each voter on the moral values dimension, as described above, and the vertical axis does the same for the economic dimension. The ideological coordinates of those most likely to vote for the Democratic presidential candidate fall in the black region, and those most likely to vote for the Republican candidate are in the white

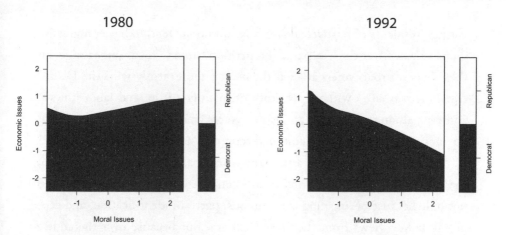

Figure 3.3: The Shifting Divide between Democrats and Republicans on Economic versus Moral Issue Preferences

region. If the dividing line between Democrats and Republicans were exclusively about economics, we would expect to see a horizontal line dividing the black and white areas. If it were exclusively about moral values, we would expect to see a vertical line.

The first graph is for the 1980 election, when Ronald Reagan challenged Jimmy Carter, and the second is for the 1992 election, when Bill Clinton challenged George H. W. Bush. We find that before the Reagan era, the dividing line between Democrats and Republicans was essentially a flat horizontal line. That is, Democratic and Republican voters were notable for their different economic policy preferences, but their preferences on moral values issues were indistinguishable. Twelve years later, however, after Reagan's embrace of the Evangelical movement, the dividing line had shifted to become diagonal, and it has remained so ever since. By the 1990s, economic moderates—and even those with center-left economic preferences—were more likely to vote for the Republican candidate if they also had conservative preferences on issues like gay rights and abortion. And those with liberal preferences on these issues were more likely to vote for Democrats. The latter were concentrated in cities and, increasingly, their suburbs. The former were mostly located outside of the large cities.

As with the rise of the knowledge economy, the net result was a gradual growth in the correlation between population density and Democratic voting. Residents of relatively dense neighborhoods tend to have progressive social values. Over time, as party competition came to focus increasingly on these issues, urban voters aligned themselves more firmly with the Democrats, even in cities without a history of manufacturing and labor unions, and even among relatively high-income voters whose class interests were not obviously aligned with the traditional economic agenda of the left.

In sum, after becoming a partially urban party during the New Deal, the Democrats maintained and even strengthened their support in cities not only because of lingering labor unions, partisan identification, and economic policy views from the New Deal era, but because over the course of the last century, the Democrats have become associated with a variety of additional urban issues ranging from civil rights, to investments in science and education, to gay marriage and abortion rights. When Americans speak of "the left," they now have in mind a bundle of policies not only about taxation and redistribution, but also about urban infrastructure, race, gender, immigration, trade, and support for the knowledge economy. The Democrats, quite simply, have become a heterogeneous coalition of urban interests, many of which would be quite unrecognizable to Earl Angstrom and other New Deal Democrats.

Along the way, they have developed a clear reputation as an urban party. Even though votes for Democratic *presidential* candidates had been relatively concentrated in cities since the New Deal, in the 1960s and 1970s, the party labels were still quite fluid, leaving plenty of room for *congressional* candidates to stake out their own positions. This was especially valuable for Democratic candidates running in congressional districts outside of city centers. Prior to the slow evolution of party platforms and reputations that started in the 1980s, in the era of denationalized political competition,[20] Democratic congressional candidates could credibly craft their own distinctive platforms in support of local industries, including manufacturing, farming, and natural resource extraction. Since the party's national platform was still inchoate, they could espouse racial, social, and cultural views that were consistent even with very rural constituents. For decades in the middle of the twentieth century—now seen in the rearview mirror as a golden era of bipartisanship—Democratic congressional candidates were able to win in nonurban districts that were carried by Republican presidential candidates, and they often voted for legislative proposals favored by their Republican colleagues.

However, as the party's platform has evolved and its urban reputation has solidified, it has become far more difficult for such candidates to escape the urban tint of their party label. Some scholars argue that this urban-rural partisan divide now goes beyond mere interests or policy preferences. As individuals with similar demographic characteristics and issue preferences sort into the same party, some might come to experience partisanship as a form of social identity that provokes increasing feelings of anger and mistrust of the opposite party.[21] In a study of rural Wisconsin, Kathy Cramer reports a confluence of partisan and place-based rural identity, whereby partisanship is driven as much by resentment of urban elites as by specific policy preferences.[22]

As a result of all this, split-ticket voting has declined. As urban-rural polarization has increased, so has the correlation between presidential and congressional voting. Nonurban districts that were once represented by "boll weevils," "blue dogs," and other socially conservative Democrats are now represented by Republicans. As a result, roll-call votes in Congress have also become polarized: Democratic and Republican members of Congress rarely vote across party lines.[23]

IN SHORT, URBAN-RURAL polarization in the United States has come to look more similar to that in Britain and in some of its other former colonies. If anything, the original New Deal Democratic alliance with rural Southern segregationists and the subsequent decades of party platform flexibility only delayed the full-fledged emergence of urban-rural political polarization in the United States relative to its peers. In most other industrialized countries with winner-take-all electoral systems, the urban concentration of the left emerged on a national scale much earlier. Labor parties gained strength among urban workers during the era of heavy industry in Britain, New Zealand, and Australia. Their support has been highly concentrated in dense, urban working-class enclaves since the industrial revolution. The core support for the New Democratic Party in Canada is now also overwhelmingly urban.

In these parliamentary democracies, party discipline and highly polarized voting behavior in the legislature have always been the norm. It has never been possible for individual Labor candidates to craft their own idiosyncratic platforms, and no one expects Conservative or Labor members of parliament to vote across party lines. The treasured American notion of bipartisanship is an outgrowth of our unique presidential system, which frequently produces divided government, and thus often requires cross-party deals to fulfill basic functions. In the current era of urban-rural polarization, these deals are now more difficult to cut, and the voting behavior of legislators is beginning to look more similar to that in a parliamentary democracy.

Today, the United States and its parliamentary peers have a basic geographic structure of political competition and representation that is strikingly similar. Let us take a brief look at England and Wales, where Labour's support map today is essentially a map of industrialization and city growth during the period of rapid industrialization in the nineteenth century. Figure 3.4 maps Labour's vote share in the 2015 parliamentary election, focusing on the level of parliamentary constituencies. The map also represents the locations of early nineteenth-century coal mines and railroads,[24] demonstrating that in most of England and Wales, cities grew as a result of nineteenth-century industrial activity—much of which took place in proximity to coal mines—and Labour support is overwhelmingly concentrated in the modern working-class neighborhoods of those old manufacturing cities. This includes large cities like Manchester and Birmingham, and smaller cities like Barnsley. Labour support is still clearly concentrated along the rail network that emerged to support nineteenth-century industrialization.

Maps of Canada and Australia are strikingly similar. Votes for the Canadian NDP and Australian Labor Party today are concentrated in the city centers along the canals, lakeshores, coastlines, and rail networks of the nineteenth century, and in areas with a history of mining.

As in the United States, the departure of manufacturing from city centers has left poverty, low-wage service sector employment, and strong

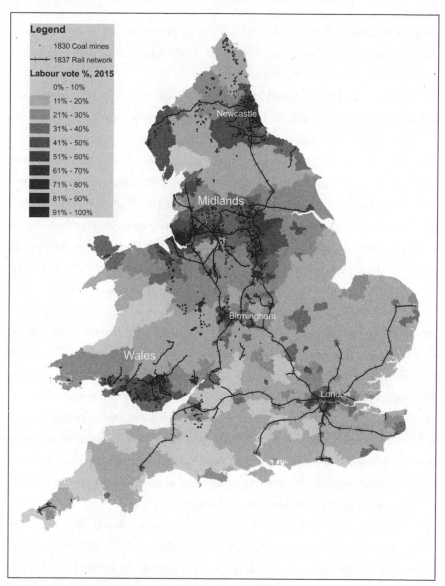

Figure 3.4: The Geography of 2015 Labour Support and the Location of Historical Railroads and Coal Mines

demands for government assistance in many postindustrial cities, like those of the British North, Midlands, and Wales. The same is true of southern Ontario and the Maritimes in Canada. Just like Reading, Cleveland, and Akron, struggling urban neighborhoods in old industrial cities like Burnley, England, and Sudbury, Ontario, still vote very reliably for the left. In many cases, the dense, affordable housing units in proximity to early twentieth-century factories are now home to racial and ethnic minorities and immigrants who vote reliably for the left.

However, as in the United States, the story of contemporary urban-rural polarization in Britain and its former colonies is not merely a story of lingering class-based attachments. In another group of cities, manufacturing has given way to knowledge-economy employment where strong universities and associated technology firms have facilitated rebirth. Examples include London, Manchester, Cambridge, and Oxford. Or think of Toronto, Ottawa, and Waterloo; Sydney and Melbourne; Wellington and Auckland. As in the United States, left parties were already dominant in these places, and candidates for these parties came to embrace the new urban knowledge economy. As part of the rebranding as "New Labor" in Britain and Australasia, they became advocates for investments in urban infrastructure, technology, and universities, and adopted liberal approaches to immigration and free trade. In the United Kingdom, Labour became the champions of the European Union. And as with the Democrats in the United States, left parties in Britain and its former colonies became associated with a set of progressive, cosmopolitan social values. As working-class voters were priced out of central urban neighborhoods of London, Sydney, and other successful cities and a new set of well-compensated young professionals moved in, vote shares of labor parties remained remarkably constant and sometimes even increased.

In sum, these countries went through similar economic and cultural transformations as the United States during the post–World War II period. They experienced the decline of urban manufacturing and the rise of the urban knowledge economy. They also experienced the cultural and social upheavals of the 1960s and 1970s, and the growth of political contestation around a new class of social issues. In these countries as well, the parties that had built strength in cities during the industrial era came to embrace a new set of interests and issues. This had the effect of perpetuating, and in the cases of the United Kingdom and Canada, increasing the level of urban-rural partisan polarization.[25]

In each of these countries, the overall correlation between population density and left voting is broadly similar to that in the United States in the early twenty-first century. To place the United States in direct comparative perspective, Figure 3.5 displays data on the relationship between population density and the vote share of the left for recent national elections in several industrialized countries with winner-take-all electoral districts.[26] Each dot is a national-level electoral district.

The United States is clearly not unique. At the beginning of the twenty-first century, support for parties of the left is highly concentrated in dense urban districts in Britain and its industrialized former colonies. The relationship between population density and left voting is just as strong in Britain as in the United States. As with the Democrats, most of the dense, overwhelmingly Labour districts are those with a historical legacy of working-class housing and labor unions dating back to the era of heavy industry. But some are also in urban neighborhoods that can be classified as "brain hubs"[27] or "creative class"[28] enclaves. The same thing is true of Labor voting

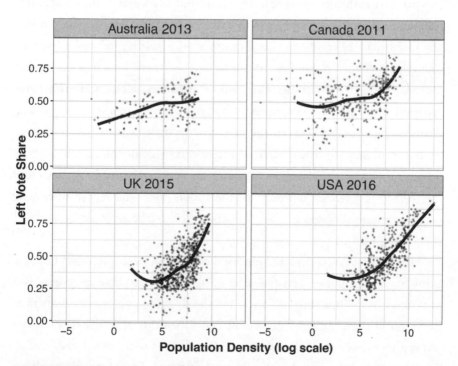

Figure 3.5: Population Density and Left Voting across Legislative Districts in Four Majoritarian Democracies

in Australia, which is concentrated not only in old industrial towns like Wollongong, but also in the gentrifying central cities of Sydney and Melbourne.

Even in Canada, with its diversity of party systems across provinces and a much-delayed nationalization of electoral competition, it is clear that left voting today is highly concentrated in urban districts. In fact, the relationship is especially pronounced *within* provinces.[29] This is true not only in heavily industrialized Ontario and Quebec, but also in the west. For instance, although the rural peripheries of Manitoba, Saskatchewan, and Alberta vote overwhelmingly for the right, left parties routinely receive large majorities in downtown Winnipeg, Regina, and Edmonton. This is reminiscent of the United States, where Republicans now win large overall majorities in rural western states like Idaho and Utah, while Democrats win concentrated majorities in cities like Salt Lake City and Boise.

IN SUM, THE transformation of left parties from advocates of the nineteenth-century industrial working class to catchall urban parties in the modern era is a broad phenomenon in countries with winner-take-all districts. The heterogeneous mix of urban interests represented by left parties today includes the urban working poor, union members, racial and ethnic minorities, immigrants, educated knowledge-economy workers, and young cosmopolitan progressives. In the early twenty-first century, national electoral competition in industrialized majoritarian democracies has become a battle that pits cities against the exurban and rural periphery. A victory for the left is a victory not only for the urban poor who rely most heavily on government services, but also for universities, laboratory scientists, and social progressives.

This spatial arrangement of electoral competition has profound implications for representation and policy making when legislative representatives are chosen via winner-take-all districts. The drawing of electoral districts in and around cities matters a great deal, but to see this, it is first necessary to paint a picture of the political geography of cities with finer brushstrokes. Democrats in the United States—and left voters in other industrialized societies—are concentrated not only in urban areas in general, but in specific neighborhoods within cities. At the same time that the parties' platforms and reputations were shifting in the postwar period, large population shifts were also taking place. Rural areas were losing population. Many urban areas were also experiencing population loss as they deindustrialized. Suburban and exurban areas were growing rapidly. As people moved within metropolitan areas, and across regions, the resulting settlement patterns created a fascinating distribution of political behavior *within* modern cities. By explaining these patterns, the next chapter puts into place the last piece of the puzzle needed to understand the contemporary political underrepresentation of urban parties.

CHAPTER 4

Urban Form and Voting

DEMOCRATS AND LABOR voters are concentrated not only in metropolitan areas, but they have also become highly concentrated *within* those metropolitan areas. Let us return once again to John Updike's fictionalized postindustrial Reading. The row houses of Harry Angstrom's youth, "built solid by German workingmen's savings and loan associations," were taken over by Poles and Italians, and then later by African Americans, Puerto Ricans, and other Spanish-speaking migrants. As a young adult, Harry bought a car and moved to the suburbs. After achieving success in business, he eventually joined a country club, only occasionally venturing into the city center, which he viewed with increasing disdain and detachment. Along the way, his fondness for the party of the New Deal faded. He rejected his father's partisanship and started voting for Republican presidential candidates.

The story of industrial decline, poverty, immigration, and suburbanization is familiar throughout the United States. Updike's description of Reading resonates in many postindustrial places: "These acres of dead railroad track and car shops and stockpiled wheels and empty boxcars stick in the heart of the city like a great rusting dagger. All this had been cast up in the last century by what now seem giants, in an explosion of iron and brick still preserved intact in this city where the sole new buildings are funeral parlors and government offices."[1]

The urban cores of US cities have been in decline for decades, and more than half of the American population now lives in a suburb. The process of urban decline and suburbanization created a striking pattern of political geography, not just in Reading, but also in cities around the United States and around the industrialized world. In many of the urban neighborhoods where dense housing was constructed for industrial workers in an earlier era, the population now consists of poor people, the young, immigrants, and racial minorities. Many are renters with unstable residential histories. These groups are highly concentrated within cities, and they tend to display (1) high rates of voting for parties of the left, and (2) relatively low voter turnout. These urban voters are often surrounded by a ring of politically heterogeneous suburbs, which give way to exurban and rural areas that provide comfortable majorities for the right.

This basic theme also displays some interesting variations from one metropolitan area to another. For instance, large Democratic majorities spill out even into the distant exurbs in some large American cities—especially those with a large knowledge-economy sector—whereas the suburban transition from Democratic to Republican is sharper in smaller postmanufacturing cities like Reading. The transition from Democratic urban core to Republican periphery is also less dramatic in some newer, auto-focused cities, like Orlando, that developed after the era of heavy industry and dense working-class housing.

Largely due to the nature and timing of industrialization, Democratic urban clusters are also arranged in different ways within and across US states. Some states are characterized by a single, gigantic Democratic enclave, or a hierarchy of such enclaves. Some states never developed a large city, and as a result, their Democrats are more dispersed across smaller enclaves. Sometimes the enclaves blend together into corridors.

Remarkably similar spatial patterns of voting behavior can be found in the cities of Canada, the United Kingdom, and Australia. And as in the United States, younger cities that came of age in the automobile era, like many of those in Australia, tend to exhibit more sprawl and lower levels of spatial concentration of left voters.

AMERICANS OFTEN THINK of suburbanization as a process that began in the 1950s with whites like Harry Angstrom. However, in his classic description of Manchester, England, in the 1840s, Friedrich Engels described a basic pattern of an urban form that came about much earlier as cities industrialized. He described a central commercial district that was surrounded by "unmixed workingpeople's quarters, stretching like a girdle, averaging a mile and a half in bredth [sic]," which was surrounded by the residences of the middle class, with "the upper bourgeoisie in remoter villas and gardens . . . in free, wholesome country air, in fine, comfortable homes."[2]

Suburbanization and residential sorting by income are as old as industrialization itself. Prior to the industrial revolution and the development of horse-drawn omnibuses, the rich and poor lived cheek by jowl in towns and cities. But once it was possible to commute by omnibus rather than on foot, "the old patterns, such as living above the shop, or a vertical social gradient with the 'noble' and 'servile' floors in a single multi-story building, gradually (though not fully) gave way to the more homogeneous blocks of flats, row houses, or detached villas."[3]

Urban sociologists and economists have discovered that while there is tremendous diversity in the world's cities, Engels was largely correct in his assessment that the segregation by income and class of nineteenth-century Manchester was a feature of all industrial cities. When factories were first built in places like Manchester, they were in close proximity to the city center. For many factories, it was important to be close to the river, warehouses, rail hubs, and other firms. Long hours, the need to share tools, and expensive transportation meant that porters, builders, dock hands, tailors, and other workers had no option but to live in very close proximity to their places of employment.[4] This imposed a tremendous demand for housing near factories, and workers had to endure high rents and live in tight, cramped quarters. In 1880s London, almost half of workers lived within one mile of their place of employment.[5] For these families, suburbs were of little use. In the words of a casually employed London worker in 1882: "I might as well go to America as go to the suburbs."[6]

In the initial period of industrialization, cities were transformed by the development of modest working-class housing, often forming the "girdle" described by Engels around the central business district. This took a number of forms. In cities that had an ancient pre-industrial residential section, like Manchester, its former inhabitants "removed with their descendants into better-built districts, and left the houses, which were not good enough for them, to a working-class population."[7] These old districts were characterized by "irregular cramming together of dwellings in ways which defy all rational plan, of the tangle in which they are crowded literally one upon the other. . . . Every scrap of space left by the old way of building has been filled up and patched over until not a foot of land is left to be further occupied."[8]

When there was open space in proximity to a factory, or where the old buildings were removed, developers designed innovative ways to build as many dwellings as possible within walking distance to the factories. In Britain, the innovation was the development of identical rows of six to ten back-to-back terrace houses that were erected around ten feet apart. This came to represent most of the housing stock in Birmingham, Nottingham, Liverpool, and other parts of the northern and Midland regions of Britain in the 1840s, as well as a significant share of the housing in South London. Elsewhere, like the northeastern United States as well as Ontario and Quebec, the construction techniques involved brick and stone tenement houses and row houses, and in New England, the innovation was the affordable, narrow wooden triple-decker.

Demand for housing in proximity to factories was strong during industrial booms, and profit-seeking developers and speculators built much of the housing. In some cases, especially when firms built new factories away from the city center, the firms invested in building their own dense housing developments in the shadow of the factories. In Germany, labor unions became actively involved in financing the construction of working-class housing developments. Eventually, the demand for affordable working-class housing attracted government involvement, and immense low-income housing projects were constructed by the government in proximity to industrial jobs. In some cities, once a public transportation network was in place, these housing projects were built on bus or train stops on the periphery of the city rather than directly in the shadows of factories.

When the area around the central business district and the factories became crowded with low-income workers, higher-income families sought out the fresh air and larger, newer houses of the suburbs. This was facilitated first by the horse-drawn tram, then by the streetcar and other forms of rail transportation and in some cases the motorized bus, and ultimately by the automobile. Initially, interurban transport was a means for the rich to escape the squalor of the rapidly growing industrial agglomerations.

Some variation on this theme can be found in many of the world's industrialized cities. From mid-nineteenth-century slum clearance efforts in London to the recent destruction of public housing in Chicago, national and city governments make frequent attempts to remove the more squalid remnants of earlier housing construction and make the city more attractive for higher-income residents. Yet for the most part, the dense working-class housing constructed during the era of heavy industrialization has been extremely resilient, and it is still the heart and soul of the urban landscape in many industrialized areas. In fact, when such housing was destroyed during World War II in Europe, it was often rebuilt in a very similar form thereafter. More generally, population density is self-perpetuating.

Buildings were rapidly constructed in the nineteenth and early twentieth century to keep up with exploding demand. That demand quickly went away, but the housing and urban form did not. When a city's manufacturing base shrinks and economic activity dies down, as has been the case with the painful deindustrialization of northern England and the northeastern and midwestern manufacturing belts in the United States, population loss is much slower than one might expect, in large part because of the durability of Updike's "explosion of iron and brick, still preserved intact" from an earlier era. Even as cities deindustrialize and the manufacturing-oriented urban proletariat described by Engels fades away, the affordable working-class housing from an earlier era has continued to attract poor migrants from other cities, regions, or countries, and the spatial distribution of income described by Engels remains.

It is no longer the case that workers must live in close proximity to the city center in order to walk to their factory jobs. Employment in the service sector is spread throughout the city and surrounding suburbs, and manufacturing jobs have, in many cities, moved to the suburban and exurban periphery. Yet the poor tend to be quite geographically clustered, often in the old working-class neighborhoods, and as described by Engels in Manchester, the wealthiest residents often live in suburbs.

There are several compelling explanations for this. First, there is the "flight from blight" argument that resembles Engels's claim: the poor had little choice but to live in the city center initially, and the wealthy chose to flee the social problems associated with the urban poor.[9] Second, relatively wealthy individuals often move to suburbs because they have a preference for more land and larger houses.[10]

Third, as with the rise of the horse-drawn omnibus in the mid-nineteenth-century, transportation technology is probably still an important part of the story. Automobiles are often too expensive for the poor, who are better off in residential settings that are near public transportation.[11] Even though public transportation was developed initially to facilitate the escape of the rich from the city center, in an era of widespread automobile ownership among the middle and upper classes, public transportation networks that serve city centers may be a part of the explanation for the urban clustering of the carless poor. And suburbanization was facilitated to a great extent by investments in highways in and around cities.[12] Other government policies—above all related to the construction of housing—have also played a role.

THE END RESULT is that the vast majority of postmanufacturing cities—whether in Pennsylvania, Ontario, or the English Midlands—are characterized by a remarkably similar economic and political geography: the city center is dominated by some mix of poor people, immigrants, and minorities, and they vote overwhelmingly for the parties of the left.

Once again, Reading is a good representative example. Let us consider Reading City Hall to be the center of the city, and measure the distance of each census block group in the Reading area to City Hall. This distance is plotted on the horizontal axis of each graph in Figure 4.1. On the vertical axes are median family income, then the share of the population with a bachelor's degree or higher, and then whites as a share of the population, and finally, Donald Trump's share of the two-party vote in 2016. Each dot is a census block group—the smallest geographic unit at which such information is available from the US Census—and the size of the dot corresponds

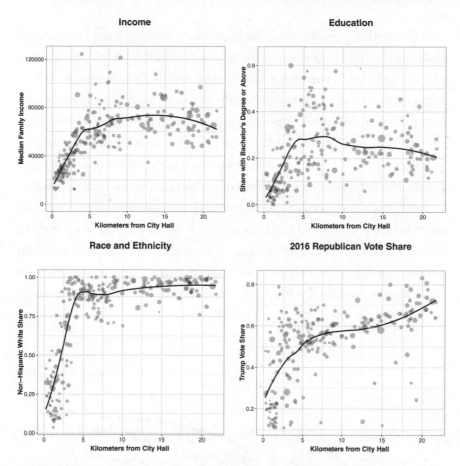

Figure 4.1: The Geography of Urban Form, Demographics, and Voting Behavior in Reading, Pennsylvania

to its population. The first three graphs show that low-income voters, those without college degrees, and minorities (Hispanics and non-whites) are quite concentrated in the city center. As one moves out from the city center toward the suburbs, there is a steep rise in income and education, and the population becomes substantially whiter.

In the fourth graph, the Republican vote share—measured at the level of precincts—follows a similar pattern. Donald Trump received a very small share of the two-party vote in the city of Reading, but the Republican vote share increases rapidly in the suburbs—surpassing 50 percent in the middle-ring suburbs, and then leveling off at 60 percent in the Reading exurbs.

This striking concentration of Democratic voting in the city center is ubiquitous in postindustrial American cities. So is the increase in Republican voting as one travels to the suburbs and exurbs. Urban economists have explored the rate at which population density declines as one moves from the urban core to the suburban periphery of various cities, and refer to this as the "density gradient." For each US city, there is a corresponding "partisan gradient" as well: a rate at which Democratic voting decreases, along with population density, as we move from the urban core to the rural periphery.

The story is strikingly similar around the country: Democrats win overwhelming majorities in city centers, with the Republican vote share increasing as one exits the dense urban core and the working-class housing constructed in the late nineteenth or early twentieth centuries and moves to the inner-ring and then middle-ring suburbs, finally reaching its maximum in the distant exurbs and rural periphery.

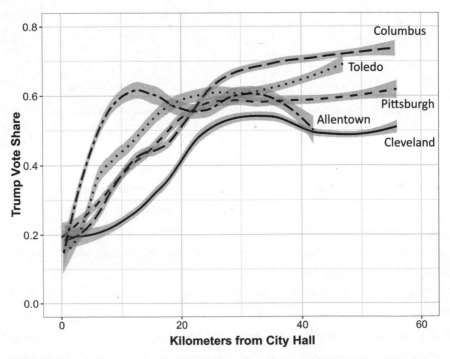

Figure 4.2: The Geography of Voting Behavior, Postindustrial Cities of Pennsylvania and Ohio

Leaving out the dots for individual census block groups, Figure 4.2 displays the relationship between distance from the city center and Republican voting in a handful of postindustrial cities in Ohio and Pennsylvania. In each city, the Republican vote share near the city center averages around 20 percent or less. The graphs display the same basic pattern of rapid increase in the Republican vote share,[13] which levels off in the exurbs at around 60 percent. The shape of these graphs looks the same whether we use data from 2000, 2008, or 2016. In small cities, like Allentown or Toledo, the increase in Republican voting as one moves away from the city center is particularly steep. In Allentown, as in Reading, one must travel only five kilometers to go from 80 percent Democratic precincts to a ring of evenly divided precincts. And in another five kilometers, one is already in the staunchly Republican periphery, with an average Republican vote share of around 60 percent. The same pattern holds even in smaller cities, like Terre Haute and Muncie, Indiana, or Johnstown and Williamsport, Pennsylvania.

The pattern is the same in larger cities, but the urban Democratic core is larger, and the transition is more gradual, such that in Columbus and Pittsburgh, one does not reach the dividing line between majority-Democratic and majority-Republican precincts until around twenty kilometers out of the city center. In Cleveland, the dividing line is at twenty-five kilometers.

Note, however, that the northeast Ohio periphery of Cleveland is more Democratic than the environs of cities like Columbus and Pittsburgh. This is in large part because in northeastern Ohio, the working-class housing from the early twentieth century is not confined to a compact girdle around the center of Cleveland. Rather, recall from the maps in Chapter 2 that the old industrial corridors—and hence Democrats—stretch out along the lake and railroad tracks to surrounding manufacturing outposts like Lorain, Elyria, Ashtabula, and Akron.

In addition to being overwhelmingly Democratic, voters in the urban core neighborhoods of postmanufacturing cities in the United States stand out in another way relative to the neighboring suburbs and the rural periphery: they are far less likely to vote. Political scientists have long understood that the groups concentrated in the urban core of postmanufacturing cities—minorities, young people, renters, and the poor—are less likely to

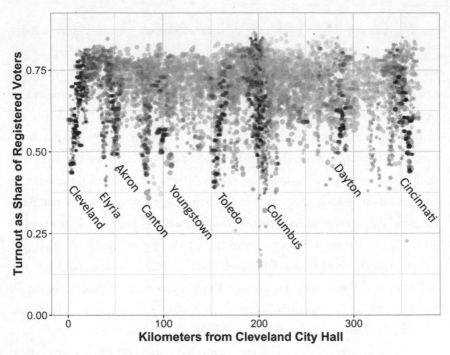

Figure 4.3: The Geography of Turnout in Ohio, 2016

participate in elections. Reading is quite typical for an American postindustrial city: turnout is around 50 percent of registered voters downtown, but it is around 75 percent in rural Berks County.

More generally, like the density and partisan gradients, there is an urban "turnout gradient" in postindustrial cities, with extremely low levels of electoral participation in the center, and a gradual increase in turnout as one traverses the suburbs. Figure 4.3 is much like the graphs of individual cities. It begins with the city hall of Cleveland, and the horizontal axis measures the distance from that point to every other precinct in Ohio. This time, instead of ending in the rural periphery of northeast Ohio, the graph continues to include every single precinct in the state. The vertical axis is turnout as a share of registered voters in the November 2016 general election. The shading of the data markers corresponds to partisanship: lighter colors of gray are associated with higher vote shares for Donald Trump, and darker colors correspond to higher votes shares for Hillary Clinton.

Each "stalactite" in the graph is a city. The wider part near the top is the suburbs; the stalactite narrows as one moves toward the center of the city, and the tip of the stalactite is the city center. The graph tells an unmistakable story about geography, partisanship, and turnout. On the left side of the graph, in the overwhelmingly Democratic precincts closest to the center of Cleveland, less than half of registered voters participated in the hotly contested 2016 election. Moving away from the city center and entering the suburbs, turnout increases, reaching well above 75 percent in the largely Republican exurbs. Next, when one reaches the other postindustrial cities of northeast Ohio, turnout falls precipitously, in each case falling below 50 percent in the city center. The same pattern repeats in Toledo, Columbus, Dayton, Cincinnati, and a variety of smaller nineteenth-century railroad towns.[14]

In fact, Figure 4.3 underestimates the extent of this massive urban-rural difference in turnout by focusing only on registered voters. In Ohio, only around 70 percent of voting-age citizens are registered to vote, and many of the unregistered are also clustered in cities. Ohio is not unique. A similar urban-rural difference in turnout rates has been present in poor postindustrial cities throughout the United States for decades.[15]

THUS FAR, WE have been focusing on postmanufacturing cities like Reading and Cleveland, where the urban core is overwhelmingly poor. The tale of US cities does not always end, of course, with decline and decay. Other cities, like Philadelphia, have managed to build a thriving knowledge-economy sector. The economic and political geography of knowledge-economy cities is notably different from other postmanufacturing cities. Above all, educated, high-income individuals in knowledge-economy cities have moved back to the city center. Figure 4.4 provides distance graphs for Philadelphia like those for Reading above. The contrast is striking. First of all, note the conspicuous "hook" on the left side of the graphs of income, education, and race. This indicates that wealthy, educated, largely white professionals have taken over the urban core of Philadelphia.

But note that there is no comparable hook in the graph of voting behavior. The political behavior of wealthy, educated whites in downtown Philadelphia is quite different from that of wealthy, educated whites in suburbs of typical postmanufacturing cities like Reading. The high-income precincts of urban Philadelphia vote overwhelmingly for Democrats. The voting

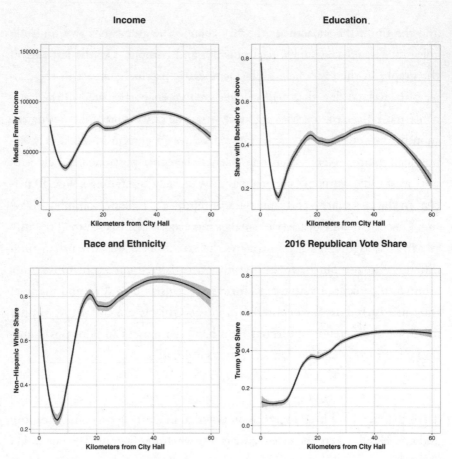

Figure 4.4: The Geography of Urban Form, Demographics, and Voting Behavior in Philadelphia, Pennsylvania

behavior of wealthy urban whites is quite similar to that of the poor African American and Hispanic service workers residing nearby in the low-income girdle surrounding the central business district.

Philadelphia is different from Reading and other postmanufacturing cities in the level of education not only of its urban core, but also of its suburban periphery. The share of individuals with a college degree in suburban and exurban Philadelphia is almost double that of suburban Reading, and substantially higher than any of the cities featured in Figure 4.2.[16] Beginning around fifteen kilometers from the city center, one enters a vast area where on average, between 40 and 50 percent of adults have a college degree. Unlike other postmanufacturing cities, this zone of high education extends fifty kilometers out into the periphery. And unlike postmanufacturing cities without a significant knowledge-economy sector, Democratic voting extends well into the outer suburbs and even the exurbs.

Strong Democratic performance in the Philadelphia periphery is partially explained by the presence of early twentieth-century working-class housing along the railroad lines reaching Reading, Lancaster, and Allentown. In that respect eastern Pennsylvania is similar to northeast Ohio. But in contrast to most old manufacturing cities, Philadelphia has a large number of high-income, high-education outer suburban precincts that are overwhelmingly Democratic. Many are in proximity to suburban colleges and universities as well as to suburban technology employers.

The same pattern can be observed in most of the large knowledge-economy hubs of the United States. The high-income urban neighborhoods near the city center—from Philadelphia's Society Hill or Boston's Back Bay, to Seattle's Capitol Hill or San Francisco's Marina District—vote overwhelmingly for Democrats. Educated professionals in the city center are surrounded by a girdle of relatively poor people who also vote almost unanimously for Democrats. In spite of very different demographics, voting behavior in the city center and its immediate surroundings is no different in the old manufacturing cities than in resurgent knowledge-economy cities. What is most distinctive about these knowledge-economy cities, however, is the fact that Democratic voting extends far out into the distant suburbs. And as a result, the partisan gradient—the rate at which Republican voting increases with distance from the city center—is typically lower in such cities. For instance, Figure 4.5 displays the relationship between distance from the city center and Republican voting in two of the cities with among the highest levels of knowledge-economy employment: Boston and Seattle. For comparison, it also includes St. Louis—a more traditional postmanufacturing city.

We see the same exponential increase in Republican voting as we move from the central city to the middle-ring suburbs. But in the outer-ring suburbs of knowledge-economy cities—the high-income zones where the Republican vote share would be well above 50 percent in a typical postmanufacturing city—the vote shares of Republican candidates are, on average,

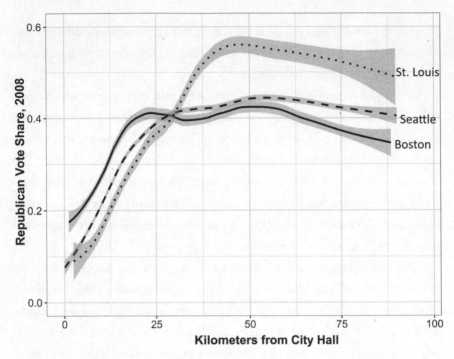

Figure 4.5: The Geography of Voting Behavior, Postindustrial versus Knowledge-Economy Cities

closer to 40 percent. Perhaps the most extreme case is the San Francisco Bay Area, where one must travel all the way to the Central Valley agricultural area to reach a substantial number of majority-Republican precincts.

On a smaller scale, one sees something similar in miniature knowledge-economy hubs like Ann Arbor, Michigan; Champaign, Illinois; Lawrence, Kansas; Charlottesville, Virginia; and Boulder, Colorado. In these cities, not only is the city center overwhelmingly Democratic, but so is the entirety of the surrounding suburbs, including the high-income subdivisions. In these cities, as in Seattle and Boston, one does not find consistently Republican precincts until reaching the rural periphery.

Knowledge-economy hubs are also different from postmanufacturing cities in another way. The urban turnout drop is far less pronounced, or missing altogether, in some of the urban neighborhoods of knowledge-economy cities. While electoral participation in San Francisco, Boston, and Philadelphia is low in poor precincts that are populated with renters and minorities, the same cannot be said for the gentrified, high-income urban neighborhoods, where turnout is similar to that of the suburbs.

NOT ALL US cities grew up around a compact nineteenth-century urban center that is filled with dense working-class housing. In fact, some of the fastest-growing cities in the United States today—especially those in the South and West—are cities that were quite small and had little industry in the late nineteenth century. For instance, Phoenix was not incorporated until 1881, and Las Vegas was not founded until 1905. Most of these rapidly growing cities of the Sun Belt, from Orlando to San Antonio to Phoenix, never developed Pennsylvania's type of compact, early working-class housing. They had neither rail-based factories nor surrounding dense urban neighborhoods designed around pedestrians and public transit. Rather, they developed in the era of the automobile and air conditioning. The growth of some of these cities is driven not so much by the presence of extraordinary labor market opportunities, but by the presence of good weather and inexpensive housing, as developers filled in vast areas with affordable single-family houses. As a result, the fall-off in population density as one moves from the city center to the exurban periphery is not nearly as steep in these cities as in the nineteenth-century manufacturing hubs of the Northeast and Midwest. In the parlance of urban economics, the "density gradient" is less steep. According to one study, if one accounts for unoccupied land, Houston has almost no density gradient at all.[17]

Similarly, in many of these sprawling cities with low density gradients, the partisan gradient is also less steep. That is, the transition from urban Democratic to exurban Republican is less sudden and dramatic. Figure 4.6 displays partisan gradients for a sample of rapidly growing automobile cities of the Sun Belt.

In each case, the familiar upward slope is present, but the gradient is not quite as steep as in the old manufacturing cities. The gray dots are individual precincts. While individual observations are rather tightly clustered around the line of best fit that follows an exponential function in most older cities, the dots in Figure 4.6 reveal far more dispersion in the newer cities. For instance, Orlando and Houston have some unusually Republican precincts in close proximity to the city center, and the first thirty kilometers are far more politically heterogeneous than we would see in any northeastern or midwestern cities of comparable size. These cities lean Democratic overall, but they contain vast, sprawling mixtures of Democrats and Republicans.

The Raleigh/Durham/Chapel Hill corridor is a dynamic, rapidly growing knowledge-economy hub. It is also a sprawling, new, automobile-oriented, multicentric urban area with rather low density gradients around each of its cities. In this respect it is very similar to Silicon Valley. It also has

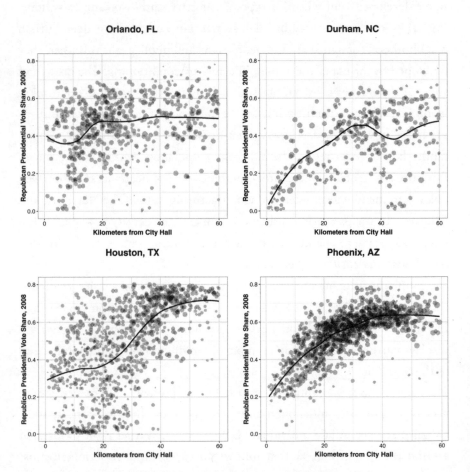

Figure 4.6: The Geography of Voting Behavior, Automobile Cities

a rather similar partisan geography. There is still a partisan gradient associated with Durham (and Raleigh), but the entire region, including the distant exurbs, leans Democratic. This produces a flatter partisan gradient than
in the old postmanufacturing cities.

On first glance, the graph for Phoenix looks rather similar to the graphs
for Philadelphia and Boston above, in that Republican voting increases
rather quickly as one moves from the city center to the suburbs. However,
there is a subtle difference. In older cities the size of Phoenix, population
density is highest in the city center, and drops off substantially as one moves
toward the periphery. In Phoenix, however, as shown in the graph, there are
relatively few dots on the left side, and they are not very close together. This
is because the urban population near the city center lives in much lower
density than in older cities. In fact, population density is relatively even
throughout the metro area. Maricopa County in Arizona is an example of
what urban economists refer to as a "polycentric city": an urban area that
has multiple centers rather than a single downtown. Some of the densest
areas, in fact, are Republican-leaning precincts that are relatively far from
the center of Phoenix. Thus Maricopa County, and Arizona as a whole, are
quite different from most of the rest of the country in an important respect:
even though Democrats cluster in the city center, the correlation between
population density and Republican voting is actually positive.[18]

ALTHOUGH THE STRENGTH of the pattern varies from one place to another,
and although there are a few exceptions such as Maricopa County, American cities are, for the most part, dense clusters of Democrats surrounded by
sparser Republicans. But these clusters are not always isolated. Some cities,
like Philadelphia and Cleveland, emerged as part of a nineteenth-century network of proximate industrial cities, joined together by a system of railroads
and waterways. Philadelphia is surrounded by a series of secondary manufacturing cities like Reading, Lancaster, Allentown, Bethlehem, and Easton.
Cleveland is surrounded by smaller satellite cities such as Elyria, Ashtabula,
Akron, and Youngstown. There is a string of manufacturing cities along the
Fox River in Wisconsin, along the Michigan Central Railroad, and along

the Illinois and Michigan Canal. Today, these old transportation corridors appear as blue veins surrounded by red on precinct-level electoral maps.

Sometimes cities spill into one another, with little or no suburban Republican periphery between them. On a large scale, this can be seen with the entire series of dense nineteenth-century industrial cities from Boston to Baltimore. On a smaller scale, this also happens when industrial cities emerged along a seam of mineral deposits, as with Scranton and Wilkes-Barre along a deposit of anthracite coal, or Bethlehem and Allentown along a deposit of limonite ore. Further afield, we see something similar in the Ruhr in Germany or the area around Lille, France. In each case, these dense urban corridors have been strongholds of the left ever since industrialization.

One of the fascinating things about cities, and hence left voters, is that they are neither randomly nor uniformly distributed in geographic space. They often emerge near harbors, river mouths, river rapids, natural resource extraction points, and man-made features like rail junctions or ecclesiastical or administrative capitals. Moreover, within an economic region, cities do not grow at similar rates over time. Typically, a "primate" city emerges and grows very quickly, and a series of lower-order cities grow more slowly. In the nineteenth century, the primate city of a region often emerged as a key conduit in the transportation of finished goods and agricultural products—a link between the outside world and the periphery of the region. Such cities experience economies of scale in the development of banking, credit, and information about markets, and their merchants were able to stock a much wider range of goods and services than lower-order cities. Competition for this primate status is often intense, but once a city becomes the focal point for investors in real estate, banking, and especially transportation infrastructure, the primate city becomes the core of a regional center-periphery arrangement. This leads to increasing returns for the primate city, which gains a set of advantages that attract investors, real estate developers, and workers.

This dynamic of urban growth is part of the explanation for a fascinating hierarchy of city sizes that has become known as Zipf's Law. Linguists have discovered that the most commonly used word in a language is typically used twice as frequently as the second-most common word, three times as frequently as the third-ranked word, and so on. Something similar is true of city sizes within economic regions. The largest city is typically twice as large as the second-ranked city, three times as large as the third-ranked city, and so on.

There is considerable evidence that Zipf's Law works extraordinarily well within countries and economic regions. However, these hierarchies of cities in the United States emerged in ways that often do not fit neatly within state boundaries. For instance, after Chicago emerged as the primate city of the upper Midwest, Iowa began to specialize in feedlot cattle and agricultural products destined for Chicago.[19] Thus the entire state of Iowa emerged in the periphery of Chicago, and it never developed a major city of its own. As a result, Iowa's population is less concentrated in a single metro area than is the population of Illinois, and hence its Democrats are far less geographically concentrated. Connecticut and New Hampshire cities are in the economic orbits of New York City and Boston, and they do not have any large metro areas of their own. Instead they have a series of lower-order cities, and as with Iowa, their Democrats are less concentrated in one place.

At the opposite extreme are states like Maryland, where much of the state is part of a vast urban corridor, and a rather small share of the state's population lives in lower-order cities or rural areas. In states like Maryland, where most of the state's population today lives in urban areas along the nineteenth-century railroad tracks, the statewide Democratic vote share is very high.

Within some states, Democrats are relatively evenly dispersed in the cores of small cities, as in New England, Iowa, upstate New York, and much of Wisconsin. And sometimes they are concentrated in larger regional primate cities, as in Missouri. But in most of the states of the old manufacturing core, and increasingly in the states of the New South, they can be found in a mixture of large cities, second-order cities, and small cities and towns.

THE UNITED STATES is often portrayed as a uniquely suburbanized country. Comparative research by urban economists, however, reveals what Engels already noticed in nineteenth-century England: suburban sprawl is a feature of cities everywhere. The population density of city centers, as well as the density gradient, are typically quite similar in British and American cities.[20] Moreover, suburban sprawl has been expanding at similar rates in the two countries over the course of the twentieth century. The level of suburbanization of the cities of Ontario and Quebec is roughly similar to the cities of the American manufacturing core.[21] And suburbanization is even more advanced in Australia than in Britain, Canada, and the United States.

Remarkably, it is also the case that in each of these countries, the density gradient corresponds to a partisan gradient that is strikingly similar to American cities. In almost every old industrial city, the urban core votes overwhelmingly for the left, and the vote shares of right parties steadily increase as one exits the city and enters the rural periphery. Only in Australia, with its newer cities and their distinctive sprawling urban form, do we see a substantial variation on this theme.

Let's start by crossing the border from the US manufacturing core into southern Ontario, which also industrialized rapidly in the late nineteenth and early twentieth centuries. In addition to the large industrial agglomeration of Toronto, southern Ontario developed a web of closely connected industrial cities like Hamilton, Kitchener, and Sudbury along the railroad lines, lakes, and at natural resource points of the nineteenth century.

The political geography of these cities looks remarkably similar to that of the US cities on the other side of the border. Figure 4.7 presents a map of voting behavior in Toronto and surrounding cities, using data at the level of polling places from the 2008 parliamentary election. The map also displays precinct-level results of the US presidential election held in the same year. Each dot represents a precinct or polling place, and the font becomes darker as votes for the parties of the left increase. It is not possible to discern a difference in the pattern of political geography when one crosses the Detroit River, the Saint Clair River, or the Niagara River and moves from the United States to Canada. Just as in the United States, the urban core of each industrial city along the water-borne and railroad transit routes of the nineteenth-century votes overwhelmingly for the left. Cities like Sarnia, Kitchener, Hamilton, and St. Catherines display the same electoral pattern as cities like Toledo, Elyria, Rochester, and Port Huron.

The political geography of Toronto is very similar to that of New York, Boston, Philadelphia, and other large, gentrified US cities. It has a ring of

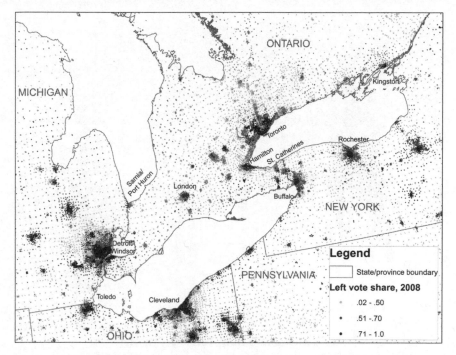

Figure 4.7: Voting Behavior in the Great Lakes Region of Canada and the United States

dense and relatively poor neighborhoods that vote very reliably for the left, as well as a fashionable central core where voters are educated and wealthy but overwhelmingly leftist in their voting behavior. Hamilton, Ontario, exhibits a very similar political geography on a smaller scale. In fact, the same can be said for virtually all the other agglomerations of Ontario, though most of them do not have a fashionable, high-income city center.[22]

It is helpful to view the southern Ontario data using the same display as Figure 4.6, where partisanship is portrayed as a gradient in relation to the city center. The horizontal axis of Figure 4.8 captures distance from Toronto City Hall, and the vertical axis captures the vote share of the Conservative Party. Instead of stopping at sixty kilometers, the displayed distance extends further into Ontario, allowing us to observe the partisan gradient around Ontario's other cities as well.

For the first sixty kilometers, the graph looks exactly like that of a major US city. It shows that the center of Toronto votes overwhelmingly for the left, but the vote share of the right increases steadily as one moves to the suburbs, with a mean that then hovers slightly above 50 percent in

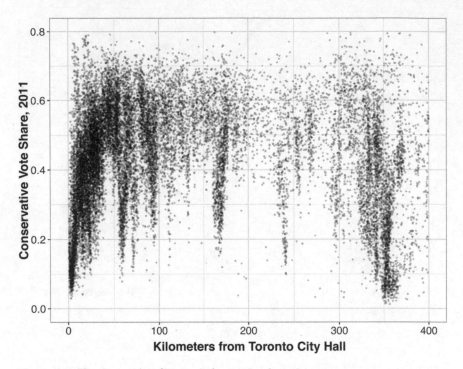

Figure 4.8: The Geography of Voting Behavior, Southern Ontario

rural southern Ontario. Next, the graph displays what, as in Figure 4.3, appear to be a series of stalactites, each of which corresponds to one of southern Ontario's cities. The lowest point at the tip of the stalactite is the left-dominated city center, with a small suburban periphery that grows increasingly conservative as one moves out in either direction until one reaches the moderately Conservative periphery again. Toronto is thus at the center of a system of lower-order industrial cities, much as Philadelphia or Cleveland are, with left voters arranged in tight clusters in early twentieth-century working-class housing near waterways, railroad tracks, factories, and warehouses.

Toronto is now one of the most important knowledge-economy hubs in North America, and as in Boston, San Francisco, and Seattle, Toronto's knowledge-economy employment is concentrated not only in the city center, but also in diverse, highly educated suburban areas like Mississauga. As in the United States, Toronto's knowledge-economy suburbs are more likely to vote for the left than are suburbs of manufacturing cities. The stalactite on the right side of the graph is Ottawa. Note that with its mix of knowledge-economy and government employment, Ottawa's suburbs and exurbs are politically competitive but lean to the left. Like the United States, southern Ontario also has a series of small, left-leaning university-based knowledge agglomerations like Waterloo and Guelph.

Further to the east, electoral behavior in the Maritimes resembles parts of New England. Like New England, the Maritime Provinces were the initial seedbed of the industrial revolution in Canada, in part because of the location of coal in Nova Scotia. The downtown areas of cities like Halifax, Sydney, and St. John's vote overwhelmingly for the parties of the left. However, as with Massachusetts, Connecticut, and Rhode Island, the increase in right voting as one moves to the rural periphery is less dramatic. In Nova Scotia, industrial activity was spread throughout the regions around Halifax and Cape Breton, and left voting is common in smaller communities with histories not only of manufacturing, but also of commercialized fishing, forestry, mining, and other natural resource extraction.

As in the United States, stark urban-rural polarization in Canada is not limited to the old manufacturing core. Figure 4.9 displays partisan gradients for several additional cities west of Ontario. Urban-rural polarization is especially stark in the Prairie Provinces. For instance, the urban core of Winnipeg, with its history of early twentieth-century labor organization and unrest, still votes overwhelmingly for the parties of the left, but the Conservative vote share increases rapidly as one exits the city center and moves into the suburbs, already reaching well above 50 percent after only ten kilometers. The city of Saskatchewan is quite similar. While rural Alberta is remarkably homogeneous in its Conservative voting behavior, the suburbs are more politically heterogeneous, and the urban cores of Calgary and Edmonton vote reliably for the left.

While much of rural British Columbia leans toward the Conservatives, smaller cities and towns, like Kelowna and Vernon, vote reliably for the left. Finally, greater Vancouver—including its surrounding edge cities and Victoria—is a diverse, high-income knowledge-economy corridor with electoral geography that looks similar to Seattle's and San Francisco's, where support for the left extends quite far from the city center.

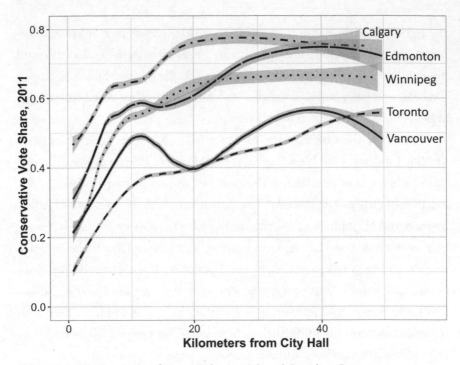

Figure 4.9: The Geography of Voting Behavior, Selected Canadian Cities

A large share of the Canadian population is foreign born. Its cities are quite diverse, and immigrants, who are clustered in the urban core, are core supporters of the Liberals and the New Democratic Party (NDP). Yet, it is important to note that Canada lacks a history of slavery and US-style white flight, and it lacks the concentration of urban poverty seen in many postindustrial US cities. This simple cross-border comparison should put to rest any suggestion that the stark urban-rural political divide in the United States is driven exclusively by its history of slavery or the unique social isolation of the urban poor.[23]

As indicated already in the map depicted in Figure 3.4 in the previous chapter, the story is quite similar in the United Kingdom. Labour voters are concentrated in the centers of both struggling postmanufacturing cities and successful knowledge-economy hubs. As one travels from the center of virtually any British city to the suburbs, exurbs, and into the countryside, one observes the same partisan gradient as in US and Canadian cities. In most of central London and the city centers of the British Midlands—including

Liverpool, Manchester, and Sheffield—the Labour vote share is very high—typically exceeding 80 percent. The Conservative vote share increases gradually with distance from the city center, surpasses 50 percent in the middle-ring suburbs, and levels off at around 70 percent in the distant exurbs and rural areas.

Some isolated cities along the nineteenth-century rail lines, like Leicester and York, appear as red Labour islands surrounded by Tory blue on election-night maps.[24] The same is true of Oxford, Cambridge, and other small knowledge hubs. In much of the Midlands, the nineteenth-century industrial cities and towns blend together in a corridor of densely populated constituencies running from Liverpool on the west almost all the way to Hull to the east, and this urban corridor votes overwhelmingly for Labour. In this respect it is reminiscent of the corridor of industrial cities running from southern Maine to Baltimore in the United States, or the industrial corridor of southern Ontario. The massive cluster of overwhelming Labour support in London is reminiscent of the Democrats' support in New York.

FINALLY, THE SAME basic pattern can be found in Australia, but with some interesting differences. Unlike Engels's Manchester model, where the city already had a distinct urban core at the time of industrialization, Australian cities were quasi-suburban from their birth in the middle of the nineteenth century. These grew up as collections of independent towns, each with its own town hall, and each with its own building codes and regulations. These towns were built around the template of the quarter-acre suburban block containing a detached single-family home. Instead of the dense clumping of terraces and alleys that characterized many British cities, working-class housing in Australia consisted of detached, low-density single-family houses. Some cities had a relatively small density gradient as one moved from the urban core to the periphery, resulting in a sprawling Australian urban form that led one observer to characterize Australia as "the most suburbanized nation on earth."[25]

In fact, the desire to escape the urban squalor described by Engels and own a single-family home was an important part of the reason skilled laborers in the early twentieth century, if they could afford the passage, left England and chose Australia rather than the United States or Canada. The areas in close proximity to warehouses, docks, ports, and factories became independent working-class towns, while other parts of the sprawling metropolis were promoted by developers as quarters for capitalists, merchants, and traders.

Instead of developing outward from a high-density urban core, Australian cities emerged as sprawling, low-density collections of neighborhoods that were rather starkly segregated according to class. Since its founding in the late nineteenth century, the core support base of the Australian Labor Party has come from the working-class neighborhoods of the large capital cities of each state, including Sydney, Melbourne, Adelaide, Hobart, Brisbane, and Perth, along with their surrounding industrial satellite cities.

The right side of the political spectrum has been divided between the National Party, which has dominated virtually all of the rural constituencies in Australia throughout the last century, and the Liberal Party, which competes in Australia's sprawling cities and in their exurban fringes.[26] Its core support base is in higher-income neighborhoods of metropolitan areas.

As in the United States, Canada, and the United Kingdom, left voting in Australia today is still highly concentrated in the neighborhoods that were built for the working class in the nineteenth and early twentieth centuries. Labor voters still live in the workers' cottages built near nineteenth-century ports and railroad tracks. Some of these are working-class voters with long family histories in the neighborhood. Some are immigrants and minorities. And some are well-compensated knowledge-economy professionals. As in Boston, San Francisco, Toronto, and London, the working-class housing from the early twentieth century in Sydney and Melbourne is now the most desirable real estate for an influx of young, affluent knowledge-economy professionals. As the class and age composition of these neighborhoods has radically changed, the Labor vote share has stayed the same or even increased.

The story about urban working-class housing and the left in Australia is strikingly similar to the other countries discussed thus far, but the spatial arrangement of that housing is somewhat different. Instead of an overwhelmingly leftist urban core and a gradual increase in right voting with distance from the city center, one sees a pattern of political segregation, such that there are concentrations of Labor voters in neighborhoods near docks, rail hubs, and old factories, but these can give way rather suddenly to high-income strongholds of the right that are akin to American suburbs— all within the same central city area. The building sites for elegant neighborhoods near the city center were usually chosen in areas with a nice view of water, and often separated from industrial facilities and working-class neighborhoods by a body of water or some other natural barrier. Unlike North American and English cities, most Australian cities have high-income, low-density neighborhoods in close proximity to the city center—often near the ocean—with high vote shares for the party of the right.

Figure 4.10 displays the vote shares of Labor and the Liberal-National (right) Coalition along the coast of New South Wales in the federal parliamentary election of 2013, and the insert zooms in on Sydney. The dots go from black to white as voting shifts from Labor to the Coalition. First, it is clear that the nexus of coal, rail, heavy industry, and left voting discovered in the northeastern United States, Canadian Maritimes, the British Midlands, and South Wales is also evident in New South Wales. On the north side of the map is Newcastle, which has a history of coal mining, heavy industry, and Labor voting quite similar to its English namesake. Wollongong to the south is quite similar. In both cities, the urban core and old mining communities along the surrounding rail lines vote overwhelmingly for Labor.

In Sydney, Labor voting is concentrated in the nineteenth-century core and the old working-class neighborhoods hugging the rail lines and docks to the south and west. However, the city is rather starkly segregated, such that Liberal voters are concentrated along the banks of the Sydney Harbor, and the Parramatta River creates a stark divide between Labor neighborhoods to the south and Liberal suburbs to the north. An interesting contrast between Australian cities and many North American ones is the presence of Labor voters in the distant exurbs in the former case. This can be explained in part by the construction of entire neighborhoods of public terrace houses in the outer-ring exurbs of Australian cities. Many of the polling places displaying large Labor vote shares along the ribbons reaching to the west and south

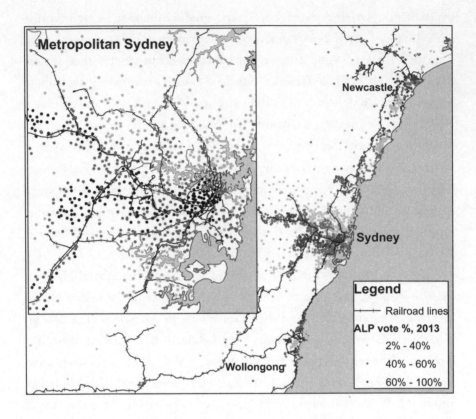

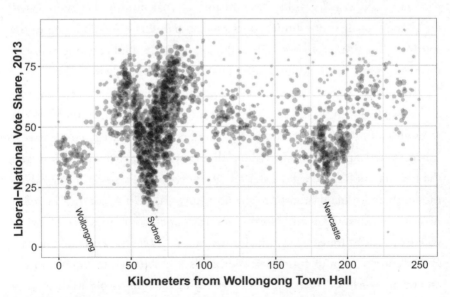

Figure 4.10: The Geography of Voting Behavior, Sydney and Surroundings

of Sydney are in neighborhoods where relatively large-scale investments in public housing were made after World War II.

Figure 4.10 also includes a graph that depicts the partisan gradients of these coastal cities of New South Wales, beginning in the center of Wollongong and ending with the periphery of Newcastle. Once again, we see the familiar "stalactite" arrangement, where the vote share of the right is well above 50 percent in the rural periphery, and dips below 25 percent in each of the city centers.

However, this pattern is more pronounced in Sydney than in the rest of Australia. To demonstrate this, Figure 4.11 provides a similar map and graph for the Melbourne area. Labor voters are clustered in the port and manufacturing town of Geelong, and in the traditional working-class areas near docks and along the rail lines built during the gold rush era in and around Melbourne. As in Sydney, some of the outlying Labor strongholds correspond to postwar public housing. And as in Sydney, there is a rather sudden divide between Labor and Liberal neighborhoods, though in this case, the divide is between east and west.

The figure also includes a map of the Melbourne partisan gradient, displaying the Liberal-National (right) Coalition vote share as one moves away from the Melbourne Town Hall. Note that the partisan gradient is not nearly as pronounced as in the industrial cities of North America and Britain. There are high-income Liberal neighborhoods in close proximity to the city center. And in the eastern suburbs, polling places with large Labor vote shares are in close proximity to polling places with very large Liberal vote shares. The overall increase in the vote share of the right as one moves further from the city center is clear, but the partisan gradient is much less steep, and the urban space is more politically heterogeneous in Melbourne than in most North American or British cities. In this respect, Melbourne has more in common with the sprawling, polycentric cities of the American Sun Belt, like Houston or Orlando, than with old nineteenth-century manufacturing cities.

Moving north to Queensland, the partisan gradient is a bit flatter in Brisbane, and the pattern of partisanship is even more dispersed. Labor voters are concentrated along rail lines and in working-class neighborhoods, but they are rather spread out, again in part due to the construction of outlying

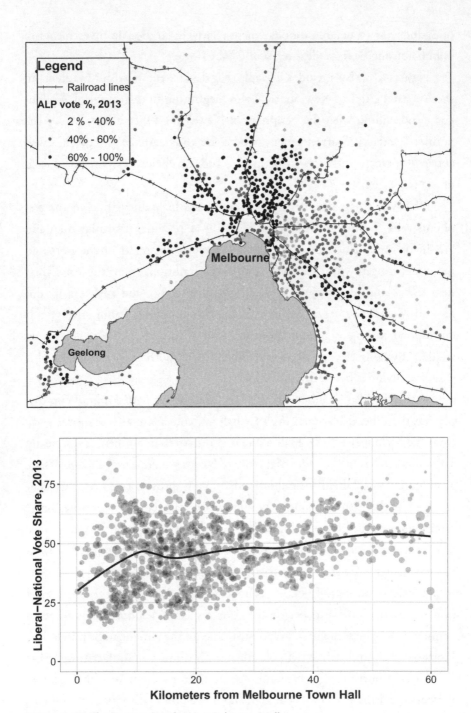

Figure 4.11: The Geography of Voting Behavior, Melbourne

public housing. Most Labor strongholds are in relatively close proximity to neighborhoods that vote for the Liberals. In Adelaide and Perth, the story is similar, but the partisan gradient is completely flat. In other words, as in Orlando, Florida, there is no discernable relationship between distance from the city center and voting behavior.

In sum, major Australian cities display many of the same features as North American and British cities. Whether they are chic boutique owners, hipsters, or low-income service workers, inhabitants of the old workers' cottages still vote reliably for the left. However, unlike the monocentric nineteenth-century cities of North America and Britain, Australian cities are large, sprawling, medium-density regions, where left-leaning working-class and creative-class neighborhoods, outlying public housing complexes, and higher-income conservative suburbs are more often interspersed.

This chapter has taken a whirlwind tour through the political geography of North American, British, and Australian cities. It revealed some striking commonalities. In the early twenty-first century, votes for parties of the left are highly concentrated in neighborhoods that were built for the industrial working class a century ago. The most typical pattern is one where the urban core provides overwhelming majorities for the left, with a dramatic increase in right voting in the suburbs, and comfortable majorities for the right in the exurban and rural periphery. This pattern can be found in large, global cities like London, New York, Sydney, and Toronto, as well as in small postmanufacturing cities like Sheffield, Allentown, Geelong, and Hamilton. It is also present in university towns like Oxford, Ann Arbor, and Waterloo.

There are also interesting cross-city differences. While still segregated on a micro scale by neighborhood, left and right voters tend to be more interspersed in newer cities that did not adopt the nineteenth-century monocentric urban form described by Friedrich Engels. This is true of the sprawling cities of the American Sun Belt and of many Australian cities.

Under some conditions, concentrations of left voters can be found far outside the urban core of a regional primate city. Sometimes an old manufacturing city is surrounded by a series of smaller satellite cities along the nineteenth-century rail network. Sometimes a series of old manufacturing cities—and hence left voters—blend together in an unbroken urban corridor. In knowledge-economy hubs like San Francisco and Vancouver, left voters can be found in large, ethnically diverse suburban and exurban swaths. Alternatively, left voters can be found far from the city center in cases where governments built public housing complexes in the exurbs.

These commonalities and subtle differences in urban political geography are fascinating in their own right. But as the rest of this book will show, they are also quite consequential for representation and ultimately for policy making. Once winner-take-all districts are drawn, this basic pattern of political geography can create a deep, structural bias against the representation of urban political parties. But to understand when and where this happens, it is necessary to appreciate these subtle differences across cities, regions, and countries. The following chapters will show that the underrepresentation of the Democrats, and labor parties, depends crucially on the nature of suburbanization and of urban form. Winners and losers in contemporary legislative elections in majoritarian democracies are often determined not only by the popularity of the parties' candidates and platforms, but also by the size, structure, and arrangement of cities.

CHAPTER 5

What Is Wrong with the Pennsylvania Democrats?

CONTEMPORARY US ELECTIONS have turned into battles between a party that represents the downtown core and inner suburbs of cities like Reading and Philadelphia, and a party that represents the sprawling exurbs and rural periphery of such cities. As in other states of the old manufacturing core, Pennsylvania has a sufficiently large urban population that in the era of polarization, Democrats can mobilize their urban base and win statewide elections. In fact, Democratic candidates have done just that in four of the last five gubernatorial elections, and six of the last seven presidential elections in Pennsylvania.

Yet statewide majorities are of little use in legislative elections. As a result of their urban concentration, the Democrats have been unable to win control of the Pennsylvania legislature. And because they dominate the state legislature, Republicans are able to draw congressional districts that build upon their natural geographic advantage. The end result is that largely because of the deep geographic legacy of the industrial revolution, the Republican Party has maintained control of Pennsylvania's legislature and congressional delegation for decades.

To understand the severity of the Democrats' problem, consider election night on November 6, 2012. It was a very good night for the Democratic Party in all of the Pennsylvania statewide races. President Barack Obama won the state's electoral votes with around 53 percent of the vote. The Democratic candidate, Bob Casey, was elected to the US Senate with around 55 percent. Democratic candidates also won large majorities in elections for attorney general, auditor general, and treasurer.

Democratic candidates for US Congress won 51 percent of the votes that night. Yet somehow, after all of the confetti was cleaned up, the Democrats came away with only five of eighteen congressional seats (28 percent). Likewise, they fell well short of majorities in both chambers of the state legislature. This stunning countermajoritarian result was not limited to 2012. While the statewide presidential vote was very close to a tie in 2016—Donald Trump won by around forty-four thousand votes out of over six million votes cast—the Republican Party won 60 percent of the seats in the Pennsylvania House of Representatives, 68 percent in the Pennsylvania State Senate, and 72 percent of the US congressional delegation. Since the last round of redistricting, from 2012 to 2018, the Democrats have won fifteen of eighteen statewide contests in Pennsylvania, but they have never won a majority of congressional seats, and have never come anywhere near winning either chamber of the state legislature. Even in the "blue wave" of 2018, when they received 58 percent of the gubernatorial vote, 56 percent of the US Senate vote, and similar majorities of the popular vote in congressional and state legislative elections, the Democrats failed to obtain a majority of seats in Congress or either chamber of the state legislature.

But the Democrats' extraordinary problem with votes and seats in Pennsylvania did not suddenly appear after the most recent round of redistricting. The Republican Party has controlled the state senate—usually with a large majority of seats—for all but one year of the entire period spanning the last *four* redistricting cycles, even while often *losing* the popular vote. It is quite remarkable that in one of the most politically competitive US states, a party that frequently wins statewide majorities has been completely frozen out of power in the legislature for almost four decades.

In fact, the difficulty of Pennsylvania's Democrats in transforming their statewide support into legislative seats goes back much further—all the way to the New Deal era. From 1930 to 1960, Democratic presidential candidates won half of all presidential elections in Pennsylvania. But the

Democrats only controlled the state senate for one session in this entire period, when they were able to ride (very briefly) on the coattails of FDR in the 1936 election. And they only controlled the state house of representatives and the US congressional delegation around one-quarter of the time. In US congressional elections in the 1950s, the Democrats routinely won the Pennsylvania popular vote while failing to make up a majority of the delegation.

Then and now, the Democrats have been plagued by a problem with geography. In the years following the New Deal, their supporters become concentrated in the core urban neighborhoods of Pennsylvania's nineteenth-century industrial cities and along the surrounding railroad tracks. They remain so today. The story of this chapter is that when winner-take-all districts are drawn on top of this geography, Democrats end up with a distribution of support across districts that is highly inefficient. That is, they win by excessive margins in the districts they win and fall short by relatively narrow margins in the districts they lose. As a result, their seat share falls well below their vote share—sometimes even when they win statewide majorities. Because of the scale and geographic arrangement of Pennsylvania's nineteenth-century cities, the Democrats' problem is severe when districts are very small—as in the state house of representatives—and even worse when they are medium-sized, as in the state senate. But small cities string together in such a way that the Democrats' geography problem, while still present, is somewhat less pronounced at the larger scale of US congressional districts.

This chapter will show that it is difficult to place all of the blame for the Democrats' consistent woes in the state legislature on partisan gerrymandering, especially since these state legislative districts are drawn by a bipartisan commission. But Pennsylvania's *congressional* districts were drawn by the Republican-dominated state legislature and approved by the governor, who also happened to be a Republican for each of the last two rounds of redistricting. The only way to explain recent Republican supermajorities in Pennsylvania's congressional delegation is to appreciate the artful gerrymandering efforts of state legislators, especially in eastern Pennsylvania. In fact, the Pennsylvania Supreme Court—an elected body with a Democratic majority in 2018—has recently ruled that these gerrymandering efforts were in violation of the Pennsylvania Constitution, and has thrown out the congressional map that had been in place since 2012.

This court decision justifiably received a good deal of attention. But by focusing on the short-term political implications of the new map, it is easy to lose sight of the Democrats' deeper, older geography problem—one that allowed Republicans the opportunity to gerrymander the state's congressional districts in the first place.

LET US START by exploring the extent of the Democrats' geographic concentration in Pennsylvania. The best way to appreciate it is to expand the distance graphs from the previous chapter to cover the entire state.

Figure 5.1 treats Pittsburgh City Hall as the origin of the graph, and the horizontal axis represents the distance of each precinct in Pennsylvania from Pittsburgh City Hall. On the left side of the graph, as in virtually every

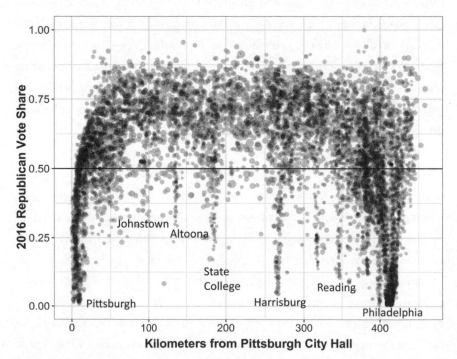

Figure 5.1: The Geography of Voting Behavior, Pennsylvania

large US city, the downtown Pittsburgh area provides almost no support for the Republican candidate, and as we move from the city center out to the exurbs, the Republican vote share rapidly increases, eventually settling at an average of around 65 percent in the most rural parts of the state. Note that Donald Trump's performance in nonmetropolitan areas was quite exceptional, and in the 2018 "blue wave" midterm election, the Republican vote share fell substantially everywhere, including in rural areas. It is also evident from the graph that while leaning Republican, rural areas are quite heterogeneous, falling in a rather wide range around the 65 percent mean. In general, nonmetropolitan areas—where scattered colleges, universities, hospitals, and unionized public employees can be found—are far more heterogeneous than urban areas. As with the graph of Ontario in the previous chapter, every time we approach another city, the graph shows something that looks like a stalactite hanging from the roof of a cave. The thicker part of the stalactite at the top is the exurban area around the fringes of the city; moving down each stalactite, we traverse the inner suburbs and reach the city center, where the support for Democrats is overwhelming.

The largest of these stalactites, on the right-hand side of the graph, is Philadelphia, but there are also miniature stalactites for all of the old industrial cities along the railroad tracks surrounding it: Reading, Lancaster, Bethlehem, Allentown, Easton, and a little further from the Philadelphia orbit, the Scranton/Wilkes-Barre corridor and Harrisburg. In western Pennsylvania, there are smaller and less proximate stalactites associated with the downtown cores of Johnstown, Altoona, and State College.

Drawing electoral districts is a process of grabbing individual precincts and joining them with some number of their neighboring precincts to form winner-take-all units. Figure 5.1 allows us to visualize the concentration of Democrats and dispersion of Republicans, and think about what happens when proximate dots are joined together to make equal-population clusters. Drawing US congressional districts requires making eighteen such clusters. State senate districts require 50, and house of representatives districts require 203.

The Democrats' basic problem is simple: their supporters are highly concentrated in the tips of the stalactites, while Republicans are spread out in surrounding areas that are more heterogeneous but majority Republican. But the implications for representation depend crucially on the size of districts relative to the size of these stalactites.

First consider a scenario where the scale of districts is *smaller* than the size of even the smallest stalactites. This is the situation in the Pennsylvania House of Representatives and its 203 districts. When pulling together clusters of precincts to make winner-take-all districts, one is likely to pull together a number of precincts in cities with very large Democratic majorities. In the biggest cities, this is simply unavoidable. Several overwhelmingly Democratic districts will emerge from the tip of the Pittsburgh and Philadelphia stalactites no matter what. There are simply no Republican neighborhoods anywhere near the urban Democratic neighborhoods.

But the same thing will happen in the smaller cities as well, especially if, because of laws or political incentives, one must try to avoid subdividing municipalities. When pulling together proximate groups of precincts in areas *outside* cities, one is likely to select a more heterogeneous group of Republican-leaning precincts closer to the top of the graph (the ceiling of the cave). Even if the overall statewide vote is evenly divided, Democrats will then end up racking up surplus votes in less than half the districts, while Republicans will end up winning smaller majorities in a larger number of districts.

One might imagine, then, that it would be a good thing for the Democrats if districts were slightly larger—as in the state senate with its fifty districts. But this turns out to be even worse. Once the districts are a bit larger than the smaller stalactites, the smaller Democratic cities are subsumed by their Republican periphery, and they cannot win seats at all, other than the overwhelmingly Democratic seats in the big cities.

Finally, consider the much larger scale of the eighteen congressional districts. At this scale, things finally get better for the Democrats, at least in eastern Pennsylvania. On the right side of the graph, the small stalactites are sufficiently close to one another, and sufficiently close to Philadelphia, that they can join together in the same district, and thus overwhelm the surrounding Republicans.

Before adding flesh to the bones of this argument by examining each legislative chamber in further detail, it is important to know how districts are actually drawn in Pennsylvania. The state legislative districts are drawn by the Pennsylvania Apportionment Commission, which is bipartisan in that it is staffed with one legislative leader from each party in each chamber. These four commissioners must choose a fifth and final commissioner, and if they cannot agree, the Pennsylvania State Supreme Court appoints one. The supreme court, in turn, is composed of justices selected via competitive, partisan elections. A court with a Republican majority appointed the tie-breaking member of the Redistricting Commission in 2002 and 2012. The Pennsylvania Constitution requires these districts "be composed of compact and contiguous territory as nearly equal in population as practicable" and that dividing a "county, city, incorporated town, borough, township or ward" should be avoided unless absolutely necessary for the purposes of population equality. Neither the legislature nor the governor has a vote on these plans, and in practice, the leaders of the two parties have a great deal of power.

The process for drawing congressional districts is completely different. As in many other states, congressional districts are drawn by the state legislature and approved by the governor as a normal piece of legislation. There are no constitutional restrictions about compactness and municipal boundaries in the case of Pennsylvania congressional districts. When the legislature and governor are controlled by the same party, this arrangement gives partisans a much freer hand to seek partisan advantage when drawing boundaries. However, a successful legal challenge to the 2012 redistricting plan led to the creation of a new plan—drawn by a special master under the supervision of the Pennsylvania Supreme Court—in time for the 2018 congressional election.

LET US BEGIN with the Pennsylvania House of Representatives, returning once again to Reading—one of the small stalactites in the graph above— and its neighboring cities. Recall that ever since the Reading Socialists became Democrats, the votes for Democratic candidates in Berks County have been highly concentrated in the city of Reading. As the population of Reading has fallen relative to that of exurban Berks County, the county as a whole has trended toward the Republican Party. In 2008, Barack Obama won 55 percent of the Berks County vote. In 2016, Donald Trump won 55 percent, but in the 2018 midterm, the Democrats were back on top in Berks County, where the Democratic gubernatorial candidate, Tom Wolf, received 54 percent of the vote. In Reading itself, the Democratic candidate received over 80 percent of the vote in each of these elections.

The top panel of Figure 5.2 displays the 2016 precinct-level election results for Berks County and its surroundings, and superimposes the boundaries of the districts of the state house of representatives. There are nine districts either completely or partially in Berks County. For the most part, it appears that the commission tried to align county and municipal boundaries with district boundaries to the extent possible. The boundary of District 127, for example, largely follows the boundary of the city of Reading, but the city is larger than the size of a single district, so part of the city spills over into District 126 to the north and west.

Recall that Democrats are concentrated not only in downtown Reading, they are also scattered in small postindustrial enclaves along the nineteenth-century rail lines heading out in each direction from Reading. We can see, however, that none of these are sufficiently large to produce a Democratic district. Like the Reading Socialists in the early twentieth century, Democrats are outnumbered everywhere except for the urban core of Reading. Summing up the precinct-level votes for Trump and Clinton displayed in Figure 5.2 to the level of Pennsylvania House districts, Clinton won a majority only in the two Reading districts—126 and 127—but fell short in all the others. Likewise, in the 2016 state house elections in Berks County, the Democratic candidates won only the two urban districts.

In a county where voters have been, on average, rather evenly split between the parties in presidential, US Senate, and gubernatorial elections, and where there are substantially more registered Democrats than Republicans, the Democrats in recent years can win only 22 percent of the seats in the Pennsylvania House of Representatives. This was true once again in 2018, when the Democrats received a solid countywide majority in the US Senate and gubernatorial contests, but could only win the two Reading seats in the Pennsylvania House of Representatives.

In neighboring Lancaster County, their problem is worse. They win a dominant victory in the single district that corresponds to the boundaries

PA House of Representatives Districts

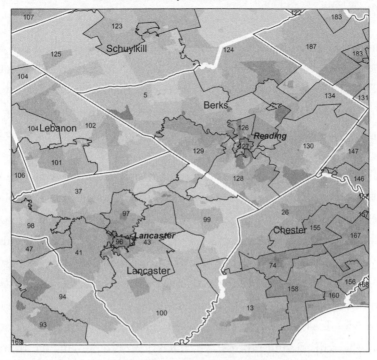

PA Senate Districts

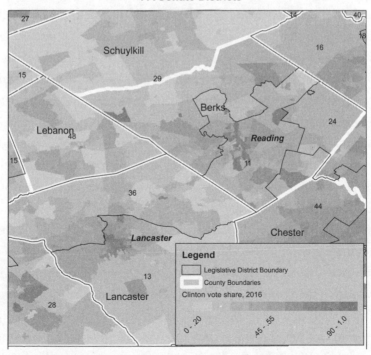

Figure 5.2: 2016 Precinct-Level Election Results and State Legislative District Boundaries, Reading and Lancaster, Pennsylvania

of the city of Lancaster, District 96, but consistently lose all of the other districts. Thus with 48 percent of the countywide gubernatorial vote in 2018, the Democrats only won 10 percent of the Lancaster County districts. Clearly, the concentration of Democrats in cities like Reading and Lancaster makes it difficult for them to translate votes into legislative seats in the region.

That is not to say that *any* system of districts containing sixty thousand people must *necessarily* produce such stark overrepresentation of Republicans in these counties. It would be possible to produce more majority-Democratic districts if Reading and Lancaster were subdivided. If parts of the urban core were combined with parts of the suburbs, there could easily be more districts with 55 or 60 percent Democratic majorities rather than a single urban district with a 70 or 80 percent majority.

So why don't Democrats push harder for the creation of such districts during the redistricting process? The Democratic representative from the Pennsylvania House of Representatives on the Apportionment Commission helped draw these districts and voted in favor of them. First of all, the Pennsylvania Constitution is very clear about the importance of respecting city boundaries, and such districts would likely invite a legal challenge in state court. In fact, the Pennsylvania Supreme Court rejected the first set of districts proposed by the Pennsylvania Redistricting Commission in 2012 on the grounds that they were insufficiently compact and respectful of jurisdictional boundaries. Moreover, Reading is a majority-Hispanic city, and any effort to dilute the Hispanic urban core by splitting it up and combining urban Hispanic fragments with white suburbs would have potentially invited a legal challenge associated with the Voting Rights Act.

However, even without these state and federal legal constraints, there is another more general reason why Democrats might find it difficult to draw such districts. Urban incumbents often grow quite fond of their safe seats. Partisans from the Pennsylvania or Berks County Democratic Party pushing for smaller Democratic majorities in Reading or Lancaster might find themselves up against longstanding urban incumbents. Thomas Caltagirone has represented District 127 in Reading for over forty years, and Mike Sturla has represented District 96 in Lancaster for over twenty-five years. Such urban incumbents often get their start in city politics and have a strong attachment to their longstanding constituents. Understandably, they may not be interested in exchanging their old urban bailiwicks for unknown suburban strip malls to help copartisan upstarts get elected on their turf.

This is an important larger observation. When they get involved in debates about redistricting, individual legislators in winner-take-all systems are often far more concerned with their own neighborhood, and their own political career, than with the overall representation of their party in the state or in the country. Recall that in nineteenth-century Europe, some safe urban incumbents voted for the retention of single-member districts that were disastrous for their parties. Remarkably, in Pennsylvania, thirty-six urban Democrats in the Pennsylvania House of Representatives voted in favor of the 2012 congressional redistricting plan—discussed in further detail below—that was eventually struck down by the Pennsylvania Supreme Court as an extreme Republican gerrymander. In all likelihood, based on relationships built up over years, many of them were protecting the safe seats of their urban congressional copartisans.

If given unfettered power to draw districts as they saw fit, unencumbered by the need to worry about compactness, municipal boundaries, or self-interested incumbents, if they could behave cohesively, the Democrats could conceivably achieve a more efficient distribution of voters across districts by artfully subdividing cities—like Erie, Scranton, and Reading—that are larger than the size of a state house district. They might also work to draw more majority-Democratic districts in the suburbs of the major cities. However, there is little they can do about the large number of urban core districts of Philadelphia and Pittsburgh, which will be extremely Democratic no matter how they are drawn. And it would not be in their interest to subdivide small cities like Chester, York, Johnstown, Newtown, and Lock Haven, where urban Democratic incumbents have been able to hold onto seats—appearing as small blue islands surrounded by a sea of red on electoral maps—even though each city's population is below the size of a state house district. In sum, Democrats would likely be able to improve their representation in the state legislature if they had a free hand to redraw partisan districts, but political geography would still make things quite difficult for them.

NEXT, LET US examine the Pennsylvania Senate, where instead of drawing districts of around 60,000 individuals, the Apportionment Commission must draw districts of around 250,000. Not much changes in the large cities of Philadelphia and Pittsburgh. A large number of overwhelmingly Democratic districts in the urban core of the primate cities is still inevitable. However, the difference is quite consequential in the smaller, secondary cities. One can appreciate the scale of Pennsylvania State Senate districts by looking at the second panel of Figure 5.2. The very Democratic city of Lancaster is swallowed up into District 13, which is quite internally polarized but produced a 54 percent majority in favor of Donald Trump and reliably elects Republicans to the state senate. Reading is a larger city than Lancaster, and its surrounding railroad enclaves are more substantial. It ends up in a more competitive district—District 11, where Trump won only by a slim majority in 2016, but where a Democrat with strong roots in the Berks County agricultural community, Judy Schwank, was elected to office in 2011.

But Senator Schwank is quite unusual. Virtually all of the small blue islands that produce Democratic seats in the state house of representatives—traditionally Democratic industrial towns like Johnstown, York, and Erie—are too small to elect Democrats when the larger state senate districts are drawn. While the map of legislative seats in the house of representatives is dotted with a series of small blue islands along the nineteenth-century railroad tracks around the state, these nonmetropolitan areas are almost uniformly red on state senate maps. After the 2016 and 2018 elections, other than Senator Schwank's Reading district, there were only three senate districts outside of the Philadelphia and Pittsburgh metro areas where the urban population was sufficiently large to produce a Democratic victory: one in Scranton, one in Wilkes-Barre, and one straddling Bethlehem and Easton. The Democrats' geography problem in the senate has only gotten worse as postindustrial Pennsylvania cities lose population relative to their Republican surroundings.

To summarize, the Democrats have an obvious problem of geographic concentration in Philadelphia and Pittsburgh. It is simply not possible to avoid drawing state legislative districts that pack large numbers of "surplus"

Democrats—far beyond what is required for victory—in a number of heavily urban districts. This is true in both the lower and upper chambers. But they also have a problem in the smaller cities—one that varies as we move from one geographic scale to another. Democrats in smaller cities along the nineteenth-century rail network are packed into overwhelmingly Democratic state house districts. These are surrounded by exurban and rural districts won by Republicans with smaller margins. However, as we move up to the level of state senate districts, the Democrats' problem changes and intensifies. Small stalactites on the graph in Figure 5.1—cities like Lancaster and York—are now too small relative to the size of districts, and they are swallowed up by their surrounding neighborhoods, which generates districts that are heterogeneous but lean Republican.

To see the Democrats' statewide problem more clearly, it is useful to look at a histogram representing the distribution of votes for the two parties across districts. To make a histogram, we place the districts into "bins" according to their partisanship, with the bins arranged horizontally, such that

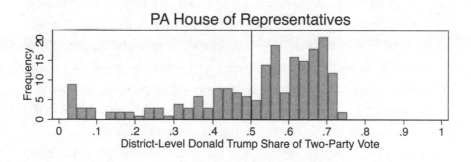

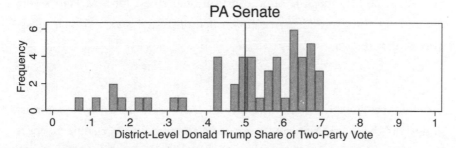

Figure 5.3: Histograms of 2016 Republican Presidential Vote Share across Pennsylvania State Legislative Districts

the vertical height of the bar for each bin corresponds to the number of districts falling into the specified range. To create Figure 5.3, I have summed up the precinct-level votes for Hillary Clinton and Donald Trump to the level of state legislative districts, and made a histogram for each chamber, with Trump's statewide vote share marked with a thin vertical line.

These histograms show very clearly what an inefficient geographic distribution of votes looks like. The Democrats win very large numbers of "surplus" votes beyond 50 percent in the left "tail" of the distribution. Each of these extremely Democratic districts is located in a city center. Note that the right-hand side of the graph is empty: there are simply no Republican districts—even in the most rural parts of the state—that are anywhere nearly as homogeneous as the urban, Democratic districts on the left-hand side of the graph. There is a large density of districts above 50 percent, where Republicans win comfortable, but not overwhelming, majorities.

When a party has a support distribution like that of the Pennsylvania Republican Party in Figure 5.3, it can win a seat share substantially beyond its vote share. In this case, Donald Trump received only a razor-thin statewide majority, but he received a majority in around 65 percent of the districts. One simple way to gauge this type of asymmetry in a party's support across districts is to contrast the mean vote share with the median. While the mean Democratic vote share across districts was just shy of 50 percent, the median district in both chambers was around 44 percent Democratic.

This striking asymmetric distribution of partisanship across districts did not appear out of nowhere in 2016. Nor was it unique to the most recent round of redistricting. Under the previous state legislative districts, implemented in 2002 under the same constitutional rules, John McCain's vote share in the 2008 presidential election demonstrated a very similar cross-district distribution.

BUT RECALL THAT the state legislative districts were drawn by a commission where the tiebreaking vote was cast by an appointee of a supreme court that had a slim Republican majority. One might suspect that this commissioner had partisan motivations, and conspired with the two Republican members to produce a favorable Republican gerrymander—packing Democrats into overwhelmingly Democratic districts in the left tail of the distribution and strategically breaking up clusters of Democrats to achieve partisan gain.[1] In other words, one might suspect that the Democrats have a problem in the state legislature not so much with political geography, but with gerrymandering.

Indeed, some of the senate districts seem to have been drawn to bolster potentially vulnerable incumbents, and some of the districts on the edges of cities could have been drawn to give Democrats better opportunities. For instance, Harrisburg was separated from some of its more Democratic suburbs and connected with the most Republican part of its rural periphery. Perhaps the Lehigh Valley could have been districted in a way that produced two Democratic districts rather than one.

This raises an important question. Are the Democrats poorly distributed across districts because of intentional gerrymandering by the commissioners, or because of their residential geography? To answer this question, we need to find ways of comprehending the parties' geographic support that do not rely on the actual, enacted districts that may have been drawn with partisan intent. I have collaborated with Jowei Chen and Nicholas Eubank on the development of two such approaches. First, we examine partisan neighborhoods. We take each individual voter in the state in the 2008 election, and for the size of the Pennsylvania lower chamber, we ask: What is the partisanship of his or her nearest 60,000 neighbors? For the upper chamber, what is the partisanship of his or her nearest 250,000 neighbors? This approach allows us to, in effect, draw bespoke districts around each individual in Pennsylvania and ask some questions about the type of partisan neighborhood people live in.[2]

This approach allows us to quantify the extent to which Democrats are more geographically concentrated than Republicans at the scale where districts are drawn. In 2008, almost one-quarter of Democrats lived in a (250,000-person) neighborhood that was over 70 percent Democratic, while no Republicans lived in neighborhoods that were over 70 percent Republican. In fact, only 10 percent of all Republicans lived in a neighborhood that was over 60 percent Republican. Thus, Democrats are far more likely to end up in districts where their copartisans run up excessive majorities. And Republicans are more likely to live in neighborhoods with comfortable, but not overwhelming, Republican majorities.

These statistics can be linked back to the "stalactite" graph in Figure 5.1. To be sure, there were some overwhelmingly Republican precincts in exurban and rural areas—some even higher than 75 percent—in both 2008 and 2016. But they do not string together to form overwhelmingly Republican neighborhoods at the scale of state senate districts. Recall from earlier chapters that rural counties almost always contain some Democratic pockets. Sometimes these are small postindustrial cities like Lancaster or York. Sometimes they are towns with colleges and universities, like Bloomsburg, East Stroudsburg, or State College. Sometimes they are county seats with unionized municipal workers and schoolteachers. Even in the most staunchly Republican exurbs of Pittsburgh and Philadelphia, there are Democratic enclaves associated with the rental housing located where nineteenth-century railroads cut through on their way to Reading or Allentown, or to Youngstown or Morgantown. All of these isolated Democratic votes tend to be subsumed by surrounding Republicans at the geographic scale of Pennsylvania State Senate districts. But at the same time, we never see overwhelming Republican majorities in these districts.

In short, if we draw bespoke districts around each Pennsylvania voter, we end up seeing the same phenomenon captured in the histograms above. Democrats tend to end up either in districts with Democratic supermajorities, or in districts with smaller Republican majorities.

A second way of disentangling geography and gerrymandering is to draw a complete, alternative redistricting plan. Better yet, one can use a computer algorithm to draw hundreds or thousands of such plans, ignoring partisanship and focusing only on drawing compact, contiguous districts with equal population. We can then look at a large number of alternative Pennsylvania redistricting plans, each with fifty relatively compact districts and equal populations. Like redistricting commissions and state legislatures, we used precincts as the building blocks in developing such plans, and then examined the partisanship of each district we created by simply summing up the precinct-level votes.[3]

Even when we draw four hundred separate districting plans in this party-blind way, we discover that Democrats almost always end up with a terrible geographic support distribution. As with the districts drawn by the Apportionment Commission, Democrats end up highly concentrated in the districts in the tail of the distribution. The top panel of Figure 5.4 presents a histogram of the McCain vote share produced in each of the fifty districts in each of the four hundred simulations. The vertical lines correspond to McCain's statewide (44.8 percent) and national (46.3 percent) vote shares. For purposes of comparison, the second panel presents a histogram of the McCain vote share when aggregated to the level of the *previous* districts, enacted in 2002, and the third panel displays the distribution of the Mc-Cain vote share across the districts implemented after the 2012 round of redistricting.

The distribution of Democrats across the simulated districts is not very different from what we see in the enacted districts. If anything, it appears that the Democrats may be slightly *more* packed in the tail of the distribution

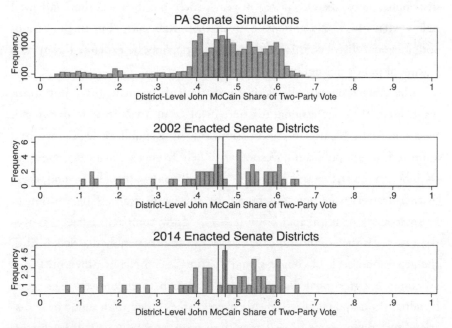

Figure 5.4: Histogram of 2008 Republican Presidential Vote Share across Simulated and Enacted 2002 and 2014 Pennsylvania State Senate Districts

in the plans drawn by the Pennsylvania Apportionment Commission, and the Republican advantage in the enacted plans might be a bit larger than in the simulated plans, but the overall picture is very similar. The distribution of partisanship across simulated districts is quite skewed: a large number of simulated districts are more than 70 percent Democratic, but the simulations never produce districts that are more than 70 percent Republican.

In short, whether we look at partisan neighborhoods or simulations, it is difficult to sustain the argument that the Democrats' problem with representation in the Pennsylvania State Senate in recent years can be blamed exclusively on the partisan machinations of the redistricting commission. The problem appears to be driven by a deeper, structural aspect of Pennsylvania's political geography.

GIVEN THE SEVERITY of the Democrats' geography problem in the state legislature, one might imagine that something similar happens to them when congressional districts are drawn. Indeed, Democrats have been very badly distributed across districts in recent years, such that their seat share falls well below what one would anticipate given their vote share. But in the case of congressional districts, this pattern cannot possibly be explained away as a feature of political geography.

The congressional redistricting process is different in three important ways. First, the congressional districts in place up to 2018 were drawn not by a nominally bipartisan commission, but by Republican legislators, and approved by a Republican governor, with help from a sophisticated group of Republican redistricting experts with avowedly partisan goals. Second, these district-drawers were not constrained by the Pennsylvania Constitution to honor county or municipal boundaries or draw compact districts, as was the case with the commission that drew the state assembly districts. Third, the geographic scale of congressional districts is completely different. Pennsylvania's congressional districts must be drawn to encompass over seven hundred thousand people. They are eleven times larger than state house districts, and almost three times larger than state senate districts. It is difficult to comprehend the truly massive scale of American congressional districts without comparing them to those used in other industrialized democracies. The districts used in the United Kingdom, Canada, and France are roughly comparable in scale to those used in the Pennsylvania House of Representatives, while those used in Australia are somewhere between the scale of the Pennsylvania House and Senate districts. In those countries, small cities on the scale of Reading, Pennsylvania, or Guelph, Ontario, or Huddersfield, UK, would have one or perhaps even two of their own federal electoral districts. In the United States, the scale of congressional districts is sufficiently large to be able to contain several such cities and their suburbs and rural surroundings.

In eastern Pennsylvania, this completely changes the implications of urban concentration for the Democrats. The concentration of Democrats in downtown Reading and other railroad towns is no longer such a problem for them. The entirety of Berks County is much smaller than the size of a contemporary congressional district, and Berks can easily be joined with parts of Chester or Montgomery Counties to the south, or with Lehigh to the east. Due to a combination of nineteenth-century railroad strongholds and knowledge-economy suburbs, each of these is majority Democratic.

Philadelphia is surrounded by a large number of geographically proximate, very Democratic mining and industrial towns along the dense nineteenth-century rail network of eastern Pennsylvania. Furthermore, as Philadelphia has become a knowledge-economy city, its suburbs and even many of its ex-urbs have trended toward the Democratic Party. At the scale of US congressional districts, these Democratic communities can easily string together and overwhelm the surrounding rural Republicans. This can be intuited from the "stalactite" graph in Figure 5.1, but perhaps a better way to see it is by returning to the "nearest neighbor" approach, this time using a picture.

Figure 5.5 displays a "heat map" that captures the share of each voter's seven hundred thousand nearest neighbors who voted for Obama in 2008. Above all, we can see that virtually all of industrialized eastern Pennsylvania is a dark shade of gray, indicating that people live in majority-Democratic congressional-scale neighborhoods. This is true not only of Philadelphia, its suburbs, and its immediate industrial satellite cities, but also of the Lehigh Valley and the Scranton/Wilkes-Barre area. For the most part,

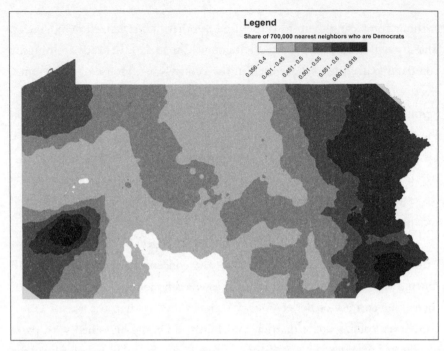

Figure 5.5: Heat Map of Partisanship of Nearest Neighbors in Pennsylvania

the Democratic outposts along the nineteenth-century rail lines are sufficiently close so that they can easily be strung together to generate majority-
Republican districts in eastern Pennsylvania.

The same lesson emerges if we draw hundreds of simulated districts.
In simulations that draw eighteen Pennsylvania congressional districts,
majority-Democratic seats always emerge in suburban Philadelphia and
many of the industrial cities to its north. The configuration of each simulated plan is slightly different, but in the eastern part of the state, the simulations usually produce six to eight seats where a Democratic victory is likely.
In the redistricting plan enacted by the Pennsylvania legislature in 2012,
there are only four—an outcome that simply does not emerge under a party-
blind approach to simulations.

In contrast, on the western side of the state, the simulations indicate
that the Democrats *do* suffer from a concentration problem at the scale
of congressional districts. Unlike Philadelphia, Pittsburgh does not have
such expansive Democratic-leaning knowledge-economy suburbs, and the

partisan gradient is rather steep. That is, the Republican vote share increases rather rapidly as one traverses the middle-ring suburbs. Pittsburgh does have outlying Democratic railroad enclaves—for instance, Altoona and Johnstown to the east, and some of the communities along the Ohio River to the northwest—but they are too small, and too far from one another, to string naturally together into Democratic districts in the fashion of the Lehigh Valley or the Wyoming Valley in eastern Pennsylvania. Most of the simulations produce only a single, extremely Democratic district in Pittsburgh, though in at least some of the simulations, an additional Democratic district emerges among the mining communities to the southwest. In other words, at the scale of congressional districts, Democrats in western Pennsylvania suffer from the same underrepresentation as Democrats in Berks and Lancaster Counties do at the scale of state assembly districts.

The difference between western and eastern Pennsylvania reveals that the extent of Democratic underrepresentation depends on the nature of nineteenth-century industrialization and city formation. At the scale of congressional districts, where early industrial activity was highly concentrated in a single city, as in western Pennsylvania, contemporary Democrats are likely to end up losing out in the transformation of votes to seats. If western Pennsylvania was a separate state, and its districts were drawn without regard for partisanship, it would be a state where Republicans would win slim overall majorities of the vote while receiving around five or six out of seven congressional seats (depending on how one defines the east-west dividing line). However, if eastern Pennsylvania, with its dense network of nineteenth-century railroad cities, were an independent state, the distribution of Democrats would be relatively propitious at the level of congressional districts; they would win a comfortable majority of statewide votes and perhaps six or seven of eleven districts.

Putting all of Pennsylvania together, the geographic distribution of Democrats at the scale of congressional districts is certainly not ideal for the Democrats, but it is better than at the scale of state legislative districts.

The top panel of Figure 5.6 is a histogram of John McCain's vote share in 2008 across the eighteen districts in each of four hundred simulated congressional districting plans. The next two panels display the distribution of votes across the actual, enacted congressional plans drawn up by Republican legislators in 2002 and 2012. Once again, vertical lines correspond to McCain's national and statewide vote share, to provide a guide to the region of the cut-point between Democratic and Republican victories in legislative races.

The top panel in Figure 5.6 indicates that as with the Pennsylvania State Senate, the Democrats have a highly skewed distribution of support in the congressional district simulations. Unsurprisingly, the simulation algorithm ends up generating extremely Democratic Philadelphia and Pittsburgh seats. But the simulations produce a very large density of seats just to the left of the cut-point, which means they produce a healthy number of highly competitive but Democratic-leaning seats. These are mostly in parts of eastern Pennsylvania outside of urban Philadelphia, where Democratic suburbs and old industrial enclaves often come together in districts where they outnumber exurban and rural Republicans.

Overall, because of their very poor distribution of support in western Pennsylvania, the simulations end up somewhat favorable to the

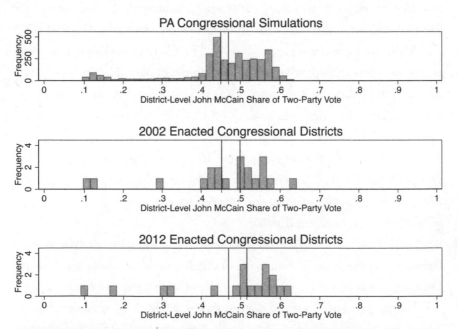

Figure 5.6: Histogram of 2008 Republican Presidential Vote Share across Simulated Congressional Districts and Enacted 2002 and 2012 Congressional Districts

Republicans. Averaged over hundreds of simulations, McCain's 2008 vote share was higher than his statewide vote share in around eleven districts.

But in the plan enacted by the legislature in 2012, there were thirteen such districts. Furthermore, the gerrymandered 2012 plan looks nothing like the nonpartisan simulated plans. The large density of moderately Democratic districts that appears in the simulations is missing in the enacted plan. In fact, the entire middle of the distribution is missing. Rather, there is a clump of thirteen solidly Republican districts on the right side of the graph. And in the elections carried out in those districts, Republicans have indeed won comfortable majorities on every occasion from 2012 to 2016, and the Democrats have been left with five extremely Democratic districts. Even a very substantial electoral tide of six percentage points would have led to zero additional seats.

All of these points were made by the plaintiffs in a recent trial that was ultimately decided by Pennsylvania's Supreme Court. The plaintiffs successfully challenged the constitutionality of the state's congressional districts, and they were subsequently redrawn under the supervision of the court. The expert witnesses for the plaintiffs showed that the districts drawn by the Republican legislature were severely biased against Democrats, and they used redistricting simulations like those presented above to convince the court that the bias went well beyond what one might expect from the geographic concentration of Democrats. Thirteen solidly Republican seats simply could not have emerged under a nonpartisan approach to redistricting that focuses on drawing compact, contiguous districts.

The original districting plan from 2012—now thrown out by the court—had artfully prevented the emergence of Democratic seats outside of urban Philadelphia, Pittsburgh, and Scranton. Above all, the Republican redistricting plan aimed to prevent the nineteenth-century railroad and mining towns from stringing together with one another, or from joining with knowledge-economy suburbs, to produce Democratic districts, taking care to surround Democratic cities with sufficient collections of rural voters. When necessary, they intentionally combined outlying nineteenth-century industrial enclaves with the larger, overwhelmingly Democratic city nearby to pack Democrats and facilitate the construction of Republican districts in the suburbs. In western Pennsylvania, their work was relatively easy. But in eastern Pennsylvania, the job took enormous creativity.

The problem for the pro-Republican legislature was that, beginning with Scranton and moving to the south, the Democratic cities of the Lehigh Valley, Reading, and several other smaller Democratic enclaves like Lancaster, Chester, West Chester, Norristown, and Coatesville are in close proximity to other nineteenth-century railroad towns dominated by Democrats, and to some of Philadelphia's Democratic suburban areas such as Wayne and the communities along the commuter railroad known as the Main Line.

In the northeastern part of the state, the gerrymandering strategy involved concentrating Democrats in one meandering, noncompact northern district that included Scranton and parts of Wilkes-Barre, and then reached over to the Easton area. This cleared the way for the careful construction of surrounding Republican districts. One artful district circumvented the Democratic precincts of Scranton, reaching from the easternmost point in the state all the way to the center of the state. Another managed to link the Republican suburbs of Wilkes-Barre with the eastern suburbs of Harrisburg, well over a hundred miles away. The legislature prevented the emergence of a Democratic district in the Lehigh Valley by splitting it and extracting part of Bethlehem, and then surrounding Allentown with a long, overwhelmingly Republican rural corridor reaching all the way to the exurbs of Harrisburg.

The Reading area was a lynchpin of the gerrymandering strategy. Many reasonable districting configurations in the Reading area would have combined it with other surrounding Democratic enclaves to the east or south. The 2012 solution was to draw an extremely narrow corridor to extract Reading from its suburbs and place it in a rural district that reached far to the west. Reading, Lancaster, and Coatesville were all extracted from the eastern industrial corridor and surrounded with enough rural Republicans to neutralize their urban Democrats. Harrisburg was bisected so as to make sure that its overwhelmingly Democratic population could not contribute to a Democratic majority.

Pennsylvania Congressional District 7 was one of the most infamous districts in the United States. On the east side, it began with a set of surgically extracted Republican exurbs, circumnavigated Norristown via an exceptionally narrow corridor, and then grabbed a swath of western suburbs, taking care to avoid Chester and West Chester, before forming another narrow corridor to avoid Coatesville and reach the rural Republican area south of Reading.

This highly gerrymandered map was replaced with a map drawn by a special master who was instructed by the court to simply draw compact, contiguous districts and avoid unnecessary splits of counties or municipalities. In the run-up to the 2018 election, Republicans complained bitterly that the new map was too favorable to the Democrats. Yet the results showed once again the powerful role of geography. In spite of a truly historic 10 percentage-point swing in the vote share in their favor from 2016 to 2018, and receiving over 55 percent of the votes cast, Democratic candidates won only half of the seats in 2018. They won only two seats in western Pennsylvania and seven in the eastern part of the state. This was viewed by many as a resounding success for the Democrats, but this only makes sense when compared with the previous gerrymandered map. It is difficult to envision a scenario in another state where Republicans could conceivably win 55 percent of the vote and not win a majority of seats, and even more difficult to envision a scenario in which they would celebrate such an outcome.

In sum, Pennsylvania's experience reveals that the concentration of Democrats in cities can easily undermine their representation, even if districts are drawn without regard for party, but as we saw in eastern Pennsylvania, this is not *always* so. The details of political geography are crucial. In a context like western Pennsylvania at the scale of congressional districts, where Democrats are highly concentrated in a big city, to achieve a seat share that is anywhere near its vote share, the Democrats would need a redistricting process that intentionally carved up large cities like pizza slices or spokes of a wheel, so as to combine some very Democratic urban neighborhoods with some Republican exurbs in an effort to spread Democrats more efficiently across districts. Democrats might also need to draw very oddly shaped districts along nineteenth-century rail lines and rivers to string together some of their isolated supporters. Such districts are often either illegal, unpalatable to Democratic incumbents, or both.

Where Democrats are highly concentrated, Republican map-drawers have a head start in the game of congressional redistricting. They can achieve impressive results without breaking a sweat. Meandering, noncompact districts are unnecessary. Republicans need only take care that large cities remain whole, and that not too many outlying postindustrial and college towns fall into the same district—goals that often align with traditional districting guidelines. However, there are also settings, like eastern Pennsylvania at the scale of congressional districts, where the size and distribution of Democratic cities are such that a nonpartisan redistricting process would serve them reasonably well. Without partisan manipulation, Democratic suburbs and cities in eastern Pennsylvania would string together to form Democratic districts. In that setting, the only way to produce substantial Republican advantage is through artful gerrymandering.

In Pennsylvania, both intentional and unintentional forms of gerrymandering reinforce one another. The very inefficient distribution of Democrats across state assembly districts is an important part of the explanation for the Republicans' stranglehold on the Pennsylvania General Assembly in recent decades. This, in turn, has provided the Republican Party with the opportunity to draw the congressional lines to their advantage in 2000 and again in 2012.

SINCE IT WAS such an aggressive and successful partisan gerrymander, and because it was the subject of high-profile lawsuits, Pennsylvania's 2012 congressional redistricting plan has received a good deal of national attention. Hopefully it is now clear, however, that the Democrats' problem with representation in Pennsylvania is substantially deeper than the misfortune of having been in the minority in the state legislature when census data were released and new districts were drawn. In fact, the Republicans have controlled the state house of representatives for every session but two since 1990, and for 63 percent of the years since 1938. And with the exception of a brief interregnum in the 1970s and part of 1993, the Republicans have controlled the state senate continuously since 1938.

It is simply not conceivable that a party would experience a lucky streak that lasts for eighty years. It also seems unlikely that, in a competitive

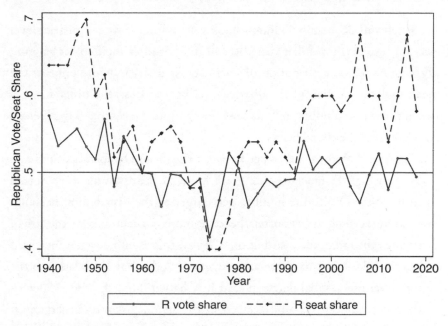

Figure 5.7: Republican Seat Share and Vote Share (Adjusted for Uncontested Seats), Pennsylvania State Senate, 1938–2018

two-party system where the parties split the votes evenly for other offices, a party could lose for eighty years because its candidates are of lower quality or less skilled at campaigning. Figure 5.7 contrasts the vote share—adjusted to account for uncontested seats[4]—and the seat share for the Republican Party in every Senate election since 1938, making it clear that the Democrats' long-term problem is with seats, not votes.[5]

During the period from 1938 to 2018, Democratic candidates actually received more statewide support than Republican candidates in a little more than half of the elections. Adjusting for uncontested seats, the Democrats have won the popular vote almost twice as often as the Republicans since 1960. Yet with the exception of a brief period in the 1970s, the Republican seat share was typically much higher than its vote share. This includes fourteen occasions when the Republican Party won a comfortable legislative majority while garnering less statewide support than the Democrats.

The reason for this disjuncture between votes and seats is no mystery. In a typical Pennsylvania State Senate election, Democratic votes have been highly concentrated in urban districts. In other words, the cross-district histograms presented above—where Democratic votes were concentrated in the left tail of the distribution—look very similar if we use district-level election results from earlier years. Recall that a simple method for gauging asymmetry in the distribution of votes across districts is to compare the mean and the median of the district-level vote shares. The difference between those two numbers tells us how much more concentrated the Democrats are than the Republicans.

Figure 5.8 plots the difference between the mean Democratic vote share and the median Democratic vote share for each Pennsylvania State Senate since the New Deal.[6] The number gets larger as the distribution becomes more asymmetric and Democrats become more concentrated in the urban districts in the tail of the distribution. Clearly, this asymmetry has increased in recent years, but it has been around since World War II. Relative to the county-level presidential data explored in Chapter Two, the rise of Democratic concentration was a bit delayed in the state legislature, in large part because in state and local elections, the Republican machines in Philadelphia and Pittsburgh were still hanging on well after the Democrats started

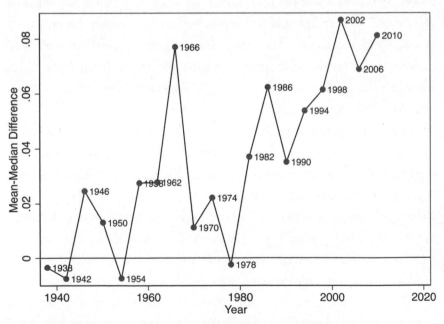

Figure 5.8: Mean-Median Difference in Democratic Vote Shares (Adjusted for Uncontested Seats) across Pennsylvania State Senate Districts, 1938–2010

to take over the urban vote in national elections. For example, Philadel-phia mayors were Republicans until 1952. However, we see that as the cit-ies became solidly Democratic over time, the difference between the mean and the median Democratic vote share increased. There was a respite in the 1970s during the era of denationalized political competition, but for the most part, Democrats have been concentrated in the urban districts, and they have suffered in the transformation of votes to seats in Pennsylvania Senate elections since World War II.

Recall that in the era of increased urban-rural polarization starting in the 1980s, when the correlation between population density and Demo-cratic voting began its rapid ascent around the country, the geographic con-centration of Democrats vis-à-vis Republicans in Pennsylvania presidential elections exploded. Here we see that what was true of presidential elections at the level of Pennsylvania counties is also true of partisan competition in the Pennsylvania Senate. Growth in urban-rural polarization since the 1980s has been associated with growth in the asymmetry in the distribution of partisanship across districts. This asymmetry, in turn, undermines the representation of the Democrats.

GIVEN THE CONCENTRATION of their supporters in a minority of urban dis-tricts, if the Democrats want to win a majority of seats in the state legisla-ture or the congressional delegation, they must do what Senator Schwank did in 2016 in her Reading-based state senate district, what Conor Lamb recently did in his western Pennsylvania congressional district, and what John Murtha was able to do since the 1970s: they must find ways to win in districts that typically vote for Republican presidential candidates.

In fact, Democratic congressional candidates in Pennsylvania have been remarkably successful in managing to do so—right up until the recent era of rapidly increasing urban-rural polarization. Recall that there was a period from the 1960s to the 1990s when congressional races were delinked from presidential races. This was the era of bipartisanship, fluid party labels, split-ticket voting, and pork barrel politics. This was also a period characterized by significant electoral advantages for long-serving incumbents like John

Murtha. When the national parties did not have such distinctive positions on issues like abortion, guns, and immigration, it was much easier for Democrats to win outside of their core bailiwicks in the major cities.

Even when the parties began to develop distinctive national platforms on cultural issues in the 1980s, many of these Democratic incumbents— some of them from relatively rural districts—were able to maintain socially conservative platforms that were distinctive from those of the national party for years. Many, like Murtha, became experts in the game of pork barrel politics, and relied heavily on claiming credit for directing federal resources to their districts. If there was something about the Democratic platform that was unappealing in these pivotal districts, so-called blue dog Democratic candidates, like Jason Altmire in western Pennsylvania and Tim Holden in exurban Philadelphia, could try to simply disavow it, often voting with Republicans.

During the period from 1968 until the election of Bill Clinton in 1992, of all the congressional seats won by Democrats in Pennsylvania, 41 percent were in districts where the Republican candidate won more votes in the presidential election. In contrast, of all the seats won by Republican candidates during this period, only 7 percent were in seats where a Democratic presidential candidate had a majority.

In that context of partisan fluidity, where self-styled Democrats were able to disavow the party's urban reputation, the geographic concentration of Democratic voters in presidential races was less consequential than it is today. In most of the years from 1960 to 2000, the Democrats made up a slim majority of the Pennsylvania congressional delegation, receiving on average around 52 percent of the votes in congressional elections, and a little less than 53 percent of the seats.

However, as the party's reputation has become more closely tied to its urban base on a wider range of issues, as split-ticket voting has faded and blue dog Democrats have exited Congress, the geographic concentration of Democrats—there since the New Deal in presidential elections—has finally come to infect congressional elections as well. To see this, consider once again the simple statistic introduced above: the difference between the mean Democratic vote share across districts and the Democratic vote share of the median district. It is useful to examine this over time, first for presidential election results—aggregated to the level of congressional districts—and then for the district-level results of congressional elections.

District-level presidential election results are useful because they provide a fixed point: everyone in Pennsylvania is evaluating the same two candidates, who are running on the same platform, which they claim they will attempt to implement if they win control of the executive. In this sense, district-level presidential votes give us a window into what the United States might look like if it had a British-style parliamentary system, where parties have national platforms, and voters cast votes for district-level party members based in large part on their evaluations of those platforms.

Figure 5.9 displays the same quantity as Figure 5.8—the difference between the mean Democratic vote share and the median Democratic vote share—but this time for congressional districts rather than state senate districts, and this time distinguishing between district-level presidential vote shares (the dashed line) and the vote shares of the congressional candidates (the solid line).

With the exception of Lyndon B. Johnson's anomalous landslide victory in 1964, in every presidential election since 1952, the average Pennsylvania congressional district has been substantially more Democratic than the median district. In other words, Democrats have been inefficiently packed into the urban districts in the tail of the distribution since the 1950s. This asymmetry in the distribution of votes across districts has been relatively stable over time, and it holds up whether the winner is a Democrat or a Republican, and whether the districts were drawn by Democrats (the 1970s), Republicans (the 1950s and since 2000), or under divided government (the 1960s, 1980s, and 1990s).[7] This asymmetry has reached new heights in recent years. If the United States had a parliamentary system with disciplined parties, the Democrats would likely have faced a disadvantage in Pennsylvania congressional elections throughout the postwar period.

The solid line in Figure 5.9 reveals something quite different in the district-level votes for congressional candidates. First, the relative concentration of Democratic congressional candidates was present for most of the 1950s—a time when district-level presidential election results were highly

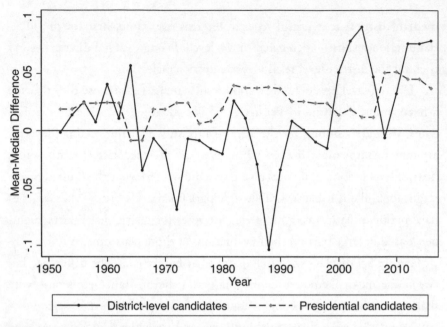

Figure 5.9: Mean-Median Difference in Democratic Presidential Vote Shares and Congressional Vote Shares (Adjusted for Uncontested Seats) across Pennsylvania Congressional Districts, 1952–2016

correlated with congressional results. In fact, the Democrats' support distribution was notably skewed in the 1950s; they received more than half of the votes cast in Pennsylvania congressional elections from 1952 to 1962, while receiving only 46 percent of the seats.[8] But the Democrats were able to overcome their inefficient support distribution in congressional races for a long period starting in the 1960s. In other words, during the era of bipartisanship, split-ticket voting, and pork barrel politics—when congressional elections became more localized, candidate-centric events—votes for congressional Democrats in Pennsylvania—were, if anything, *less* packed in the tail of the distribution than those of Republicans. Throughout this period, Democratic voters were asymmetrically packed in urban districts in presidential elections, but not in congressional races. In recent years, as congressional and presidential elections have become more tightly linked, the relatively skewed support for Democrats—there all along in the presidential data—is now once again relevant in congressional elections. It is in this setting that Republicans have taken control of the redistricting process, creating a worst-case scenario for congressional Democrats in the 2010 round of redistricting.

PENNSYLVANIA HAS BEEN useful as a case study for several reasons. First, as an early-industrializing state with a mixture of large and small nineteenth-century cities, it is an excellent demonstration of why cities so often lose in the game of political representation when winner-take-all districts must be drawn in a context of urban-rural polarization. When cities are too large or too small relative to the size of districts, the party of the urban left can be dramatically underrepresented, even without any intentional partisan manipulation of district boundaries. This problem originated well before the recent era of intense gerrymandering.

But second, Pennsylvania also demonstrates that this logic of urban underrepresentation is not universal. Under some conditions, for instance when suburbs coalesce with the urban core of large cities in voting for the left party, or when small rail-based industrial agglomerations are sufficiently close to one another and districts are very large, the party of the left can escape this trap. It can also do so if district-level contests are delinked from the larger urban-rural partisan conflict and transformed into local popularity contests.

Third, Pennsylvania demonstrates that in a context of urban-rural polarization, it matters a great deal who draws the districts, and according to what rules. It will often be disadvantageous for the Democrats if districts must be compact and drawn to honor municipal boundaries. Pennsylvania's recent history of gerrymandering demonstrates that if incumbent politicians are allowed to draw districts in a nakedly partisan way, stark urban-rural partisan segmentation allows them to make substantial improvements in their seat share. When the Republicans have this power, they can magnify their structural geographic advantage or create one that would otherwise not exist. The Democrats, on the other hand, when presented with the opportunity to redraw the districts, must often set their sights not on creating an advantage for themselves, but on neutralizing their structural disadvantage. This can be a difficult task, however, since it often involves crossing city boundaries and breaking up the bailiwicks of powerful urban incumbents, many of whom may be protected by federal voting rights legislation.

On the whole, since the Socialists and the Republican machines were pushed aside and Democrats became the party of Pennsylvania's cities, the system of winner-take-all districts has worked out quite badly for the Democrats, especially in recent years. In the next chapter, we'll see that Pennsylvania is not alone.

CHAPTER 6

Political Geography and the Representation of Democrats

THE DEMOCRATS CLEARLY face a deep-rooted problem of political geography in Pennsylvania—one that has been compounded by partisan gerrymandering. The extreme concentration of Democrats in cities is now a fact of life in other states as well. But the size, shape, structure, and arrangement of those cities can vary a great deal from one state to another, as can the scale at which state legislative districts are drawn. And while Pennsylvania is a quintessential "purple" state, the implications of geographic concentration are quite different in states that are dominated by one party or the other.

The next task is to examine the other states—each with its unique combination of Democratic urban centers, suburban partisan gradients, and surrounding Republican periphery—and see what happens when they too are divided up into winner-take-all districts. To fully comprehend the Democrats' geography problem, and isolate the role of gerrymandering, we must understand the conditions under which the Democrats' geographic support distribution is most detrimental. For instance, Connecticut has no large cities that approach the size of a congressional district, but it has a large number of proximate smaller industrial cities along the nineteenth-century rail network between Boston and New York, and an expansive, highly educated suburban area near New York City. In those respects, it resembles a swath of eastern Pennsylvania. At the other end of the spectrum, early industrialization was highly concentrated in larger cities in Tennessee and Missouri, where the outlying Democratic mining and railroad outposts are smaller, fewer, and further apart. In that respect they resemble western Pennsylvania. In parts of the Deep South like South Carolina, where cotton and slavery prevailed, large industrial cities did not emerge, and African Americans—and hence Democrats—are less concentrated in space than in the industrialized states.

In short, there is substantial variation across states in the extent to which Democrats are geographically clustered, the scale at which they are clustered, as well as the overall partisanship of the state. The Democrats' geographic concentration in cities often undermines their representation—sometimes quite dramatically—but it does not *always* do so. Sometimes Democratic enclaves string together and overwhelm surrounding Republicans. And in late-industrializing states where Democrats are an embattled minority, their concentration in cities can actually be a *good* thing for their legislative representation. The Democrats suffer in the transformation of votes to seats most clearly in states that are hotly contested, like Pennsylvania, as well as in states where they typically expect to win majorities, like New York. Most of these states are in the original eastern and western manufacturing cores and in the dynamic, urbanizing parts of the South.

The asymmetric distribution of Democrats across legislative districts is extremely common, and it cannot be explained away as an outgrowth of partisan gerrymandering. In practice, it shows up no matter who is drawing the districts. Even if compact, winner-take-all districts are drawn by a computer without regard for partisanship, the configuration would hurt the Democrats in a number of large, populous states. Even though urban clustering actually helps the Democrats in the state legislatures of a handful of Republican-dominated states, on the whole, the representational cost of urban concentration far outweighs its occasional benefit for the Democrats.

As in Pennsylvania, gerrymandering emerges as a crucial part of the story in other states as well. When Republicans gain control of the redistricting process, they are often able to make things substantially worse for the Democrats. As in eastern Pennsylvania, sometimes the geographic distribution of Democrats is not problematic, and the main explanation for pro-Republican bias is gerrymandering. When the Democrats gain control of the redistricting process, in contrast, they are sometimes able to draw lines that neutralize their built-in disadvantage, but they are rarely able to build an advantage.

Above all, this chapter shows that, although it varies across states and over time, the Democrats' geography problem is deep and enduring. Moreover, it has worsened with the recent surge in urban-rural polarization and spread from the North to the South.

DEMOCRATS AND REPUBLICANS are geographically segregated in a very specific way. Both groups are more likely to live among their own kind, but there is a fascinating asymmetry to their segregation. At each geographic scale relevant for drawing state and congressional legislative districts, Democrats are more likely to live in homogeneous Democratic neighborhoods, and Republicans are more likely to live in mixed neighborhoods. Recall that Democratic presidential votes are far more geographically concentrated than Republican votes at the level of counties. But we have also now learned that most of the relevant segregation and clustering occurs *within* rather than across counties. We can get a clearer sense of the relative concentration of Democrats by applying the "nearest neighbor" technique introduced in the previous chapter to a national precinct-level data set from the 2008 election.

Figure 6.1 communicates the extent to which Democrats are more geographically concentrated than Republicans in each state, focusing on the geographic scale of state senate districts.[1] The horizontal axis captures the share of the average *Republican's* nearest neighbors who are *Democrats*, where the "neighborhood" is the size of a state senate district in that particular state. The vertical axis captures the share of the average *Democrat's* nearest neighbors who are *Democrats*. As we move to the right on the horizontal axis, and as we move up on the vertical axis, neighborhoods are becoming more Democratic overall, meaning that we are moving from the most Republican to the most Democratic states. The key insight of the graph is that

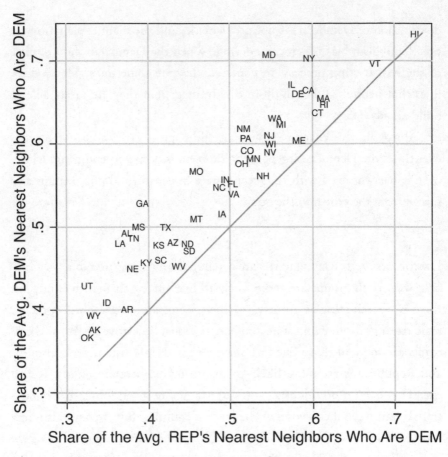

Figure 6.1: The Relative Geographic Concentration of Democrats

every single state is above the 45-degree line. This indicates that no matter the level of statewide partisanship, Democrats live in more homogeneous partisan neighborhoods than Republicans.

If partisans were randomly distributed in space, or if they were segregated in a symmetric way, we would expect to see observations clustered around the 45-degree line, some above and some below. For example, consider Indiana, where the 2008 presidential election was almost a tie. If partisans were evenly distributed in space, we would expect to see that the average Democrat lived in a 50 percent Democratic neighborhood, and the average Republican also lived in a 50 percent Democratic neighborhood. However, because Democrats are clustered in Indianapolis as well as in second-order cities like Fort Wayne, Terre Haute, Muncie, South Bend, and Gary, we see that the average Republican lives in a neighborhood that is slightly Republican, but the average Democrat lives in a neighborhood that is almost 56 percent Democratic.

In general, we can see that states with large, very Democratic cities—like Georgia, Missouri, Illinois, and New York—are quite far from the 45-degree line. States without regional primate cities—where the population is more evenly distributed throughout the state—are closer to the 45-degree line. Examples include Arkansas, West Virginia, the Dakotas, and the New England states. But in all cases, Democrats are more likely to live in homogeneous copartisan neighborhoods than are Republicans. The story is very much the same if we use the scale of state lower chamber districts or US congressional districts to define neighborhoods.

Let us take the obvious next step and ask what happens when we draw legislative districts. Here as well, Democrats end up highly concentrated within urban districts. First, to hold constant any possible effects of partisan gerrymandering, let us consider hundreds of simulated districting plans generated by my collaborator, Jowei Chen, for each state. And to evaluate whether Democrats are relatively more "packed" into districts with their copartisans than are Republicans, let us return to the simple statistic introduced in the previous chapter: the extent to which the mean across simulated districts is more Democratic than the median in simulated districts. We can calculate this mean-median difference for the 2008 Obama vote share across all of the simulated districts in each state.

Next, it is useful to also examine the actual districts that were enacted in each state. For these also, we can calculate the difference between the mean Obama vote share and the median across districts. By comparing the actual and simulated districts, we can examine whether Democrats are either more or less concentrated in the enacted districts than in the baseline districts that were drawn without regard for partisanship. Figure 6.2 facilitates this comparison by plotting these measures of Democratic concentration against each other across states. The mean-median difference in the *simulated* districts is on the horizontal axis, and this quantity for the *enacted* districts is on the vertical axis. The top panel focuses on state upper legislative chambers, and the bottom panel considers congressional delegations for states with more than three districts.[2]

Let us begin with the state senate districts, and focus first on the simulated districts, for which the mean-median difference is displayed on the horizontal axis. The first thing to notice is that the mean-median difference is positive for almost all of the states. This means that the average simulated district is more Democratic than the median in almost every state. This is because in each of these states, a group of exceptionally Democratic urban districts emerges when the computer draws simulated state senate districts. Note that Pennsylvania's mean-median difference is right around the average of all states.

Since Democrats are clustered in the urban districts even in the simulations, it is not possible to blame partisan gerrymandering for the existence of this phenomenon. However, the graph also allows us to see what happens when politicians, courts, and redistricting commissions—rather than a computer algorithm—draw the districts. Not surprisingly, the positive values on the vertical axis reveal that Democrats are also more concentrated than Republicans in the enacted redistricting plans. By comparing the value on the horizontal and vertical axis for each state, we can compare the mean-median difference in the simulated, nonpartisan districts with that in the enacted districting plan. If a state is above the 45-degree line, Democrats are *more* concentrated in the enacted plan than in the simulated plans. The states where districts were drawn under unified Republican control are represented by light circles. Those drawn under Democratic control are plotted with dark circles in the background. Those where districts were drawn by bipartisan or nonpartisan commissions, by divided legislatures, or by courts are plotted without circles.

Notice that with the exception of New York, the bipartisan/nonpartisan group of states is arranged nicely along the 45-degree line. That is, the relative concentration of Democrats in the enacted plans looks very similar to that of the simulated plans in the states where districts were not drawn under unified party control. However, many of the states where Republicans drew the lines are above the 45-degree line, indicating that Democrats are substantially *more* clustered than in the simulated plans. This is consistent

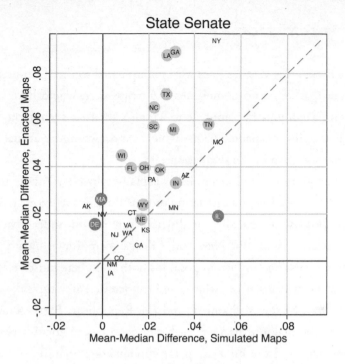

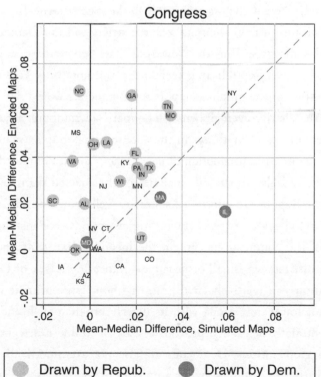

Figure 6.2: Mean-Median Difference, Simulated and Enacted Maps, State Senates and US Congress

with the notion that district lines were manipulated so that Democrats were even more "packed" into homogeneous districts than would have been the case under a nonpartisan approach. We also see that Democrats are *less* packed in the Illinois enacted plan—which was drawn under unified Democratic control—than in the simulations.

Partisan gerrymandering also likely explains why New York is an outlier from the 45-degree line. Its districting process is treated as "nonpartisan" on the graph because technically, the districts were drawn under divided government. More specifically, New York's districts are drawn by a bipartisan advisory commission, and its proposal for both chambers must be approved as one law by the legislature, where the Democratic Party typically controls the assembly (the lower chamber) and the Republican Party controls the senate. But the majority party of each chamber gets to appoint two of the commissioners, and the minority party appoints one. A norm of logrolling has emerged, whereby the majority party in the state senate—for many years the Republicans—draws the state senate districts and the Democrats draw the assembly districts. Thus the New York State Senate districts are widely understood to be a Republican gerrymander. But note New York's horizontal positioning on the graph—support for Democrats would still be highly skewed if the districts were drawn by a nonpartisan computer algorithm.

We see some similar things in the congressional graph. Again, there is a similar asymmetric distribution of partisanship in the simulated plans for most states, and also in the vast majority of the enacted plans. And again, many of the Republican-controlled states are well above the 45-degree line. But there are also a number of interesting exceptions. For instance, on the left side of the congressional graph, the mean-median difference for the simulated districts was small or negative—indicating a lack of Democratic concentration—in relatively small states without large primate cities, like Kansas and Iowa; in Arizona with its diverse urban sprawl; and in Ohio, with its unusually dense and proximate array of sizable nineteenth-century railroad agglomerations. Democrats are also not asymmetrically clustered in the redistricting simulations for a number of southern states with many rural African Americans.

As with state senates, there are many states well above the 45-degree line, meaning that Democrats were far more packed in the enacted congressional districting plans than in the simulated plans. As indicated by the light gray circles, Republicans drew the districts in almost all of these. In some of the southern states with large rural African American populations, for example, South Carolina, the simulated congressional plans, which paid no attention to race, did not produce an asymmetric clustering of Democrats. In some cases, they produced the opposite, indicated by a negative value on the horizontal axis in the graph. Yet in many of these cases, the familiar asymmetric clustering of Democrats was nevertheless present in the enacted districts, as indicated by high positive values on the vertical axis.

This is because of a complex combination of racial and partisan gerrymandering. In many of these cases, the Voting Rights Act (VRA) required the state to draw one or more majority-minority districts that would not have emerged without a conscious effort to link far-flung minority communities. In some cases, however, like Virginia and North Carolina, the Republican legislatures used the VRA as a pretext to draw districts that had far larger African American populations—and hence larger Democratic majorities— than required by federal law, leaving the remaining districts with a much lower Democratic population. On some occasions, this was done with the explicit consent of urban incumbents who saw these districts as personally beneficial.

North Carolina is an especially striking case. The nonpartisan simulations did not lead to any asymmetric packing of Democrats. Due to the presence of a sprawling knowledge-economy corridor, a series of smaller automobile cities with relatively low partisan gradients, and the distribution of rural African Americans, Democrats are relatively efficiently distributed in North Carolina at the scale of congressional districts. Nevertheless, the enacted plan demonstrated one of the most extreme mean-median differences of any state. Just as the Pennsylvania gerrymander was overturned in state court, the North Carolina plan was recently overturned by a federal district court. As in Pennsylvania, expert witnesses used redistricting simulations to convince the court that the dramatic overrepresentation of Republicans was the result of gerrymandering rather than geography.

In short, Democrats are often, but not always, more concentrated than Republicans at each of the spatial scales used for drawing electoral districts. Republican gerrymandering, sometimes in tandem with the Voting Rights

Act, often exacerbates this. Democratic gerrymandering sometimes ameliorates it. The next task is to explore what this means for representation.

IN PENNSYLVANIA, IT was very clear that the asymmetric concentration of Democrats undermined their legislative representation. However, Pennsylvania is a highly competitive state. The dynamic is different in the South and the Mountain West, where early twentieth-century industrialization and city growth did not happen, and where the Democrats today are an embattled minority. If a party receives 30 percent of the statewide vote and its voters are evenly distributed in space, it will lose every single district in a landslide. In this context, the minority party's only hope for legislative representation is if its supporters are clustered, such that they form majorities in one or more districts. For instance, the geographic clustering of Democrats in Nashville and Memphis is not necessarily a bad thing for the Democrats in Tennessee. With a statewide vote share that is typically around 40 percent, Democrats are able to win two congressional seats. If their support were more dispersed across smaller cities—as in West Virginia—they would perhaps not win any.

Utah is an extremely Republican state, but Salt Lake City—like every other American city of its size—is very Democratic. It would be a *good* thing for the Democrats in Utah if there were a reasonably large difference between the mean Democratic vote share and the median—a *good* thing if there were a long left tail in the distribution of Republican vote shares across districts. In a state where Republicans win very large majorities overall, and thus the cross-district mean is extremely Republican, it is a blessing for the Democrats if the distribution of vote shares is highly skewed, such that at least one Salt Lake City district is less than 50 percent Republican. Note that in Figure 6.2, at the scale of congressional districts, the simulated districting plans do indeed produce a sizable mean-median difference in Utah because of the clustering of Democrats in the Salt Lake City region. However, we can also see, by looking at the vertical axis, that the mean-median difference was negligible in the plan drawn by the Republicans. In Utah, the best strategy for Republicans was not to further pack Democrats in an urban district, but to break up the Salt Lake City metro area in a way that would prevent a sufficiently Democratic cluster from emerging. However, this strategy was not built to withstand the "blue wave" of 2018. Too much of Salt Lake City was placed in District Four, and the Democratic candidate, Ben McAdams, was able to win this district by seven hundred votes.

This is also quite relevant in southern states where the Voting Rights Act is an important consideration. Alabama's largest city, Birmingham, is the largest Democratic cluster in Alabama, but the simulations reveal that it is insufficiently large to produce a Democratic congressional district on its own. And African American Democrats are geographically quite dispersed elsewhere in rural Alabama. In other words, in a state where they are a minority, Democrats are insufficiently clustered in Alabama to win any congressional seats. In this instance, by linking Birmingham together with far-flung African Americans in a noncompact majority-minority district, the Voting Rights Act may have reduced the Republican seat share by producing a Democratic district in a setting where one might otherwise not emerge. This is quite different from North Carolina—a highly competitive state— where, by drawing gerrymandered districts that artificially packed far-flung Democrats, the Republican legislature substantially *improved* its seat share.

THE NEXT TASK is to put all of these insights together and get a full picture of the relationship between votes and seats in the US states. We cannot do this without first gaining a basic understanding of the way votes are transformed into seats in two-party systems with winner-take-all districts. It may seem fair and reasonable, at first glance, to expect that if neither party is more clustered than the other, a party's seat share will be proportionate to its vote share. One might imagine, for instance, that 60 percent of the vote should translate into 60 percent of the seats. However, for reasons that will be clear in a moment, this is not how majoritarian democracies work. Because of the way voters are typically distributed across districts, the winning party typically receives a seat share that is substantially higher than its vote share.

Before moving on, we need to first understand this dynamic. This will give us a baseline to determine whether a particular seat share in a state is good or bad for a party given its vote share, and whether it is typical or anomalous. Abstracting away from the details of a specific state, we need to know what type of seat share a party might expect if it typically loses by a lot, like the Democrats in Tennessee; wins or loses by a small margin, like the Democrats in Pennsylvania; or if it typically wins by a large margin, like the Democrats in New York. In each of these scenarios, we would like to contrast the seat share we would expect if the parties' support was skewed across districts, as in Pennsylvania, with what we would expect if it was distributed more symmetrically across districts. This will allow us to understand the impact of geographic concentration in different types of states.

In other words, we need a gentle introduction to electoral geography. The most painless way to achieve this is with a simple example. Imagine a hypothetical democracy, portrayed in Figure 6.3, with only forty-eight voters, twenty-four of whom are predisposed toward the urban left party—let's call them Democrats (D)—and twenty-four typically prefer the rural right party—the Republicans (R). Voters living close to one another in city centers typically vote for the D Party, suburbs are evenly split, and those living further from one another in rural areas typically vote for the R Party. There are three D voters in each city, and three R voters in each surrounding rural periphery. Let us imagine that this polity must be apportioned into six districts of equal size, the boundaries of which are portrayed with vertical bars. Each district contains eight voters and is hence larger than the scale of the D and R clusters. The two parties are evenly matched in four of the resulting

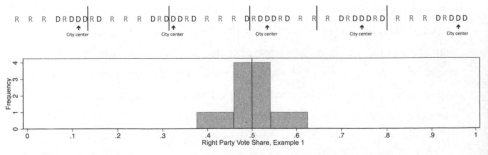

Figure 6.3: A Hypothetical State with Small, Evenly Spaced Cities, Symmetric Distribution of Partisanship

districts, which inevitably contain urban, suburban, and rural areas, while the D Party can expect a majority in one district that ends up slightly more urban, and the R Party can anticipate a majority in one district that ends up slightly more rural. The distribution of expected partisanship across districts is then symmetric with a large peak in the middle. With 50 percent of the votes, a party can expect 50 percent of the seats.

Next, consider scenarios in which one of the parties suffers from a scandal or benefits from a strong economy, and the election is not tied. To do so, let's simulate ten thousand elections in which one voter is randomly selected to switch from D to R, then do the same for two voters, three voters, and so on until the R Party wins all of the votes. And let's also conduct the same exercise in the opposite direction. For each scenario, we can calculate the average seat share across all simulations that would be produced

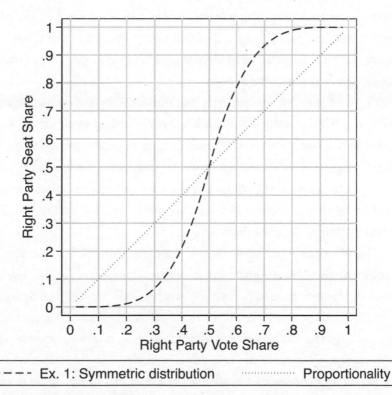

Figure 6.4: Votes and Seats with a Symmetric Distribution of Partisanship

by the districting scheme displayed in Figure 6.3. The resulting relationship between votes and seats is displayed with the dashed line in Figure 6.4.

This dashed line in Figure 6.4 is what election scholars have long identified as the standard votes-to-seats curve in a winner-take-all majoritarian system. As a benchmark or starting point for thinking about votes and seats in a system of winner-take-all districts, election scholars imagine a distribution of partisanship across districts that resembles something like the symmetric histogram in Figure 6.3. That is, they imagine a large density of competitive districts in the middle of the distribution, and symmetric "tails" of the distribution on each side; neither of which is further from the median than the other. And as a result, they assume that the standard transformation of votes to seats looks something like Figure 6.4.

An important feature of this is often referred to as the "winner's bonus." When a party wins 52 percent of the votes, it receives substantially more than 52 percent of the seats. For comparison, the dotted 45-degree line represents proportionality. The winner's bonus exists because, in the pivotal districts near the middle of the distribution, a victory by even a single vote will deliver the seat, and when a party benefits from a tide in its favor, this can happen in several seats at once.

Figures 6.3 and 6.4 help clarify that under the right circumstances, spatial segregation between the urban left and rural right need not provide an advantage for one party or the other. In this example, the cities are small relative to the size of districts, but not so small that the left party is overwhelmed, as happens to Lancaster at the scale of Pennsylvania State Senate districts. In this example, cities are also similar in size and spaced with a uniform distance between them.

This example might come close to capturing some US states, like West Virginia or the New England states, where Democrats are not especially clustered. However, most US states—and indeed most industrialized democracies with winner-take-all districts—do *not* resemble Figure 6.3. And as a result, the standard, benchmark votes-to-seats transformation imagined by election scholars since the 1950s does not quite capture reality.

Let us now consider a hypothetical example that more closely resembles Pennsylvania and other US states with large cities, where instead of being clustered in a series of small, evenly spaced agglomerations that do not quite reach the size of districts, there is at least one cluster that reaches or surpasses that size along with other smaller agglomerations that do not. For instance, Philadelphia is larger than the size of a congressional district, while Reading is not. Reading is larger than the size of a Pennsylvania House of Representatives district, but neighboring Birdsboro is not. Recall that within regions, city populations are often arranged in hierarchies, such that the largest city is twice as large as the second-largest city, and so on.

A stylized example of this more realistic pattern of political geography is presented in Figure 6.5. It has one large city that votes overwhelmingly for the D Party, surrounded by heterogeneous suburbs and a rural periphery that vote for the R Party. It also contains a smaller city and a small town, both surrounded by right-leaning suburbs and a rural periphery.

Again, let us examine what happens when this evenly divided polity is partitioned into six districts of equal size, the boundaries of which are captured with the solid vertical lines. Because its supporters are inefficiently packed into the large city and the cross-district distribution has a left skew, the left party wins only 42 percent of the seats in spite of winning half the votes. This is akin to the long-term experience of the Democrats in the Pennsylvania Senate.

Now, using the same technique described above, let's imagine elections that are not tied, and examine how this type of geographic distribution translates into seats at different levels of statewide support. Figure 6.6 adds a

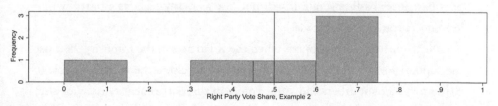

Figure 6.5: A Hypothetical State with a Hierarchy of City Sizes and a Skewed Distribution of Partisanship

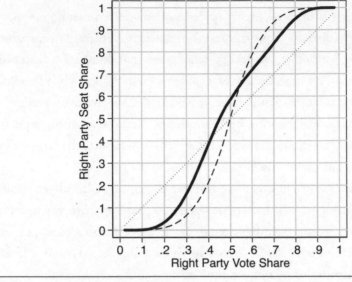

Figure 6.6: Votes and Seats with a Skewed Distribution of Partisanship

thick, solid line to the vote-seat graph that captures the vote-seat curve associated with the example above.

Several features of this curve are noteworthy. First, the curve is flatter and closer to proportionality than the dashed curve. Because of the greater relative clustering of the D Party, it is able to win more seats when it performs badly (on the right side of the graph) than if it had a more even distribution of support across cities. It is able to win seats in its urban core support area even when it performs very badly overall. This is precisely the story told above about Utah and Tennessee. We can think of this as the "silver lining" of geographic concentration. When a party with a highly concentrated support base loses badly overall, it will not lose as many seats as a party with a less concentrated support base.

Next consider what happens when the R Party is in the minority. Because the support for the D Party is so concentrated in cities, the R Party is able to string together suburban and rural voters in districts that it wins with slim majorities, and relative to the more even distribution of cities portrayed by the dashed line, it is able to win a seat bonus when it is in the minority. This is the story of the Republicans in the state of New York in recent decades.

From a normative perspective, perhaps the most striking feature of Figure 6.6 is the large seat bonus enjoyed by the party of the right in the case of a tied election. The bold curve displays an asymmetry that is not present in the dashed curve. In general, the R Party can expect a larger seat bonus than the urban D Party. Most notably, the R Party can expect a majority of seats with only 45 percent of the votes. Likewise, it achieves proportional representation with 40 percent of the votes, while the D Party can only expect 30 percent of the seats with a similar vote share.

As we learned from these examples, to understand a party's representation advantage, we must compare its seat share *not* with its vote share, but with the dashed line in the graphs above—the seat share that *would* be obtained if voters were symmetrically distributed across districts. While there are interesting exceptions, the overall relationship between votes and seats across the American states is exactly what we would expect given the clustering of Democrats in urban districts. In other words, as captured by the bold line in Figure 6.6, there is a remarkable overrepresentation of Republicans in highly Democratic states, hotly contested states, and moderately Republican states, but this advantage fades away in extremely Republican states.

To see this, consider Figure 6.7, which captures overall statewide partisanship on the horizontal axis, as measured by the average statewide vote share of Republican candidates in US Senate and presidential elections from 2012 to 2016.[3] On the vertical axis, it displays the average Republican seat share during the same period. As in the graphs above, when the district map was drawn by Republicans, the state is surrounded by a light gray circle; when it was drawn by Democrats, the state is surrounded by a dark gray circle. The dashed line captures the "benchmark" vote-seat transformation described above—the one we would expect if the distribution of Republican vote shares across districts were symmetric with a large peak in the middle. The solid gray line represents proportional representation.

The graphs tell a remarkable story about Republican advantage. If we connect the dots, we get a line that looks very much like the bold line in Figure 6.6. On the left side of each graph, in states where the Democrats dominate in statewide elections, most of the observations are well above the

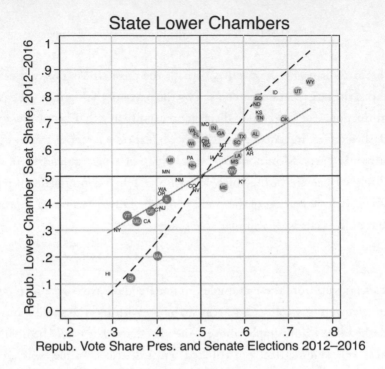

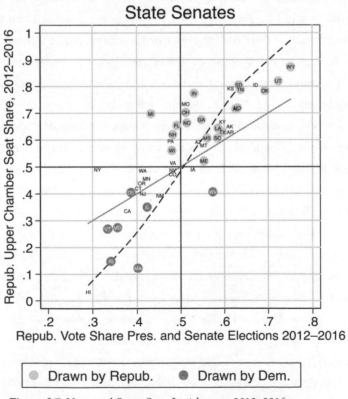

Figure 6.7: Votes and Seats, State Legislatures, 2012–2016

dashed line. This indicates that the Republican seat share in states where they receive a minority of the vote share is higher than we would expect from the benchmark. Remember that this benchmark is one in which neither party is more geographically clustered than the other—where the vote share of the average (mean) district is identical to that of the median district. But we have learned that in virtually every US state, at the scale of state legislative districts, the benchmark assumption of symmetry does not capture reality. Democrats are clustered in overwhelmingly Democratic districts, and the average (mean) district is more Democratic than the median district.

In the very Democratic states on the left side of the graph, this translates into a surprisingly favorable outcome for Republicans. In fact, the Republican seat share in many of these states is in the vicinity of proportionality with the statewide vote share. The only exceptions are (1) a handful of states where Democrats drew the districts (for example, the New England states, Maryland, and Illinois), and (2) states where Democrats are not especially clustered at the relevant spatial scale (for example, the New Mexico Senate). And in the New York State Senate, up until 2018, the Republican Party has actually been able to win a majority of seats in spite of losing by very large margins in typical statewide races.

Compare these very Democratic states on the left side of the graphs with the very Republican states on the right side of the graphs. As in the simple hypothetical example above, we see that in states where the Republicans dominate, the Democrats begin to enjoy the silver lining of geographic concentration. Because the Democrats' support is highly clustered in the cities of states like Tennessee, Oklahoma, and Utah, Democrats are able to win a substantial number of urban seats in spite of their low statewide support, and the Republican seat share falls a bit short of the benchmark we would expect in the absence of asymmetric clustering. All in all, however, the graphs suggest that the Republicans have obtained a larger seat share in deep blue states—those like New York that are more than 60 percent Democratic—than Democrats have in deep red states—states like Utah that are more than 60 percent Republican.

The most remarkable Republican advantage, however, is to be seen in the most competitive states in the middle of these graphs. Once statewide

Republican support surpasses 40 percent, the Republican vote share typically exceeds proportionality. In fact, there are two states—Minnesota
and Michigan—where Republicans have been able to win legislative majorities with less than 45 percent statewide support. Note that the districts
in Minnesota were not drawn by Republicans. There are several additional
states—including New Hampshire, Pennsylvania, Wisconsin, Florida, and
Virginia—where Republicans have won large legislative majorities while
losing statewide elections. And there is another group of states—including
Missouri, North Carolina, Ohio, and Indiana—where Republicans have
won very large legislative supermajorities on the order of 65 percent or more
while winning only rather slim statewide majorities. These legislative outcomes are well beyond the typical winner's bonus discussed above.

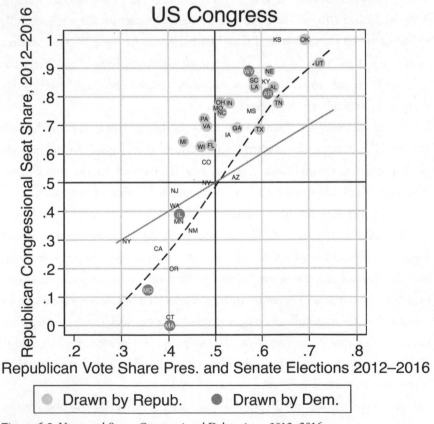

Figure 6.8: Votes and Seats, Congressional Delegations, 2012–2016

Next, let's turn to a similar graph for each state's congressional delegation, focusing only on states with at least three congressional districts.

In Figure 6.8, the advantage for Republicans is even more pronounced. Above all, the silver lining of geographic concentration has largely disappeared for the Democrats at the congressional level. With the exception of a couple of New England states, the *best* the Democrats can do is end up right around the dashed line associated with a standard, symmetric vote-seat curve. Very few observations fall below the dashed line, which would indicate an advantage for the Democrats. The vast majority of states fall well above the dashed line, indicating a substantial Republican advantage. This Republican advantage has been present even in very Democratic states, like New York, New Jersey, Washington State, and Illinois, where the Republicans are typically able to achieve a seat share that is actually proportionate to their statewide support. This proportionality may not seem remarkable at first glance, but it is important to understand that in a two-party majoritarian system, these are exceptionally good seat shares for a party with such weak statewide support. To appreciate this, simply contrast these states with those on the right side of the graph. There is not a single solidly red state where the Democrats come anywhere near proportional representation. The Democrats would be happy to win, for instance, 45 percent of the seats in Georgia, 40 percent in Texas, or 30 percent in Oklahoma. Even in the wave election of 2018, when Democratic senate and gubernatorial candidates came quite close to victory in Georgia and Texas and overperformed in Oklahoma, they were unable to come close to such seat shares.

The role of political geography in the surprisingly strong representation of Republicans in congressional delegations is especially difficult to deny in states where extreme pro-Republican gerrymandering is unlikely: for example, New York, where the congressional districts were drawn by a court-appointed special master; New Jersey, where they were drawn by a bipartisan commission; or Illinois, where they were drawn under unified Democratic control. As in the state legislatures, the most striking Republican advantage is found in the competitive states in the middle of the graph, where Republicans win large legislative supermajorities even though their statewide support is in the vicinity of 50 percent.

THE EXTENT OF Republican overrepresentation indicated in the graphs above is quite remarkable. The Democrats often fall well short of the legislative representation we would expect, given their statewide support. While partisan gerrymandering is not the only explanation, it plays an important role in the magnitude of this phenomenon. The gray dots in the graphs reveal quite clearly that Republican legislators drew the districts in many of the states with the most striking levels of Republican overrepresentation. These include several states of the nineteenth-century manufacturing core, including Michigan, Indiana, Ohio, Pennsylvania, Wisconsin, and Missouri, in addition to some of the rapidly urbanizing southern states including North Carolina, Florida, Georgia, and Virginia. If we estimate a statistical model that controls for political geography, we see that, as suggested by the graphs above, Republican seat shares are significantly higher in states where Republicans controlled the redistricting process.[4]

Additionally, as in the case study of Pennsylvania, the importance of partisan gerrymandering is crystal clear when we contrast the partisanship of redistricting simulations with that of the enacted districts. In 2010, the people of Florida adopted an amendment to the state constitution that, while keeping the redistricting process in the hands of legislators, forbade them to consider partisanship when drawing the districts. Headed by the League of Women Voters, a group of plaintiffs successfully sued in 2013, arguing that the legislature's 2012 congressional map had in fact been drawn for the most part by partisan operatives for partisan gain. At trial, Jowei Chen and I presented evidence from redistricting simulations, indicating that although Florida's geography slightly favored the Republicans at the scale of congressional districts, the bias in the map created by the legislature was far beyond anything that would emerge from nonpartisan simulations. In later trials in North Carolina and Pennsylvania, this same approach was successfully used by plaintiffs to demonstrate that gerrymandering led to partisan bias beyond what might be explained by the geographic concentration of Democrats. Even though Democrats are clustered in ways that often produce a seat bonus for Republicans in the simulated plans, the court can be confident that a gerrymander has occurred when the enacted plan goes further, such that the enacted plan is a statistical outlier when compared with the simulated plans.[5]

This approach reveals that gerrymandering and geography are usually not substitutes but complements. The clustering of Democrats in cities often provides Republican map-drawers with an excellent starting point, such that they could achieve a disproportionate seat share without much effort or skill—simply by drawing compact and contiguous districts, as the law often demands. However, as demonstrated in the Pennsylvania congressional example in the previous chapter, they can often build on that advantage by taking care to pack Democrats to a greater extent than would occur with a nonpartisan redistricting process, break up medium-sized isolated cities, and prevent smaller Democratic cities and suburbs from stringing together to facilitate potential Democratic victories.

The most controversial states are those in the middle of the graphs above, where Republicans win large legislative majorities in spite of very competitive statewide elections: Michigan, Ohio, Indiana, Missouri, Pennsylvania, Wisconsin, Florida, Virginia, and North Carolina. In each of these states, well beyond half of the simulated state senate districts had Republican vote shares larger than the statewide Republican vote share, indicating that we would expect to see some level of Republican advantage even in the absence of gerrymandering. The same can be said about the simulated congressional districts in each of these states, with the exception of North Carolina and Ohio. In those states—each of which has a number of medium-sized cities as well as proximate clusters of smaller cities—the congressional simulations do not produce substantial pro-Republican bias. In general, the presence of pro-Republican bias in the simulated redistricting plans should not be understood as evidence that gerrymandering is somehow unimportant. On the contrary, redistricting simulations allow us to quantify its extent.

In sum, gerrymandering often makes things worse for the Democrats when the Republicans draw the districts, and the Democrats improve their seat share somewhat when they have the opportunity to draw the districts. But by no means can we conclude that the overall representation problem faced by the Democrats was conjured out of thin air by skilled redistricting operatives.

BY NOW IT should be quite clear that in the early twenty-first century, the Democratic Party has a political geography problem. This problem is most pronounced in the states of the original manufacturing core, like Pennsylvania, where due to patterns of nineteenth-century industrialization, Democrats are most geographically concentrated. But this lurking geography problem has not always been discernable. Looking at overall votes and seats in the US Congress from the 1960s through the 1980s—prior to the recent rise of urban-rural polarization and the nationalization of politics—the Democrats often received larger seat shares than their vote shares and consistently controlled Congress. However, this was largely an artifact of (1) the "winner's bonus" described above, (2) the relatively efficient distribution of Democrats in the South prior to the partisan realignment of nonurban Southern whites from the Democratic Party to the Republican Party, and perhaps most importantly, (3) the ability of the Democrats to win in Republican districts throughout the era of partisan fluidity.

In the previous chapter on Pennsylvania, we learned that in *presidential* elections, Democratic votes have been inefficiently concentrated in urban districts ever since the New Deal. The same observation can be made about the United States as a whole. In presidential voting, the concentration of Democrats in urban congressional districts across the United States emerged far earlier than the last couple of rounds of redistricting and the Republican-led Redistricting Majority Project (REDMAP).

Let's return once again to our simple summary statistic for assessing the distribution of partisanship across congressional districts: the difference between the mean and median. A simple approach is to calculate the mean-median difference in the district-level presidential vote for each individual presidential election, and then compute averages for each decade, which are presented using the solid line in Figure 6.9.[6] As above, this difference is calculated so that positive values correspond to higher levels of Democratic concentration in the tail of the distribution. We can see that the

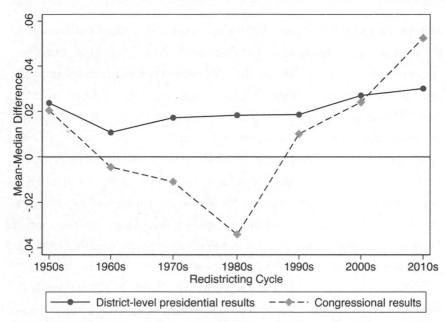

Figure 6.9: Mean-Median Difference in Democratic Presidential Vote Shares and Congressional Vote Shares (Adjusted for Uncontested Seats) across US Congressional Districts, 1950s–2010s

relative concentration of Democrats within districts has been quite stable throughout the postwar period. There was a slight dip in the 1960s, which can be explained by the landslide victory of Lyndon B. Johnson in 1964, and there has been an uptick in the last two redistricting cycles, but the basic pattern has been around all along.

But if support for the Democratic Party was so badly distributed in space for so long, how did Democrats manage to control the House of Representatives for so much of the postwar period? First, for decades Democrats could rely on a large chunk of seats in the South. And second, as established in the Pennsylvania case study, they were able to win a large number of seats in districts won by Republican presidential candidates even outside the South. In other words, presidential and congressional elections became uncoupled in the 1960s. The dashed line in Figure 6.9 shows this. It captures the mean-median difference for each redistricting cycle, but it uses actual congressional election results rather than presidential election results.[7] In the 1950s, district-level presidential and congressional results were highly correlated, and the cross-district distributions of support for Democratic presidential and congressional candidates were virtually identical. However, the two lines started to diverge in the 1960s after the historic loss of Republican Barry Goldwater to Democratic incumbent Lyndon B. Johnson in 1964. For the better part of three decades, up through the Reagan administration, the Democrats were able to make their geography problem disappear in congressional elections. This was the era of lingering Southern Democrats, denationalized politics, and overall partisan fluidity. As urban-rural partisan polarization has taken off since the 1980s and the correlation between congressional and presidential elections has grown, the relative concentration of Democrats in urban congressional districts has come to resemble what has *always* been the case in presidential elections.

The Democrats' problem is deep and structural. It did not suddenly emerge in the last decade. But it has been hidden from view by the presence of Southern Democrats and the success of "boll weevils" and "blue dogs" in Republican districts. To verify and expand upon this insight, let's move beyond the mean-median difference and take a look at a concept that has become known as "the efficiency gap." The concept is simple: count up all the *wasted* votes received by a party in districts that it loses, then combine this with all the *surplus* votes for the party beyond the winning threshold in districts it wins. For each party, tally these numbers over all the districts, and divide by the total number of votes cast. The number conveys how efficiently a party uses its votes: the lower the number, the more efficient. The efficiency *gap* is then the difference between the two parties. A party with an inefficient support distribution will have the problem that relative to its competitor, too many of its voters are stuck in districts that it either loses by small majorities or wins by large majorities.[8]

Let's examine the efficiency gap for each congressional election since 1950. Here, we use congressional, not presidential election results, and the gap is constructed so that as with the mean-median ratio, higher positive numbers correspond to a more efficient support distribution for Republicans, and negative numbers correspond to an advantage for Democrats. Using every district in the country, Figure 6.10 displays averages for each redistricting period with a bold line. The "U" shape of the graph—and the

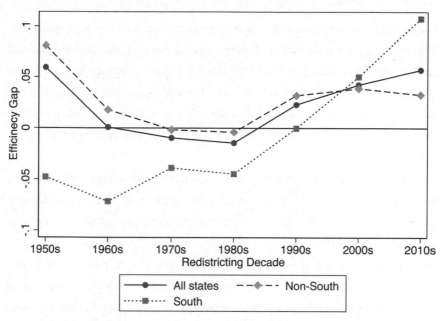

Figure 6.10: Efficiency Gap, South versus Non-South, 1950s–2010s

conclusions drawn from it—should now be quite familiar. The Democrats had a relatively inefficient support distribution in the 1950s, which went into abeyance for three decades during the era of partisan fluidity, and then returned again in the 1990s in the era of invigorated urban-rural polarization.

Recall from county-level data presented earlier that the rise of relative geographic concentration for the Democrats was radically different in the South than in the North. Even though Democrats were becoming quite geographically concentrated in the North in the New Deal era, they were relatively dispersed in the South in the era of the segregationist Southern Democrats. The efficiency gap, then, should also be examined separately for southern and non-southern congressional districts. Accordingly, these are represented on the graph with dotted and dashed lines, respectively.

Outside the South—especially in the manufacturing core—the Democrats suffered from an inefficient support distribution in the 1950s, wasting too many votes in urban manufacturing districts, and not winning enough to form majorities in the pivotal nonurban districts. Their saving grace during that period was the solidly Democratic South. From the 1960s to the 1980s, Democratic candidates were able to win many of the pivotal districts outside the South by adopting a very flexible approach to the party platform. But their relatively inefficient support distribution in the North returned in the 1990s and has prevailed ever since. In spite of aggressive gerrymandering by the Republicans in states like Pennsylvania and Michigan in the last redistricting cycle, the overall efficiency gap outside the South has not increased notably since the 1990s, and the gap has still not returned to the level of the 1950s.

In the South, however, we see a dramatic transformation. Initially, the Southern Democrats were a rural party with a relatively efficient support distribution. But as the partisan realignment progressed, they became an increasingly urban party—especially in growing states with big cities like Georgia and Texas—and by the end of the 1990s, patterns of political geography started to look very much like those in northern states, with overwhelmingly Democratic city centers and an increasing Republican vote share as one moved from the city center to the countryside. In such states, a northern-style efficiency gap emerged. By the 2000s, the pro-Republican efficiency gap in southern districts was very similar to that of northern districts.

But the explosive growth of the efficiency gap in the South has as much to do with the way districts are drawn, as it does with the concentration of Democrats in cities. In many southern states, one legacy of slavery was a dispersed, rural African American population, leading to spatially dispersed Democrats today. If districts were drawn merely according to traditional criteria like compactness and contiguity, as in the simulations above, we would not expect to see a large pro-Republican efficiency gap in states like the Carolinas. However, the Voting Rights Act requires the construction of districts that provide African Americans with sufficient opportunity to influence the outcome. Not surprisingly, as described above, southern Republican legislatures have interpreted this as requiring them to draw overwhelmingly Democratic districts. In this way, southern states have replicated the problem of excessive Democratic concentration even in rural areas.

One of the most interesting observations emerging from this long-term analysis of the efficiency gap is that outside the South, it completely disappeared for three decades, only to reappear in the 1990s. Because of the

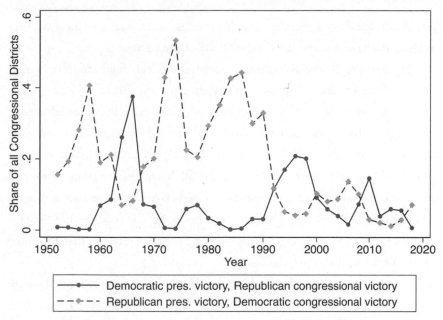

Figure 6.11: Share of US Congressional Districts with a Partisan Split between Congressional and Presidential Winner, 1952–2018.

skew in the distribution of presidential votes across districts, the median district in presidential elections was solidly Republican for virtually the entire period from 1950 to 1992. Thus, the *only way* for Democrats to win the median district—and win control of Congress—was to win in Republican districts. And that is exactly what they did.

Figure 6.11 examines so-called split congressional districts, where the party winning more votes in the presidential election was different from the party winning more votes in the congressional election. Districts won by Democratic congressional candidates and Republican presidential candidates are represented with a dashed line, and those where the opposite was true are indicated with a solid line.

With the exception of 1964 and the following midterm election, Democrats were far more likely to win congressional seats in split districts than were Republicans until the 1990s. Thus, the golden era of bipartisanship in Congress was one in which Democratic candidates in heterogeneous districts successfully wriggled free of a party label that would have undermined their chances if they had embraced it. During long stretches with Republican presidents, these "boll weevils" and "blue dogs" were able to strike deals that avoided the gridlock and debt showdowns of the current era.

In districts where Republican candidates like Richard Nixon and Ronald Reagan were winning majorities between 50 and 65 percent— Democrats were able to field candidates who successfully eschewed the increasingly urban national party label and crafted their own idiosyncratic platforms, especially on issues like race, civil rights, abortion, and women's rights. Riding on the coattails of Lyndon B. Johnson's landslide victory in 1964, a large number of moderate or conservative Democrats were victorious in Republican-leaning districts, and thereafter, the "class of 1964" managed to exploit the advantages of incumbency and survive in office for many years in spite of their party label.[9]

The districts represented by blue dog Democrats often contained small, shrinking nineteenth-century manufacturing towns, with their history of labor unions and strong support for Democrats dating to the New Deal, as well as surrounding rural areas. During that thirty-year period, these Democratic representatives often adopted platforms closer to Democrats on economic issues, and closer to Republicans on the social issues that were becoming more salient at the time.

In short, the Democrats were temporarily able to solve their geography problem by diluting the party's brand and running candidates who successfully disavowed the party's national reputation. Such candidates were especially likely to win during anti-Republican wave elections like 1964, and they were then able to hold onto power through artful use of the perks of incumbency. These ideologically flexible Democrats often voted with Republicans, and are thus largely responsible for what, in retrospect, seems like a golden era of bipartisanship in Congress.

As we can see in the graphs above, that era came to a close in the 1990s. In the 1994 midterm election, the Republican Party, under the leadership of Georgia congressman Newt Gingrich, pursued an explicit strategy of focusing not on individual congressional races but rather a single national policy agenda called the "Contract with America." This ushered in a period of hotly contested battles for control of the legislature. Since then, the correlation between district-level congressional and presidential votes has grown dramatically, and split districts have mostly disappeared from the map. Boll weevils are extinct, and blue dogs have become an endangered species. Figure 6.11 shows that the Democrats have been able to increase their haul of seats in Republican-leaning districts in the pro-Democratic 2006 and 2018 midterm wave elections, but they are nowhere near the levels of the 1980s.

Individual candidates and incumbents can no longer escape blame for their party's actions. High-stakes battles for partisan control of Congress now involve activists and donors from outside the district, and it is increasingly difficult for idiosyncratic local notables with a district-tailored platform to win. Because of this nationalization, the distribution of Democrats across districts in congressional elections has come to resemble the distribution that has been there all along in presidential elections. And as a result, since the 1990s, Democrats have been losing out in the transformation of votes to seats.

As a legacy of the process of city formation and growth in the industrial era, and the subsequent formation and transformation of the New Deal coalition, Democratic voters have been inefficiently distributed across districts for decades, first in the manufacturing states of the North, and now in many southern states as well. Although there are important exceptions, this often undermines the representation of Democrats in Congress and state legislatures. Their problem has become more severe in recent decades, as politics has nationalized and Democrats have lost their ability to win in Republican districts. At the same time, bolstered by their geographic advantage in state legislatures, Republicans have been able to go even further by gerrymandering.

As demonstrated by the midterm elections of 2006 and 2018, the Democrats' problem is not so severe that they cannot win control of Congress. On both occasions, they benefited from a massive electoral wave in response to an unpopular president, allowing them to win victories in some pivotal Republican-leaning districts. On both occasions, they were able to win around 54 percent of the seats in Congress with around 54 percent of the votes cast for the two major parties. However, this chapter has shown that in a system of winner-take-all districts, a party with 54 percent of the votes should typically expect a much larger seat share. In fact, in the elections of 2012 and 2014, the Republican Party won around 53 percent of the votes cast for the two major parties, while winning 57 percent of the seats on both occasions. In 2016, the Republican Party won less than 51 percent of the two-party vote, but well over 55 percent of the seats. By no means does the result of the 2018 midterm indicate that the Democrats' geography problem has come to an end.

Nationalized congressional elections are good for the Democrats in years like 2006 or 2018 when a Republican president is highly unpopular. However, absent such conditions, it appears that the Democratic national policy reputation—perfectly fine for winning the national popular vote in presidential elections—has been perceived as too far left, or too "urban," by the decisive voters in the pivotal suburban and mixed legislative districts. If this is the case, in the absence of events like wars, financial crises, or unpopular Republican presidents, Democrats have no choice but to nudge their platform to the right in pursuit of victory. But in this effort, the Democrats face a classic dilemma that has also plagued socialist and labor parties from the nineteenth-century to the present. They are pulled in one direction by their urban purists—and by their desire to win statewide and presidential elections—and in a different direction by candidates seeking victory in the pivotal congressional and state legislative districts. To overcome their geography problem and win control of legislatures, Democrats and other urban parties of the left must first resolve the battle over their own soul.

CHAPTER 7

Political Geography and the Battle for the Soul of the Left

I N THE RECENT era of enhanced urban-rural polarization, the United States has come to more closely resemble a parliamentary democracy like Great Britain. The parties' national platforms and reputations are more meaningful than in the past, and when participating in congressional elections, many voters are thinking about their vote less as an evaluation of individual candidates, and more as part of a battle for partisan control of Congress. As in Britain, there is a clutch of mostly urban legislators under one party label who vote in a cohesive way in the legislature. And there is a group of exurban and rural legislators under a different label who rarely cross the aisle to cast votes with the urban party.

Control of the legislature is determined by the outcomes of elections in pivotal districts, which are typically in the suburbs. In the United States, given the massive scale of its congressional districts relative to smaller cities, sometimes these are also districts containing a mix of urban, suburban, and rural areas. Voters in these pivotal districts understand that a vote for the urban party is a vote for the policy agenda preferred by urban voters—for instance, secular, progressive social policies and greater investments in risk-sharing, public transportation, affordable housing, and scientific research.

We have now seen a great deal of evidence that in recent years, the Democrats lose in the transformation of votes to seats because they win massive majorities in the urban districts while falling short in the pivotal districts. This raises an obvious question that also emerges in parliamentary countries: Since the urban party is in little danger of losing the urban districts, why can't it simply shade its platform to the right to appeal to the pivotal suburban voters?

This turns out to be more difficult than it sounds. Urban parties have been fighting internal battles over the soul of the left since the industrial era. To make the party palatable in the pivotal districts, suburban pragmatists must win a credible and convincing victory over urban purists. The pragmatists face a vexing challenge that animates this chapter: the distribution of voters' ideology across districts is just as skewed as the parties' vote shares. Like the socialists in early twentieth-century Europe, contemporary voters in urban districts are well to the left of the median suburban district.

Because progressive voters are concentrated in cities, the median *voter* in the United States as a whole is to the left of the median *district*. If the Democratic Party wants to win the national popular vote, it must appeal to the national median voter. However, if the Democrats want to win a congressional majority, they must appeal to the median *congressional district*.[1] By promoting a progressive, urban policy agenda, Democrats can put themselves in a reasonable position to win the national popular vote. But under normal conditions, they would need a somewhat more conservative platform to appeal to the pivotal districts and win control of Congress.

The same dilemma exists within states as well. In states where progressives are highly concentrated in cities, US Senate candidates are trying to appeal to a relatively progressive statewide median voter, while congressional candidates in the median district are chasing after a more conservative voter. This is why we often see that within such states, the roll-call votes of the senators are to the left of those of the median member of the House of Representatives. More broadly, the Senate-House comparison demonstrates that in contrast with direct statewide elections, winner-take-all districts push elected officials to the right.

In parliamentary countries like Britain or Canada, there are no direct elections for the chief executive or for any other national or provincial offices. The only relevant elections are legislative races in the individual districts.

But in the United States, in addition to district-based legislative races, there are separate elections for statewide offices and the presidency, and these are often held on the same day. This creates a dilemma for the Democrats. If they court the median national voter in pursuit of the presidency, they can end up with a policy reputation that allows them to win a majority of the national popular vote, but that reputation will be too "urban" for the pivotal congressional districts. The high profile of presidential elections often helps give the urban purists the upper hand over suburban pragmatists in the battle for the soul of the Democratic Party, resulting in consistent victories in the national popular vote, but deep challenges in winning control of Congress.

The other side of the coin is that in recent years, Republican legislative incumbents have crafted a party reputation that allows them to consistently capture the relatively conservative median congressional district. Given the consistent overrepresentation of rural states in the US Senate, a recurring Electoral College advantage, and low turnout among urban voters, the Republican Party has had few incentives to move its platform to the left.

In the anglophone parliamentary countries, labor parties face a variant of the same problem as the Democrats. Since party leaders have no presidential election to worry about, the most important prize is a legislative majority. As a result, the party's only incentive is to develop a platform that appeals to the voters in the median district. But if the stalwart leftists of the urban core are allowed to set the party's platform and shape its reputation, they run the risk of alienating the pivotal suburban voters. This is a recipe for an inefficient support distribution that allows the party to win votes but not seats. Occasionally the suburban pragmatists are able to gain the upper hand in the battle for the soul of the left—a phenomenon that has become known in the United Kingdom as "New Labour." When this happens, Labour is able to obtain a more efficient support distribution, but only at the price of adopting a platform that is anathema to its core urban supporters.

The parliamentary countries of the Commonwealth exhibit another feature that distinguishes them from the United States: the existence of more than two parties. If Labor faithfully adopts the platform of the urban core, it opens up space for a center-left challenger in the suburbs. But if Labor is too opportunistic in seeking suburban support, it can invite a challenge on its left flank. This problem has dogged Labor and Socialist parties in systems with winner-take-all districts ever since they first entered the electoral fray in the nineteenth and early twentieth centuries. In the United Kingdom and especially in Canada, it has created a long-term partisan divide within the left.

This divide, combined with the longstanding inefficiency of support for labor parties, has generated a striking long-term underrepresentation of the urban left throughout the postwar period in the Commonwealth countries. These facts help put the US experience in comparative perspective. A phenomenon that has only recently garnered attention in the United States— the legislative underrepresentation of urban voters—has been there all along in Britain and its other industrialized former colonies.

RECALL FROM EARLIER chapters that the General Social Survey (GSS) reveals persistent urban-rural differences in political preferences in the United States. When judged on answers to a variety of questions about economic issues, respondents in urban core areas have policy preferences that are far to the left of preferences in the suburbs; and on the whole, political preferences in large metropolitan areas are to the left of those in nonmetropolitan areas. On social issues like abortion, women's rights, and gay rights, many big cities are not that different from their suburbs, but nonmetropolitan areas are far more conservative than metro areas. Having explored the construction of winner-take-all electoral districts at different geographic scales in previous chapters, we are ready to return to the public opinion data with a new question: In terms of voter ideology, are the urban Democratic-dominated districts on the left further away from the median district than are the rural Republican-dominated districts? In other words, does the now-familiar left skew in the distribution of partisanship also apply to voters' preferences?

Let's start with the distribution of ideology across US congressional districts, using survey responses from over 362,000 individuals nationwide during the period 2000 to 2012, on a wide variety of questions in several policy areas.[2] Individuals with a low score (a relatively large negative number) produce consistently progressive responses on a wide range of issues, and individuals with a high score (a relatively large positive number) provide consistently conservative responses. People with a score somewhere in the middle typically provide a combination of moderate responses or display a mixture of liberal and conservative views on different questions.

Figure 7.1 displays a smoothed histogram that captures the distribution of the measure of ideology across US congressional districts. The range for these estimates is from around -1 for the most liberal urban districts in places like San Francisco and Brooklyn, to around .5 for the most conservative districts in rural Texas and Georgia. The median congressional district in the United States during this period was the Fourth District of Colorado—a relatively rural district in eastern Colorado that includes the city of Greeley. Its ideological estimate, 0.028, is indicated with a solid vertical line. Other districts around the national median include a Texas district running from Corpus Christi to the southern border, a suburban Minneapolis district,

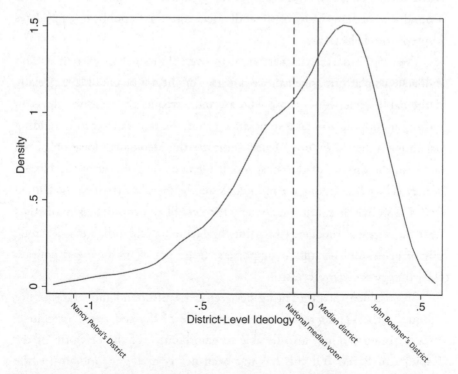

Figure 7.1: The Distribution of Ideology across US Congressional Districts

and a district that is split between Cincinnati and part of its conservative suburbs.

It is immediately clear that the distribution of ideology across congressional districts demonstrates a pronounced left skew, where Americans who give consistently left-wing answers to survey questions are quite clustered in cities. In fact, this distribution looks very similar to that of recent Republican presidential vote shares that were discussed in the previous chapter. The key insight offered by this graph is that voters in the urban core congressional districts are ideologically quite distinct from the rest of the country, and quite far away from the median district. And the most extremely conservative rural districts are actually not very far away from the pivotal districts around the median.

Figure 7.1 illustrates a difficult challenge for the Democrats. If the long-standing safe incumbents of the urban core are allowed to set the party platform in a way that is pleasing to their constituents, the Democrats will be stuck with a platform that is rather far to the left of the crucial districts around the median. Most of these districts vote for Republican candidates in presidential elections.

Even if the party tries very hard to overrule its urban extremists and moderate its platform, one can see how this might not be credible, especially if the party leadership—those who are most frequently seen on television talking about policy—tends to be drawn from the ranks of the longstanding urban incumbents. Figure 7.1 also indicates the ideological location of the voters in the district of the most recent Democratic Speaker of the House, Nancy Pelosi. It is among the most consistently liberal districts in the United States. An obvious campaign strategy for Republican candidates in districts near the national median is to paint the Democratic candidate as a strong ally of Pelosi and her urban supporters. In an era of nationalized politics, this strategy is often successful.

The problem of negotiating between extremists and moderates is not unique to the Democrats. On the other side of the spectrum, of course, rural extremists might also be able to gain control of the platform of the Republican Party. But this has not been nearly as big a problem for the Republicans—at least in congressional elections—since those districts have not been very far away from the median district. As a result, the districts of successful incumbent Republicans who have ascended to leadership positions are also likely to be closer to the median district. The ideological estimate of former Republican Speaker of the House John Boehner's district, for instance, is also indicated in Figure 7.1, and it was not far from the median district. Paul Ryan's Wisconsin district was even closer. To be attractive in the median district, the Republican purists must compromise their principles far less than the Democratic purists.

The Democrats are in trouble if they allow their long-serving incumbents to dominate the party's platform and reputation. Recall from the previous chapter that Democrats were able to win control of Congress in the past by steering clear of the party's growing urban reputation in the pivotal districts. Figure 7.1 drives home the reason Democrats have been forced to rely on blue dogs and boll weevils: Democrats must move further from the ideology of their core supporters—and often onto Republican turf—to win control of the legislature.

One might expect that the Democrats in pivotal congressional districts can solve this problem by running on the coattails of moderate presidential candidates. Perhaps a moderate presidential candidate can keep urban interest groups at bay and minimize the ideological stain of the party label in crucial districts. Figure 7.1 demonstrates why this is difficult. The median ideology score of all survey respondents is indicated with a vertical dashed line. Even if the Democratic presidential candidate were able to move the party's perceived platform all the way to the position of the national median voter—a tall feat given the importance of "true believers" among campaign donors and primary voters—this platform would *still* be well to the left of the pivotal district, and thus create a drag on the prospects of Democratic candidates in the pivotal districts around the median.[3]

Democratic campaigns in pivotal states often focus heavily on efforts to boost urban turnout. Recall that turnout is often extremely low in urban precincts, and presidential candidates—as well as statewide Democratic candidates—often focus on appeals and rhetorical strategies that help with urban get-out-the-vote operations. This is a reasonable strategy that often pays off. But by pursuing their best strategy in statewide and presidential elections, Democrats may be hurting themselves in the battle for control of the legislature. Statewide and presidential elections are important political prizes in the United States, and it is easy to see why Democratic strategists might be tempted to adopt a strategy aimed at mobilizing the urban left. However, Democrats do not always consider the collateral damage that these appeals might cause for the party's reputation in the pivotal congressional districts.

THE PROBLEM OF platform choice and reputation management bedevils the Democrats not only at the national level, but also within states. The urban districts, where Democrats typically win by large majorities, are often ideologically quite far away from the rest of the state. For instance, the distribution of district-level ideology for Pennsylvania's congressional or state legislative districts looks almost identical to the distribution in Figure 7.1. Again, the urban districts in the left tail of the distribution are composed of voters who are extremely liberal relative to the rest of the state. The median statewide voter is well to the left of the median district. If the Pennsylvania Democratic Party comes to have a statewide policy reputation that corresponds to the preferences of its core urban districts, the party faces an uphill climb in the pivotal centrist districts. Given this distribution of ideology, it is not surprising that the party has been able to win statewide elections while consistently losing the state legislature.

Pennsylvania is not unusual. Recall our simple measure of the skew of district-level partisanship: the mean-median difference. But now, let's apply it to district-level ideology. In state upper legislative chambers, the median district is more conservative than the mean in every state but five.[4] If we look at congressional delegations for states with more than three congressional districts, this is true in all states but seven.[5]

In most US states then, urban districts are far more liberal than the rest of the state. As a result, Democrats face a difficult challenge in trying to manage their statewide party reputation. If it comes to be dominated by urban incumbents, they will find it hard to compete in the pivotal districts. In a number of states of the manufacturing core and the South, most of these urban incumbents are African Americans, and the pivotal suburban districts are overwhelmingly white. In states like Alabama, Missouri, Georgia, Mississippi, and Louisiana—due to a combination of demographics, the Voting Rights Act, and racial and partisan gerrymandering—the entire Democratic US House delegation is composed of African Americans with liberal voting records. Something similar is often true of the Democrats' state legislative delegations in these states.

Based on this analysis of the distribution of ideology across districts, it should be easier for urban progressives to achieve favorable representation with a system of statewide winner-take-all elections than with a system of smaller winner-take-all districts. In statewide elections—as long as the state has enough urban voters—the Democrats might be able to craft a winning platform, and follow up on it once in office. But if their supporters are too concentrated in urban districts, that same platform is liable to undermine their chances in the median district.

Fortunately, the US constitutional structure allows us to examine this claim. Each state elects two senators via a simple winner-take-all statewide election, and a congressional delegation from a series of single-member districts. Within states, we can examine the difference between the roll-call votes of senators and those of the median member of the state's legislative delegation.

Americans are accustomed to thinking of the US Senate as a graveyard of progressive reform.[6] The Senate is famous for its supermajoritarian rules, including the filibuster, as well as its overrepresentation of rural states. Indeed, because large, urban states like California and New York have the same number of senators as smaller, more rural states like Wyoming and the Dakotas, Republicans frequently win control of the Senate while losing the nationwide popular Senate vote by a large margin. In the House of Representatives, on the other hand, rough population equality is assured by a reapportionment that takes place every decade. Focusing only on the issue of apportionment, one might expect that urban progressives would find the "house of the people" to be a better vehicle for their agenda.

However, urban political geography creates a strong countervailing logic. In a number of large, politically competitive states, the Democrats might be in a better position to win statewide Senate elections than to win the median congressional district. In the long run, within relatively competitive states, we should expect to see that senators tend to exhibit more liberal voting behavior than the median member of the congressional delegation. In early-industrializing states that are largely urban—like New York, Massachusetts, and Connecticut—Democrats are typically able to dominate both Senate and House delegations. Likewise, in late-industrializing states with smaller urban populations—like those of the South and Mountain West—the Republicans will often dominate both delegations. In these states, there is no good reason to expect the voting behavior of the two senators on the floor of the legislature to be very different from the median member of the House delegation.

More interesting are the large states in the manufacturing core, the Midwest, and the "New South," with a more even mix of urban, suburban, and rural voters. These are states where Democrats—even with a liberal urban policy reputation—can hope to win Senate seats somewhat regularly. In the states where progressives are concentrated within districts—where the distance between the ideology of the mean and median district is pronounced—we should expect to see that the Democrats find it hard to compete in the median district; meaning that on average, senators will be more liberal than the median member of the congressional delegation.

American political scientists typically examine legislative behavior in the US Congress by applying a scaling procedure to roll-call votes, the most common of which is called DW-Nominate. This widely used indicator characterizes the voting behavior of members of Congress on a scale that ranges from the most consistently liberal members of Congress, like Barbara Lee or John Conyers, to the most conservative, like Tom Graves or Jeffrey Duncan (in 2014).[7]

According to DW-Nominate, in Congresses from 2000 to 2014 in relatively competitive states—where both parties have a reasonable chance of winning statewide elections—and where liberal voters are relatively clustered in urban districts—senators tend to exhibit more liberal voting records than the median member of Congress elected from the same state.[8] To demonstrate this, Figure 7.2 focuses on the relatively competitive states, and

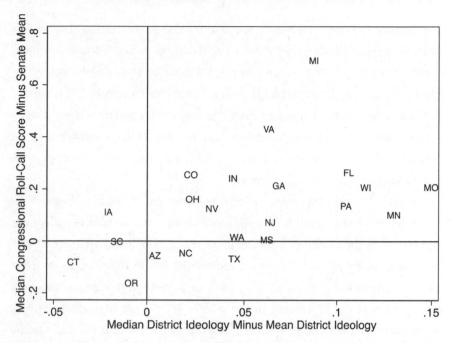

Figure 7.2: Skew in the Cross-District Distribution of Voter Ideology and the Extent to Which the Median Member of the Congressional Delegation Is to the Right of the Senate Delegation, by State

displays the ideological distance between the mean and median district—that is, the extent to which liberals are clustered in cities—on the horizontal axis. On the vertical axis, it displays the difference in the roll-call voting score between the average of the two senators and the median of the House delegation. This number gets higher as the median member of Congress is more conservative than the senators elected from the state.

There are some states, like Iowa and Connecticut, that are in the lower left corner of the graph near the origin, which means that votes of senators and House members are usually rather similar (low values on the vertical axis), and where there is not a significant geographic skew in the distribution of ideology across districts (low values on the horizontal axis). Note that these are states where nineteenth-century industrialization was not highly concentrated, and where voters are not highly clustered in large cities. But as we move along the horizontal axis to states with larger cities, where liberal voters are more geographically concentrated in urban congressional districts, a difference between the Senate and House delegations emerges. The difference is especially large in states like Michigan, where Democrats have managed to dominate the Senate delegation while consistently losing the House delegation. In states like Virginia, Pennsylvania, Florida, Wisconsin, Ohio, and Missouri, Democrats often win at least one Senate seat while consistently losing the House delegation. The median House member is quite conservative in these states, and representation in the two chambers of the US legislature is considerably different.

Figure 7.3 uses data from all of the states, and provides a better way to understand the conditions under which the Senate-House difference emerges. On the horizontal axis, it plots the survey-based estimate of the median ideology of the state. As we move from left to right, we move from the very conservative states in the South and Mountain West, to the very liberal states of the Northeast. In the middle are the ideologically heterogeneous swing states. The vertical axis represents the median roll-call voting

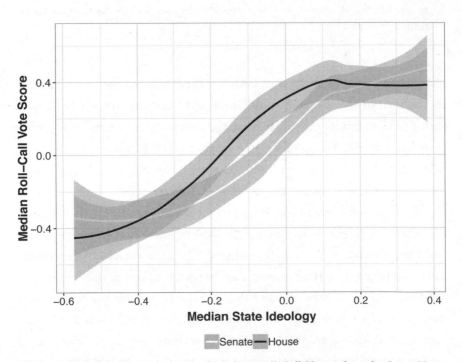

Figure 7.3: Median Voter Ideology and Median Roll-Call Voting Score by State, House Delegation versus Senate

score for the state's House delegation (in black), and for the state's senators (in white). Both lines are surrounded by gray 95 percent confidence intervals that allow us to assess whether the difference between the lines is statistically significant. We see that in very liberal and very conservative states, the voting behavior of senators and House members is indistinguishable. But for the states in the middle of the American ideological spectrum, the voting behavior of senators is significantly to the left of House members.

A strikingly similar pattern emerges when we look at differences in voting behavior between senators and House members within states over time.

Figure 7.4 plots the difference between the median roll-call voting score of the state's House delegation and the mean roll-call voting score of its two senators, so that again, a positive number indicates that a state's congressional delegation was more conservative than its Senate delegation.[9] Once again, we see the familiar U-shape that was present in the graphs from the previous chapter. In the 1940s and 1950s, when New Deal Democrats were inefficiently concentrated in cities in the large states of the manufacturing

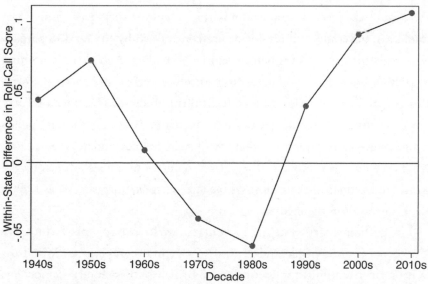

Note: Positive number indicates that the median Congressional district is more conservative than the Senate delegation.

Figure 7.4: Extent to Which the Median Member of the State Congressional Delegation is to the Right of the State's Senate Delegation, Weighted Averages across States, 1940s–2010s

core, they were more likely to win a Senate seat (or two) than to win a majority of the state's House delegation. Democrats picked up seats in a number of Republican districts in the 1964 wave election, and this had the effect of moving their states' House delegations to the left for quite a long time. However, by the 1990s, the old pattern had returned. Urban voters in large states are once again more likely to gain representation in the statewide Senate elections than in the districted House elections. This pattern was on display once again in the 2018 midterm election, when in seven states, Democrats won Senate seats without winning a majority of the US House or of state legislative seats. They also came very close to statewide wins in Florida, Georgia, and Texas without coming anywhere near legislative majorities. In contrast, Republicans always won a majority of US House and state legislative seats in states where they won Senate seats in 2018.

BECAUSE OF THE presidential system, party platforms are relatively unimportant in the United States. The state and national parties do write down platforms at their conventions, but these documents are almost immediately ignored. Everyone understands that whatever their party's platform might say, governors and presidents are constrained by the need to bargain with legislators in two fissiparous legislative bodies. And there is nothing to prevent individual candidates from running against the party platform. Pro-gun and anti-abortion candidates still run under the Democratic Party label, for instance. Yet the parties have increasingly strong national policy *reputations*—based largely on what their presidential candidates espouse and what they do when in office. The parties' reputations are also driven by the words and actions of their most visible and outspoken legislators, as well as their portrayals in the media.

In parliamentary systems, in contrast, written party platforms have always been quite visible and central to electoral competition. Woodrow Wilson, in his admiring description of British parliamentary democracy, described a system in which "the responsibility for legislation is saddled upon the majority. All legislation is made a contest for party supremacy."[10] Parties articulate clear platforms, and the winning party must implement its platform and defend it against the criticism of the opposition, stepping down if it is unable to do so. In such a system, there is no room for blue dogs or boll weevils. Individuals who run for legislative seats under a party banner will be bound to uphold its platform once in office.

As a result, the major parties in parliamentary democracies experience a battle over the party's soul each time they revisit the platform. As in the United States, this battle is especially consequential on the left. If labor parties adopt the platform preferred by their urban stalwarts, they are likely to lose in the pivotal districts and suffer from an inefficient support distribution. Moreover, because individual candidates in heterogeneous districts are stuck with a one-size-fits-all platform, the left side of the political spectrum often fractures under the strain. The battle for the soul of the left in parliamentary countries often takes place not only *within* parties, but also across parties.

Recall the basic geographic dilemma of labor parties that has plagued them from the start. As workers gained the franchise, labor parties entered the electoral arena in the late nineteenth and early twentieth centuries with a focus on mobilizing geographically concentrated workers. But these workers were clustered within districts such that labor parties could not win parliamentary majorities unless they broadened their reach beyond industrial working-class neighborhoods.

In one respect, the New Deal Democrats had it easy relative to labor parties in Australia and the United Kingdom. The malleability of party labels allowed urban Democrats to form legislative coalitions with Southern segregationists, and then later, boll weevils and blue dogs, all under the same amorphous party label. This option was not available to labor parties in parliamentary systems. They were associated exclusively with platforms like the nationalization of industries, investment in social insurance for workers, and the construction of urban public housing. In the early postwar period, labor parties ran on these platforms in Britain and Australia, winning large majorities in working-class neighborhoods, but falling consistently short in the pivotal parliamentary constituencies.

When labor parties in Britain and Australia sit down to write their platforms, it is difficult for them to avoid the influence of their sitting legislative incumbents. These are, quite naturally, some of the most decisive voices. Urban incumbents might set the platform in a way that elevates their own self-interest—or view of the world—over the goal of winning in the median district.

Once Labor loses an election or two, the problem only gets worse. After losing pivotal districts, suburban moderates are no longer among the Labor incumbents. Rather, the platform is left in the hands of a group of urban representatives with safe seats in the left tail of the distribution. This can lead to a period in the wilderness, where the platform is too far from the median district, but self-interested urban incumbents prevent changes. The only way out is something like a scandal, failed military adventure, or fiscal crisis that produces a wave election, allowing the urban party to win in the districts around the median. This in turn brings a new set of moderate suburban incumbents into the fold, allowing the party to then select a moderate platform going forward.[11]

In short, if the preferences of urban voters in the left tail of the distribution are ideologically more distant from the median district than the median district is from the rural districts in the right tail, life is more difficult for the party of the left than the party of the right. Its moderates must fight harder against its extremists to adopt a winning platform. But the mainstream left party faces an additional problem. If it fully embraces the platform preferred by its urban voters, it might open up space for an alternative center-left party in the suburban districts around the median. But if it abandons the preferences of its core supporters in pursuit of victory in the median district, it might invite competition from more "authentic" parties of the left.[12] This can lead to costly coordination failures between rival parties of the left, each hoping to marginalize the other and become the left's dominant party. Because the right tail of the distribution of district-level ideology is closer to the median, this problem is less severe for the party of the right.

This problem has not emerged in the United States because of the flexibility of party labels afforded by its presidential system. Even today, both American parties are quite heterogeneous. The Democratic Party includes candidates who emphasize free markets and some who describe themselves as socialists. They fight their battles within the party, whereas in more disciplined parliamentary systems, similar battles are more likely to result in breakaway parties and long-term splits.

Both problems—inefficient geographic support and coordination battles with other competitors on the left—have plagued the Labor Parties in Britain and Australia and the New Democratic Party in Canada. Let us begin with the experience of Britain and Australia. Recall from the previous chapter that there is a skew in the distribution of Republican vote shares in the United States, such that the median district has been consistently more Republican than the mean district throughout the postwar period. The distribution of vote shares for the Conservative Party in the United Kingdom has been strikingly similar throughout the postwar period. The distribution has a long left tail composed of urban districts in London, the North, and the Midlands that are won by the Labour Party with overwhelming majorities. And the median district has been consistently more conservative than the mean district throughout the postwar period.

In Australia, the right side of the political spectrum is divided between the Liberals—who mostly compete in urban and suburban areas, and the Australian National Party, which represents the right in rural areas. The parties typically do not compete against one another, but rather have agreed on which constituencies to contest. Collectively, they are known as "the coalition parties," and they run on a common ideological platform. The parties have formally joined in Queensland, and work closely together in other states. As with the Tories in Britain, the distribution of votes for the coalition parties has also demonstrated a pronounced left skew throughout the postwar period.

To communicate the relative concentration of left voting over time, Figure 7.5 returns to the approach used previously—it looks at the gap between the district-level mean and the median. Specifically, it takes the cross-district median vote share of the Conservatives in the United Kingdom, minus the cross-district mean vote share, and presents decade averages. It does the same for the Australian coalition parties.

On average, the magnitude of the mean-median difference in the United Kingdom is roughly similar to the United States. There was a substantial decrease in the geographic concentration of the left in Britain in the 2000s,

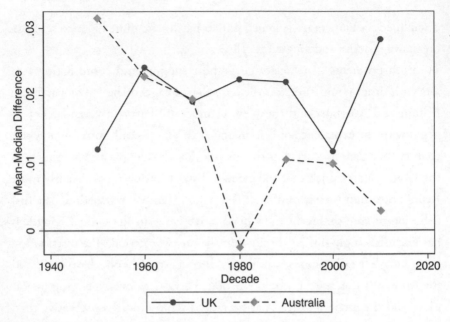

Figure 7.5: Mean-Median Difference in Labor Vote Share across Parliamentary Constituencies, Australia and Britain, 1950s–2010s

followed by a dramatic increase to new heights in the elections since 2010. Australia started the postwar period with an extremely skewed distribution of partisanship, but the skew has been steadily decreasing over time—with a decade in the 1980s when it disappeared altogether.

These trends correspond to important developments in the parties' platforms. With the exception of the early 1950s, the British Labour Party spent several decades of the early postwar period in the wilderness. With a traditional leftist platform favored by its urban incumbents, it racked up large majorities in the urban districts, while consistently falling short in the pivotal suburban districts. This was true from the late 1950s until 1997.[13]

After losing for thirty of the last forty years, a dramatic change occurred within the Labour Party in the late 1990s. A series of scandals associated with the governing Conservatives helped Labour to a landslide victory in a wave election in 1997. This brought a large group of new Labour MPs into Parliament who represented moderate suburban constituencies, thus strengthening the hand of moderates in the party for the next decade. Along with the moderate platform came a substantial improvement in the party's geographic support distribution, captured by the large dip in Figure 7.5.

But the "New Labour" moment did not last. After Labour lost power in the wake of the Iraq War, its urban stalwarts have gradually regained the upper hand, a process that culminated with the takeover of Jeremy Corbyn. Predictably, Labour's old geographic problem has returned—now stronger than ever. Once again, as in the period from the 1960s to the 1990s, Labour receives too many votes in city centers and too few elsewhere. The median district is once again reliably Conservative.

It is useful to revisit the notion of wasted votes from the previous chapter. For each party in each district, let us consider a vote to be wasted if it is either (1) cast in a district that the party lost, or (2) exceeded the vote total of the second-place party in the district.

The three panels in Figure 7.6 display the share of all wasted votes received by each party in each election. With one exception, from 1950 to 1997, the Labour Party consistently wasted a larger share of its votes than the Conservatives. After only a brief respite during the New Labour era, this pattern has returned in the most recent elections.

The Australian postwar story begins in a similar way. As in Britain, the Australian Labor Party (ALP) started the postwar period with a striking level of concentration in urban districts, as indicated by the dashed line in Figure 7.5. It won supermajorities in the working-class districts of Melbourne, Sydney, and Adelaide, but was unable to win majorities in the pivotal suburbs. Like the British Conservatives, the Australian Liberal-National Coalition had an admirable cross-district support distribution, with a large density of districts where they won comfortable but not overwhelming majorities.

Like their comrades in the United Kingdom, the Australian Labor Party also experienced a corresponding period in the wilderness after World War II, although the ALP's lasted much longer. Their period of futility began in 1949 and lasted for twenty-three years—a period during which the ALP won the popular vote but failed to win a majority of seats on *three* separate occasions. Remarkably, from 1950 to the 1980s, they were only in power for

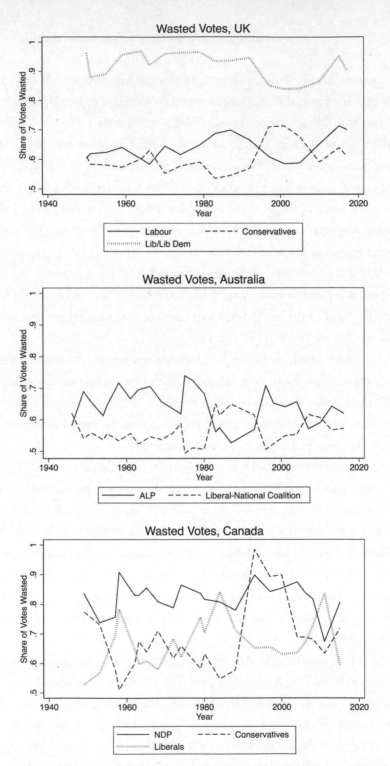

Figure 7.6: Wasted Votes by Party in the UK, Australia, and Canada, 1945–2017

three years. This was a period when the ALP wasted a large share of its votes by winning excessive majorities in districts it won but falling short in the pivotal districts.[14]

The Australian Labor Party has also struggled throughout the postwar period with an intense battle between urban labor union purists, who argue against ideological compromise, and suburban moderates who argue that a pro-business, market-oriented platform is the only way to win crucial pivotal districts in the center of the ideological distribution. There has always been a simmering conflict in the party between socialists and moderates, and for decades, the ALP has been divided into formal internal factions known as Labor Right (also known as Labor Unity), versus Labor Left (also known as Socialist Left). The ideological differences between these factions are larger than those between the Liberals and Nationals. Labor Right gained the upper hand in the party in the 1980s, and in fact, Britain's "New Labour" concept had its origins not in Great Britain in the 1990s, but in Australia in the 1980s. After decades in the wilderness, Labor benefited from a wave election in 1983 during a period of high inflation and unemployment. As with Tony Blair in the United Kingdom in the late 1990s, Bob Hawke was able to move Labor's economic platform rather dramatically to the center in the 1980s in an explicit effort to end the party's frustration in the pivotal districts in the middle of the distribution. This move was quite successful, and Labor entered a long period in government from 1983 to 1996.

This period of moderation and time in government had a powerful impact on the party's support distribution. In Figure 7.5, we can see that the urban concentration in the party's support distribution disappeared in the 1980s. It returned in subsequent decades, but today, Labor's concentration in landslide districts is far less pronounced than in the immediate postwar period. In the graph of wasted votes, we can see that throughout the postwar period, Labor has consistently wasted more votes than the Liberal-National Coalition. As in Britain, this pattern reversed during the New Labor period, only to return thereafter. But in Australia, the gap between the wasted votes for the ALP and the coalition has narrowed over time.

Unlike the other anglophone countries, the relative geographic efficiency of support for the right has declined in Australia. Part of the answer may lie in Labor's platform moderation. Moreover, upon coming to power, Labor was able to alter the Commonwealth Electoral Act so as to equalize the population of districts. This was similar to what happened in the United States with the *Baker v. Carr* Supreme Court decision of 1962, which required population equality across congressional and state legislative districts within states. Previously, urban constituencies had been much larger than rural constituencies. Reapportionment in Australia led to the breakup of large Labor-dominated working-class districts in cities.

Another explanation has to do with deeper trends in political geography. Compared with other former British colonies, recall from Chapter 4 that urban Australia is less dominated by monocentric nineteenth-century cities with a dense and overwhelmingly left-voting urban core. Many Australian cities look more like Houston or Orlando than Philadelphia or Reading. As Australian cities continue to gain population, sprawl out, and fill in, they have become increasingly heterogeneous, and Labor voters have become less concentrated. Additionally, Labor voters have become more efficiently distributed across districts as dense public housing facilities have been constructed on the outskirts of Australian cities throughout the postwar period. In fact, the Australian states of South Australia and Western Australia now have little or no partisan gradient—that is, not much clustering of Labor voters to speak of—and as a result, they exhibit no anti-Labor electoral bias.

THE GEOGRAPHIC CONCENTRATION of progressive voters hurts mainstream parties of the left not only because it undermines the transformation of their votes to commensurate seats, but also because it facilitates challenges from alternative left-wing parties. The age-old Labour-Liberal conflict in Great Britain is perhaps the classic case. In addition to battling the Conservatives, Labour has been fighting a battle for predominance on the left side of the political spectrum since the early twentieth century. By the early postwar period, Labour had emerged as the dominant progressive party, relegating the Liberals to a few rural constituencies in Wales and Scotland. In the early 1960s, the Liberals were perhaps ideologically closer to the Conservatives than to the Labour candidates.

However, the leftist urban Labour platform of the early postwar period created an opening for center-left rivals in the suburbs. The Liberals repositioned themselves in the 1970s as a party of the center-left for the educated suburban middle class. Additionally, in the 1980s, a group of breakaway Labour moderates formed the Social Democratic Party. The Liberals and Social Democrats eventually fused to form the Liberal Democrats. For a period from the 1970s to the rise of New Labour in the 1990s, the Labour Party lost ground in pivotal suburban constituencies to its center-left rivals.

In recent decades, the Liberal Democrats have positioned themselves to the left of Labour on social and international issues, and to the right on traditional economic issues. This makes them a thorn in the side of Labour in many urban and suburban constituencies. Meanwhile, the Conservatives have not suffered from a similar splintering on the right—except for a brief challenge from the UK Independence Party (UKIP) in 2015.

Perhaps the most striking thing about the UK panel in Figure 7.6 is the extent to which votes first for Liberal and now for Liberal Democratic candidates have been wasted throughout the postwar period.[15] The geographic support distribution of the Liberals could not be much worse. In a system with two major parties, a third party can transform votes to seats quite effectively if its support is highly concentrated in targeted districts—like the Bloc Quebecois in Quebec or the Scottish National Party. This was the case for the Liberals when their support was concentrated in a few districts in Scotland and Wales. However, as they attempted to challenge Labour throughout the country, they began to split the left vote, usually ending up on the losing side, and sometimes handing the district to the Conservatives. By trying to compete throughout the country as an alternative challenger to the Conservatives, the Liberals won a substantial number of votes but failed to win corresponding seats.[16]

The Australian Labor Party has suffered from fractures as well. In fact, the contemporary internal split within the party has deep roots. In 1955, a largely Catholic anti-communist group led by B. A. Santamaria split from the party, eventually forming a breakaway party called the Democratic Labor Party (DLP). Though its social origins are quite different from the British Liberals', they posed a threat that was somewhat analogous: they took votes away from the ALP in crucial districts. In fact, this was the explicit strategy of the DLP, known as "veto with a view to reunification." Whereas the Liberals in the United Kingdom hoped to force Labour into a coalition government, the DLP in Australia hoped to punish the ALP to force it to change.

Australia operates with a system of preferential voting. Voters are able to rank their choices. A left-leaning voter who prefers an alternative small party of the left, like the DLP in the 1960s or the Greens today, can rank that party first, and be sure to rank the ALP second over the Liberals. If and when the smaller party's candidate is eliminated because he or she has fewer votes than the ALP candidate, many of that party's votes are then transferred to the ALP. In this way, the coordination problem that plagues Liberals and Labour in the United Kingdom can be avoided. A voter can vote his or her true preference without worrying that the district will be handed to the Conservatives.

DLP voters, however, were instructed by the party *not* to give their second-preference votes to the ALP, which had the effect of wasting all of the DLP votes and allowing the Liberals to win several crucial districts. The hope was that, faced with this threat, Labor would be forced to accept their demands and the DLP would eventually rejoin the ALP. This never happened, and the DLP eventually disbanded in 1978. But that long-lasting split on the left was an important part of the story of Labor's long time in the wilderness, and as described above, the ALP remains internally divided today. Very recently, the Greens in Australia have been making incursions in urban districts by capturing voters to the left of Labor. In fact, they were able to deny the ALP a parliamentary majority in 2010 by winning a crucial Melbourne seat that had been held by Labor for over one hundred years.

Perhaps nowhere has this type of partisan split on the left been more consequential than in Canada, where for decades, two alternative parties of the left have been engaged in a destructive battle for supremacy. The mainstream party of the center-left—the Liberal Party—gets much of its support in inner- and middle-ring suburbs of Canadian cities, and traditionally, it has been dominant in federal elections in much of the province of Quebec. Support for Canada's social democratic party of the left—the New

Democratic Party (NDP)—has become quite concentrated in the urban core of Canadian cities. As we saw in Chapter 4, the geography of support for the Conservative Party in federal elections is similar to that of the Republicans in the United States; it is spread rather efficiently across the outer suburbs, exurbs, and rural areas throughout Canada.

In the United Kingdom, it is useful to think of Labour as the mainstream party of the urban left throughout the postwar period, while the Liberal Democrats are an insurgent center-left party in the suburban districts. In Canada, on the other hand, the Liberals emerged as the mainstream party of the left in the postwar period, and the NDP arose as an urban insurgent to its left. Like the Liberal Democrats in the United Kingdom, it is difficult for such an insurgent to transform its votes into seats—especially if it aims to be a national party. In the last panel of Figure 7.6, we can see that the NDP has wasted between 80 and 90 percent of its votes throughout the postwar period.[17] The ability of the NDP to win votes but not seats parallels the experience of the Liberals and the Liberal Democrats in the United Kingdom. In the Canadian case, the winner-take-all electoral system is especially unkind to the party of the urban left.

The battle for supremacy on the left in federal elections has played out differently in different provinces, in part because the nature of party conflict is so different at the provincial level. In British Columbia, for instance, the NDP has the upper hand, while in Ontario and the Maritimes it is typically, but not always, the Liberal Party. In general, the NDP's base is in the left-wing urban core neighborhoods, while the Liberals vie with the Conservatives to win the pivotal suburban districts in the middle of the ideological distribution, ceding the right-leaning rural districts to the Conservatives.[18]

In the past, the Liberals have been able to cede some urban districts to the NDP and still win parliamentary majorities, primarily because of their dominance in the province of Quebec. Due to their positions regarding federalism, language, and the status of Quebec, for many years the Liberals were able to win so many seats in Quebec that this province alone put them halfway to a parliamentary majority.[19]

But as Liberal dominance in Quebec has faded, the three-way division of party competition between the NDP, Liberals, and Conservatives has been a tremendous gift to the Conservatives. Recall that in early twentieth-century Europe, when the dominant Liberals faced challengers from workers' parties in the most left-leaning districts, the two leftist competitors were often able to work out strategic withdrawals so that there would be only one left-wing candidate in the district. The NDP and Liberals have done no such thing; both parties compete aggressively throughout the country. Voters who prefer a left-wing government in Canada must think not only about which platform is closer to their preference, but more importantly, which party has a better chance of winning (1) the most votes in the district, and (2) the most seats in Parliament. Both assessments require left-leaning voters to process dubious and conflicting information from polls and media punditry. And some voters will always choose to vote sincerely rather than strategically.

As a result, the left as a whole often loses. At the national level, the Conservatives can easily emerge as the largest party even though the combined vote share of the Liberals and NDP is much higher. In fact, this was the case in the Conservative victories of 2006, 2008, and 2011—a period during which the Conservatives repeatedly formed governments without reaching 40 percent of the vote.

The coordination dilemma on the left can also be seen very clearly at the district level. Conservative candidates win quite frequently in Canadian districts where a majority of voters actually preferred one of the left parties. For each postwar federal election, let's count up the seats in which a candidate of the right is victorious even though the combined votes of the candidates of the left are higher. And let's do the same for seats where a candidate of the left wins in spite of a majority of votes for candidates of the right. These are displayed, as a share of all seats, with solid and dashed lines, respectively, in the top panel of Figure 7.7.[20]

We can see that coordination failures of the left are quite common and severe in Canada. The right has been able to win seats due to vote-splitting on the left in 15 to 20 percent of all districts since the 1970s, but it is relatively rare to see the opposite occur. This asymmetric coordination problem only disappeared temporarily in the 1990s. This was a period when the mainstream conservative party of the postwar period, the Progressive Conservatives, imploded and the Canadian right was in disarray due to a

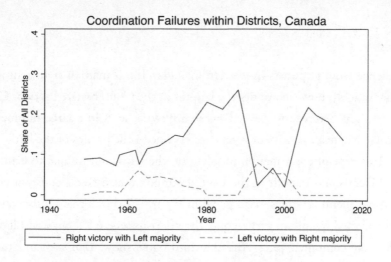

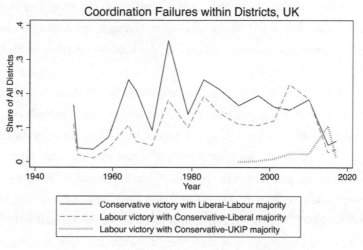

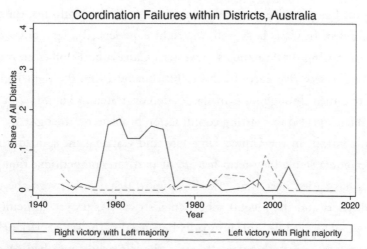

Figure 7.7: Coordination Failures in Canada, the UK, and Australia, 1945–2017

challenge from populists in western Canada. The Canadian right reunified rather quickly, however, under the banner of the Conservative Party of Canada. And as before, this party consistently wins seats in a large number of districts where a majority of voters prefers one of the parties of the left.

This type of coordination problem on the left is not unique to Canada. The Liberals and Labour in the United Kingdom also face a constant coordination dilemma. The second panel in Figure 7.7 shows that Conservatives in the United Kingdom very frequently win seats where Labour and Liberals have more combined votes. And the third panel shows that even in Australia, where one might expect that ranked-choice voting would mitigate the problem altogether, DLP voters who were attempting to punish the ALP handed a significant number of seats to the coalition parties in the 1960s and 1970s.

To be sure, there are occasional splits on the right as well. The most enduring has been the segmentation in Australia between the suburban Liberals and the rural National Party. However, as indicated by the dashed line in Figure 7.7, the parties have divided up the turf in a way that rarely generates coordination problems. The system of ranked voting—instituted by the right specifically to help avoid coordination problems between the Liberals and the National Party—has been quite helpful. In the United Kingdom, a brief split on the right emerged with the rise of the UK Independence Party, but as the Conservatives have adopted some of UKIP's platforms, the threat has subsided. In Canada as well, the right experienced a temporary divide when right-wing rural populists in western Canada broke off from the Progressive Conservative Party in the 1990s, but by 2003, the right had once again reunified throughout Canada. As demonstrated in Figure 7.7, none of these incursions led to a lasting coordination problem on the right.

In contrast, in the United Kingdom and Canada, the split on the left has become a stable long-term feature of partisan competition, though its impact has varied over time. The ideological distance between the urban core districts and the pivotal suburban districts has proven difficult for a single party to straddle. This is broadly beneficial to the right. National elections are fractious, multiparty affairs on the left, while a unified conservative party enjoys stable primacy on the right.[21] The British and Canadian

Conservatives can expect to form governments even if the combined vote for left parties is much higher.

In sum, the concentration of leftists in cities in the Commonwealth countries has had two detrimental effects for parties of the left over the course of the postwar period: an inefficient distribution of support across districts *within* parties and a costly divide *across* parties. The combined effect has been significant. Looking at the popular vote for every British parliamentary election held between 1950 and 2017, the Conservative Party has received around 41 percent of the votes cast, compared with around 40 percent for Labour. Yet the Conservative Party has been in power for 63 percent of that period. Aggregating over all elections since 1950, the Australian Labor Party and the coalition parties have split the popular vote almost exactly down the middle, yet the coalition has been in power for 68 percent of the time. In Canada, the center-left Liberal Party has parlayed its dominance in Quebec into impressive success in forming governments throughout the postwar period, but the party of the Canadian urban core has never participated in a federal cabinet.

THIS CHAPTER HAS provided a fuller accounting of the ways in which urban voters can lose in a system of winner-take-all districts when party competition is characterized by urban-rural polarization. The problem for the urban left is not merely a technical matter of votes and seats. Urban parties must resolve a vexing battle over the soul of the left.

In the United States, progressive voters are highly clustered in urban congressional and state legislative districts. When they force the Democratic Party to align with their urban values, they undermine its ability to win in the pivotal districts that determine control of Congress and state legislatures. Urban progressives face two possible scenarios. If the Democratic Party runs on an urban agenda, develops an urban reputation, and tries to maximize urban turnout, it can win statewide and presidential elections. But barring the occasional wave election, it will be positioned to consistently cede control of Congress and many state legislatures. Alternatively, as in the past, Democrats can put themselves in a better position to win Congress and state legislatures by running candidates in pivotal districts with platforms that are further to the right than those of urban voters. Either way, the system of geographic winner-take-all districts works against the legislative agenda preferred by urban voters.

The Democrats' problem is not an American anomaly or a feature of presidentialism. Labor parties in parliamentary democracies with winner-take-all districts have struggled with the same problem throughout the postwar period. Like the Democrats in the United States, they are riven internally by battles between urban purists and suburban pragmatists. But unlike the Democrats of the 1970s, they cannot solve the problem by writing a different platform in each district. When the platform of the mainstream party of the left is fully responsive to the interests of the urban core, it is able to win votes but not seats. Wave elections in the wake of scandal, war, or economic distress can usher in periods of electoral success, but usually with a moderate, pragmatist platform that is unrecognizable to the urban core. Sometimes the ideological divide on the left is simply too great, and the left side of the political spectrum is then divided between rival parties. In this case, the battle for the soul of the left takes place not only *within* parties of the left, but also *between* rival parties of the left, which can further undermine the representation of urban voters.

In addition to their parliamentary structure, the Commonwealth countries are different from the United States in another important respect. Electoral districts in Australia, Canada, and the United Kingdom are drawn by independent commissions rather than politicians. The similarity of their experience throughout the postwar period thus provides more evidence that the representational disadvantage of the Democrats in the United States is not merely a function of partisan gerrymandering, but a lasting feature of elections with winner-take-all districts in industrialized societies.

CHAPTER 8

Proportional Representation and the Road Not Taken

IN THE EARLY twentieth century, all of the industrialized democracies of continental Europe adopted some form of proportional representation (PR). Today, parties in most European parliaments receive seat shares that are roughly proportional to their vote shares. But Britain and its former colonies retained their traditional systems of legislative representation based on winner-take-all districts. We have now seen that over the ensuing century, two important things happened in these majoritarian democracies. First, electoral competition was distilled into a battle pitting urban political parties of the left against exurban and rural parties of the right. All of the new issues that arose in the twentieth century—including environmentalism, women's rights, and multiculturalism—were bundled into the overarching urban-rural dimension of political conflict. Second, because of the geographic concentration of progressives in cities, the urban political parties have been systematically underrepresented relative to their share of the vote.

This chapter examines the alternative path followed in continental Europe since its fateful electoral reforms in the early twentieth century. First, European systems of proportional representation managed to preserve the multiparty systems of the early twentieth century in spite of the rapid rise of socialists and workers' parties. Crucially, proportional representation sent a lifeline to parties with a preexisting electoral base in cities—above all, liberal parties. In other words, the parties of the early twentieth-century industrial working class did not form the type of urban political monopolies that were built by the British and Australian Labor Parties or the Democrats in the United States. As new issues emerged in Europe, because of the multiparty system, there was no reason to bundle conflicts related to class, social diversity, religion, and economics together into a single overarching urban-rural battle. As a result, urban-rural polarization has been less intense. While parties of the right have abandoned cities in Britain and North America, such parties have been quite successful in many European cities, and European center-right governments almost always contain urban representatives.

Second, when legislative districts are large and a party's legislative representation is in proportion to its overall vote share, the geographic dilemma of the left is resolved. It simply does not matter if votes for socialist or workers' parties are concentrated in the old, dense working-class housing near nineteenth-century factories, coal mines, and smelters, or scattered along the old transportation corridors. In a perfectly proportional electoral system, there is no such thing as a "wasted" or "surplus" vote. Moreover, parties of the urban left need not engage in costly coordination battles with one another.

As a result, in stark contrast with the majoritarian democracies, there has been no systematic bias for or against urban parties in industrialized countries with proportional electoral systems. These differences in representation are associated with pronounced long-term policy differences. Above all, the proportional systems of Europe have developed larger public sectors, more generous social expenditure, higher levels of redistribution, and more stringent efforts at environmental protection. Over the century since it was introduced in much of Europe, proportional representation has been a boon not only for the representation of cities, but for the policy agenda of the urban left.

Yet Democrats in the United States and labor parties in the Commonwealth countries have not pushed for electoral reform when in power. In many cases, reform is not in the self-interest of elites in the mainstream parties of the left. They embrace the majoritarian system in an effort to maintain safe seats and prevent rival parties of the left from gaining a foothold.

And parties of the right have had little interest in altering electoral systems that have been so good to them for so long.

But reform is not impossible. This chapter concludes with the remarkable story of New Zealand, where the typical logjam was broken and electoral reform was achieved in the 1990s via popular referenda that allowed voters to circumvent the opposition of the political class.

LET'S BEGIN BY clarifying how proportional representation works. There are important variations from one country to another, but in most cases, the country is divided up into a series of large multimember districts, and within each district, every party receives a number of seats that is proportionate to its share of the vote. But there are several reasons why strict proportionality is not always achieved. Sometimes small parties don't meet a fixed vote threshold and are excluded from the legislature. The combination of district magnitude—the number of representatives per district—and the specific formula for translating votes into seats is also important. As a general matter, larger districts yield a more proportionate transformation of votes to seats. In the extreme case, the Netherlands uses a single nationwide district, and achieves a very high level of proportionality. Some countries with smaller regional districts achieve the same thing by adding seats based on the national vote share to assure a highly proportionate overall result. Most of the PR systems of Northern Europe have a feature like this, and as a result, achieve a highly proportional transformation of votes to seats.

However, some systems end up with a transformation of votes to seats that is not especially proportional. Above all, this happens when the districts are small, and especially if they are asymmetric in population size. This is the case in some Southern European PR systems including Spain, Italy, and Portugal.

Another important variation is the use of so-called mixed member proportional systems like the one used in Germany since World War II, and the one recently adopted in New Zealand. In this type of system, a certain number of legislators is elected through single-member plurality districts, just as in the United States or Britain, but the rest of the legislature is elected via proportional representation. This system combines the best features of winner-take-all districts and proportional representation. Legislators represent specific localities, but highly disproportionate results are avoided.

In highly proportional systems with large districts, like those in Northern Europe, the geography of a party's support is largely irrelevant for the transformation of votes to seats. It is just as useful to have 30 percent of the vote that is highly concentrated in cities as to have 30 percent of the vote evenly dispersed throughout the country.[1] It is largely for this reason that geographically concentrated workers' and socialist parties latched onto the idea of proportional representation with large regional or national districts early in the twentieth century. And because their votes are inefficiently spread across districts, British Liberals, the Canadian NDP, and Green parties everywhere advocate for proportional representation today.

Another attractive feature of proportional representation is that it resolves the coordination and strategic voting problems that often plague rival parties whose ideological positions are relatively close to one another. Consider the dilemma of a British voter who prefers the Liberal Democrats to Labour, but much prefers Labour to the Conservatives. Such a voter must decide whether to run the risk of giving a vote to the Liberal candidate, knowing that this might split the left vote and hand the district to the Conservatives. The progressive Canadian voter who prefers the NDP to the Liberals and dislikes the Conservatives faces the same dilemma, as does the American who would like to vote for a Green candidate. In a proportional system, such a voter need not worry about strategy or coordination; she can simply vote her true preference.

As a result, voters who would support smaller parties under PR, such as the Libertarian or Green Party in the United States, must strategically abandon them in a system of winner-take-all districts. Early twentieth-century workers' and socialist parties also favored proportional representation because it absolved them of the need to negotiate and coordinate with the liberals in urban districts.

Because of this logic, proportional representation allows more parties to thrive, and political scientists have documented that more proportional electoral systems tend to have more parties represented in the legislature.

This can be seen not only via cross-country comparisons, but also within countries. The winner-take-all lower chamber of the Australian legislature is dominated by Labor and the Coalition, whereas the Australian Senate, which is based on proportional representation by state, represents around ten parties. In the mixed-member proportional systems of Germany and New Zealand, competition is whittled down to the two major parties in the district races, but a wider diversity of parties is successful in winning the proportional seats.

Recall that in many European countries, crucial support for electoral reform in the early twentieth century came not only from the new socialist and workers' parties who were gaining strength in urban districts, but from preexisting urban representatives—often liberals—who feared voters would abandon them for strategic reasons, and from urban conservatives who suspected they would be squeezed out. Proportional representation was a way for these preexisting urban parties to save themselves.

They were largely successful. Liberals and other centrist parties with an urban support base have survived and even thrived in Europe's proportional electoral systems over the ensuing century. These parties have long positioned themselves on the center or center-right on economic issues—often somewhere between the socialist and workers' parties on the left and more rural conservative parties on the right. Over time, as new social issues have been politicized, these parties have taken urban, "cosmopolitan" positions on issues like abortion, gay marriage, the environment, and multiculturalism.

Examples in Sweden include the Liberals and the Moderates, who do very well in Stockholm and other cities. These parties typically form coalitions with the Centre and Christian Democratic Parties, whose support base is more exurban and rural. A government of the right in Sweden is a mix of urban, suburban, and rural representatives. This phenomenon can be found throughout Northern Europe. In Norway, the Liberals (*Venstre*) are an upper-middle-class urban party that coalesces with the right. The Liberal Alliance plays a similar role in Denmark. The Danish Social Liberals have attempted to position themselves as the party of the knowledge economy and the urban "creative class," and have been open to coalitions with both the right and the left. In Finland, the National Coalition Party, with its center-right positions on economics and support for multiculturalism and gay marriage, has a primarily urban support base. In Belgium, this role is played by the Reformist Movement (in Wallonia) and the Open Flemish Liberals and Democrats (in Flanders). In the Netherlands, this role is played by the People's Party for Freedom and Democracy, and in Germany, by the Free Democrats.

While some of these parties are open to coalescing with the left, most of them typically join together with other parties of the right. In fact, such urban parties of the center-right have been crucial players in postwar coalition governments of the right throughout Europe. This is an important contrast with the United States and the Commonwealth countries, where a government of the right typically comprises little or no urban representation.

Proportional representation has also facilitated differentiation among parties of the left. In Sweden, many socially progressive college students and young voters in city centers opt for the Greens and the Left Party, while the Swedish Social Democratic Party maintains its traditional support in the old working-class neighborhoods in the shadows of factories, warehouses, docks, and along the nineteenth-century rail network. The Social Democrats have also maintained their electoral base in northern rural areas with a history of mining, forestry, and landless agricultural workers. Thus, a government of the left in Sweden also includes significant rural representation. Similar differentiation on the left takes place in a number of other European countries, where educated young knowledge-economy workers in city centers often vote for a mix of liberal parties, Greens, and assorted new left parties, while the socialist and workers' parties of the early twentieth century obtain most of their support in the old industrial neighborhoods, including those with new migrants from abroad.

In a European proportional democracy with six or seven parties, a voter who prefers lower taxes and legalized gay marriage, or a voter who supports labor unions but wishes to limit immigration, can find a party to vote for. In the United States, such voters must compromise and choose from one of the two options—neither of which is a good match to their own values. The ability to vote sincerely for a party with matching issue positions is perhaps the feature of proportional electoral systems that is most celebrated by their advocates. It is perhaps part of the reason voters in proportional systems display higher turnout than voters in majoritarian systems, are more likely to report that elections are fair, and are more likely to say that elected officials are responsive to their interests.[2]

But there is another advantage that has received less attention. By preventing the growth of two dominant parties, PR systems in industrialized societies have undermined the logic of urban-rural polarization described in previous chapters. The Democrats, along with labor parties in the Commonwealth countries, have come to be monopolists in cities. Likewise, the Republicans and Conservative parties are hegemonic in rural areas, and battles for legislative control focus on a handful of suburban or mixed districts. Elections have come to feel like existential battles between two very different economic sectors, ways of life, and value systems. In highly proportional systems, in contrast, the entire country is a competitive electoral battleground. Some parties of the right compete for votes in cities, and some parties of the left, in rural areas.

Thus American-style urban-rural polarization has been avoided. To be sure, there are also European parties of the right with an overwhelmingly exurban and rural support base. This includes not only traditional agrarian and Christian parties, but also a new class of anti-globalization, anti–European Union, and anti-immigrant populist parties. The rhetoric of such parties is often quite explicitly anti-urban, like that sometimes employed by Republican candidates in the United States. However, in most European countries, it would be nearly impossible to assemble a workable governing coalition of the right that did not include some Liberals or other urban-based parties of the center-right. In contrast, the entire right side of the political spectrum in the United States is represented by a single party that has given up on contesting votes in cities. Its hostility to things like interurban rail and urban infrastructure projects would be self-defeating for mainstream European parties of the right.

The point is not that urban-rural polarization is absent in Europe. On the contrary, the political orientation of voters in the urban core, sprawling exurbs, and rural periphery are quite different from one another in many European countries. Earlier I described a dynamic in the United States, whereby socially progressive residents of increasingly affluent global cities benefit from free trade and liberal immigration policies, while socially conservative residents of the periphery are left behind by the global knowledge economy. The same dynamic is at work in much of Europe, but because of proportional electoral systems, the urban-rural polarization at the ballot box is less stark.

It is illuminating to examine situations in which Europeans, like Americans, are forced to choose between two options. A recent example was the second round of the Austrian presidential election in 2017, when there were only two candidates—one from the Green Party and the other from the right-wing populist Freedom Party. The urban-rural polarization in the election results was stunning. The major cities of Vienna, Linz, and Graz voted overwhelmingly for the Green candidate, and the rest of the country returned majorities for the candidate of the right. This is perhaps a window into what Austrian politics would look like with an American-style, majoritarian two-party system. However, under the current proportional system used for its more important parliamentary elections, electoral maps in Austria are far more varied and textured. For instance, in legislative elections, the Social Democrats have pockets of strength in rural areas, and both Liberals and the mainstream party of the right—the Austrian People's Party—have significant areas of strength in cities. Because of the proportional electoral system, an Austrian government of the right typically includes Viennese and other urban ministers and depends on urban legislators for support. In the vast majority of postwar governments in Austria, neither the Social Democrats nor the People's Party have had enough seats to govern alone, and they have formed a so-called grand coalition that includes urban, suburban, and rural representatives.

Some political scientists have argued that party platforms tend to be more polarized in proportional democracies than in majoritarian democracies, in the sense that smaller, more extremist parties on both the right and left can gain a foothold as independent parties rather than being folded into one of the larger parties.[3] Systems of proportional representation do indeed sometimes give rise to extremist parties of the right and left, but also to successful, moderate parties that occupy the center of the political spectrum.

Some of these parties are centrist on a variety of issues, while others lean to the right on some issues but to the left on others.

Such parties are a crucial antidote to American-style urban-rural polarization throughout Europe. Because of the greater diversity of policy platforms from which they can choose, relative to Americans, voters in proportional democracies can find a party that comes closer to their own mix of policy preferences on different issues. In some cross-country surveys, respondents have been asked to place themselves, as well as the parties, on a simple numerical ideological scale. On average, European voters in proportional democracies see themselves as much closer to their most proximate party than do Americans. Moreover, they also see themselves as closer to their *nonpreferred* parties than do Americans. Many Democrats view Republicans as ideologically extreme, and vice versa. In fact, Americans perceive their parties as ideologically further apart than respondents in any other wealthy democracy.[4] In other words, the American two-party system is, in an important respect, more polarized than the multiparty systems of Europe.

ONE OF THE most striking features of industrialized majoritarian democracies in the postwar period has been their tendency to produce governments that are, in the long run, well to the right of what we might expect, given the parties' vote shares. We have already seen that labor parties spent a large share of the postwar period frozen out of power in the United Kingdom and Australia, and the same is true of the Canadian NDP. The experience of countries using proportional representation has been quite different. In some countries, like Sweden, Social Democratic parties have been dominant for much of the postwar period. But in other countries, like Austria, neither the left nor the right has consistently had the upper hand. And in countries like Germany and Italy, center-right Christian Democrats have dominated for most of the postwar period.

We can verify that there is no systematic bias in favor of the left or right in proportional democracies by examining some data. A group of political scientists has placed the ideological platforms of parties in industrialized countries in the postwar period (1945 to 2005) on a "left-right" scale, so that communist parties are at one end and far-right parties are at the other.[5] These assessments have been combined into a single number for each party, and I have standardized this measure so that the average is zero and the standard deviation is one. Next, for each government, I calculate three useful weighted averages. First, I take the ideological score for each party and weight it by the party's *vote share*. Next, I do this for the party's *seat share* in the lower chamber of the legislature. And finally, I weight each party's ideology score by its *share of cabinet posts* in the government. This makes it possible to see whether, because of disproportionalities in the transformation of votes to seats, legislatures tend to be to the right (or left) of voters. Moreover, we can examine whether, because some parties in the legislature are systematically left out of governments, cabinets are to the right (or left) of the legislature.

In proportional representation systems, we should expect to see that the ideological composition of the legislature is very similar to that of the voters. Indeed, this is the case. For each of the fifteen proportional representation systems in the data set, over the course of postwar elections, the representation of parties in the legislature is a very accurate reflection of the parties' vote shares. Looking across proportional systems as a whole during this period, neither the voters nor the legislatures tend toward the right or left. Taking all postwar governments in proportional systems, the weighted averages of the party scores for both voters and legislatures is almost exactly in the middle. If we simply add up the votes for parties within each PR country, and do the same for seats, we learn that each country has been quite competitive, and left parties have gained more votes (and seats) in about half of the PR countries, and right parties have been more successful in the other half.[6]

Elections do have winners and losers, however, and except for rare cases like Austria's grand coalitions, we should not expect to see that cabinets will be perfect reflections of the partisanship of the legislature. In the long run, because of the frequent victories of the Social Democrats, Swedish cabinets have been, on average, to the left of the Swedish parliament, and because of the success of the Christian Democratic Union (CDU), German cabinets have been to the right of the German parliament. If we aggregate all

European proportional representation systems in the postwar period, this cancels out. The partisanship of the average European government in the postwar period is neither right nor left, and summing all postwar cabinet seats by country, we see that parties of the right have had the edge in about half of the PR countries, and parties of the left in the other half.[7]

In short, the European experience suggests that proportional representation creates no systematic bias in favor of either the right or left. This may seem unremarkable on its own, but the contrast with majoritarian democracies is striking. In every industrialized parliamentary democracy with majoritarian electoral institutions, averaging over the postwar period, the legislature has been well to the right of the voters, and in most cases, the cabinet has been even further to the right.

For each government in the postwar period, again using the expert survey-based measure, I subtract the vote-weighted ideology of the legislature from the seat-weighted ideology. A positive number indicates that the legislature is to the right of the voters. I also subtract the vote-weighted

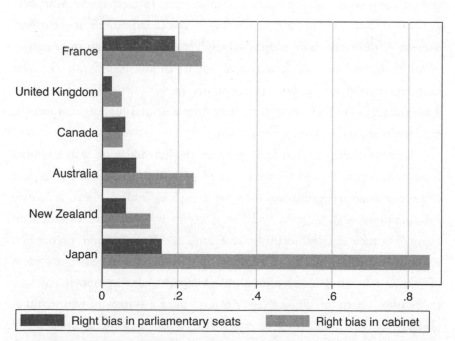

Figure 8.1: Bias in Favor of the Right in Parliament and Cabinets, Majoritarian Democracies

ideology from the cabinet-weighted ideology, which provides an indicator of the extent to which the government is to the right of the voters. Figure 8.1 displays averages over the postwar period for majoritarian parliamentary democracies.[8] It shows that in each country, the partisanship of the parliament has been, on average, to the right of the voters. And with the exception of Canada, where the center-left Liberal Party has spent much of the postwar period in government, governing cabinets have been even further to the right.

Other scholars have also noticed that during the postwar period, governments headed by parties of the left have been more common in countries with proportional electoral systems than in countries with majoritarian electoral systems.[9] While PR systems have been evenly split, two-thirds of governments formed during the postwar period in majoritarian democracies were parties of the right or center-right.[10] This striking pattern cannot be explained by some bias in favor of the left associated with proportional representation or by a special fondness for parties of the left among European voters. Nor can it be explained by an unusual admiration for parties of the right among voters in majoritarian democracies. In fact, aggregating over the period from 1945 to 2005, according to the classifications of the expert surveys, left-of-center parties received slightly more votes than right parties in all of the majoritarian democracies but Japan and New Zealand.[11] The best explanation for the poor performance of left parties in majoritarian democracies lies in their struggle to transform electoral support into seats in the legislature and to form governments.[12]

We have already explored the roots of this phenomenon in the United Kingdom, Australia, and Canada, but to get a better sense of the impact of proportional representation vis-à-vis winner-take-all districts, it is useful to briefly examine two additional countries that have experienced changes in their electoral institutions: France and New Zealand. France had a proportional electoral system until 1958, when it switched to a system of winner-take-all districts (though it switched back to proportional representation briefly in 1986). New Zealand used a system of winner-take-all districts until 1994, when it switched to a mixed-member proportional system similar to that used in Germany. In both France and New Zealand,

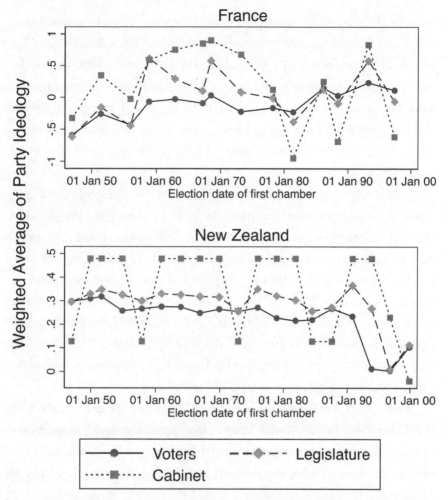

Figure 8.2: The Ideology of Voters, Legislatures, and Cabinets in France and New Zealand, World War II to 2000

periods with winner-take-all districts were associated with substantial bias in favor of the right, but this bias disappeared during periods of proportional representation.

Figure 8.2 displays the ideological classifications of the parties from the expert surveys in each of these countries, weighted by vote shares, seat shares, and cabinet shares, from World War II to 2005. In France, we can see from the first three observations that during the period of proportional representation during the Fourth Republic, votes and seats tracked one another very closely. The same was true during the PR interregnum in 1986.

However, because of its relative geographic concentration in urban indus-trial areas, the majoritarian system used during the Fifth Republic has not been kind to the French left. Throughout the 1960s and 1970s, the legisla-ture was well to the right of the voters. When the right was winning elec-tions during this period, and again in 1993, it enjoyed a large seat bonus. This is captured by the large gap between the solid and dashed lines. How-ever, when the left obtained victories in 1981, 1988, and 1997, it received minimal seat bonuses.

New Zealand is even more striking. Because of the geographic con-centration of Labour voters in cities, the party of the right—the National Party—has been overrepresented throughout the postwar period. As a result, the legislature has been consistently to the right of the voters. As in Austra-lia, this has allowed the right to govern for most of the postwar period. In New Zealand, from World War II to 1993, even though the Labour Party received more votes overall, the National Party formed twelve governments, while Labour formed only five. As in the state legislatures of Michigan and Pennsylvania, the party of the urban left became accustomed to winning the popular vote without gaining control of the legislature.

However, Figure 8.2 also reveals that this bias in favor of the right came to a sudden end in 1996—the first election contested under proportional representation. From that point forward, New Zealand has resembled a Eu-ropean democracy in that the strength of Labour and other left parties in the legislature has matched their strength in the electorate.

In sum, relative to proportional systems, the legislatures and govern-ments of industrialized majoritarian democracies have been well to the right of their voters since World War II. Moreover, they have been well to the right of the legislatures and governments of the countries with propor-tional electoral systems. In each case, the political base of these overrepre-sented right parties has been predominantly exurban and rural, and that of left parties has been concentrated in city centers. In majoritarian democra-cies, parties of the right are often able to win elections and govern without significant urban support. In contrast, when parties of the right come to power in proportional democracies, at least some urban support is usually essential.

THESE PRONOUNCED CROSS-COUNTRY differences in the geographic bases of postwar governments have shaped long-term differences in policy. Economists and political scientists have discovered very large differences between policies pursued in majoritarian and proportional democracies. Above all, governments in countries using proportional representation raise more revenue and spend more as a share of gross domestic product (GDP) than majoritarian democracies. They also spend significantly more on social policies like health, old age support, unemployment insurance, and housing.[13] Systems of taxes and transfers in countries with proportional electoral rules are also more redistributive, and overall levels of economic inequality are lower.[14] Much of this has to do with the fact that labor unions are also far more influential in countries with proportional electoral systems. Laws are more favorable to labor unions, larger shares of workers are unionized, and the process through which collective bargaining takes place is far more centralized.[15]

These cross-country differences are not new. They emerged during a period of rapid growth in government expenditures after the Great Depression and World War II. In the early twentieth century, when many voters still did not have the franchise and transitions to proportional representation had not yet occurred, social expenditures were tiny as a share of GDP everywhere. In 1910, on the eve of electoral reform, there was no discernable difference between the countries that would end up with majoritarian systems (the United States, Australia, Canada, the United Kingdom, New Zealand, and Japan) and countries that were soon to adopt proportional representation (Austria, Belgium, Denmark, Sweden, Norway, Finland, the Netherlands, Italy, and France). In fact, the United Kingdom had a larger system of social transfers than Sweden. The United States and Australia had more generous social transfers than the Netherlands.

But after the European countries adopted proportional representation, an impressive divergence took place. During a period of rapid growth in the size of government in industrialized societies after World War II, social expenditures took off much faster in the countries with proportional electoral systems. This can be seen in Figure 8.3, which plots averages for the majoritarian and proportional countries from the nineteenth century to 2016.[16]

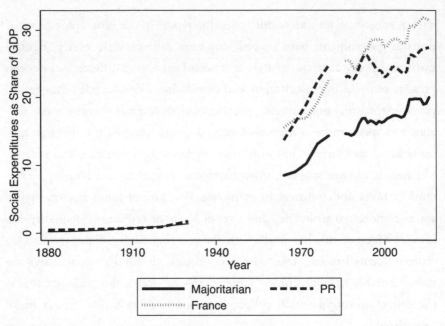

Figure 8.3: The Growth of Social Expenditure in Majoritarian and Proportional Democracies, 1880–2016

Comparable data are unavailable for the 1940s and 1950s, but by 1960, the United States, Canada, Australia, New Zealand, Britain, and Japan had fallen quite far behind the European countries.

France is displayed separately because of its shifting electoral rules. Recall that France had a proportional electoral system until 1958, by which time it had already built one of the largest systems of social transfers in the world. Once such programs are put in place, they develop strong support constituencies, and they are very difficult to reform. Social transfers have continued to grow as a share of GDP in almost all of the industrialized democracies, but the majoritarian democracies have shown no sign of catching up with the proportional democracies. France is the only exception: the programs built in the 1940s during the era of proportional representation have continued to grow at a rate similar to other PR countries even after the return of winner-take-all districts. Most of the cross-country variation had emerged by 1970, and the rankings have been relatively stable since then.

Demands for greater government involvement in social insurance went hand in hand with urbanization and industrialization. As people moved from farms to cities to work as wage laborers, the family and church became less reliable as the primary tools for individuals to reduce income risk and absorb negative shocks.[17] New types of labor contracts emerged, and unemployment and retirement became discrete and often abrupt events.[18] The demand for investment in urban infrastructure was very strong, and many countries experienced shortages of affordable housing. Labor unions mobilized urban workers not only to negotiate wages and working conditions, but to push for a political agenda of workers' rights, risk-sharing, redistribution, and investments in health and public housing. In cross-country data, urbanization is a very good predictor of the growth of government expenditures.[19]

Countries with proportional electoral systems were more responsive to the demands of urban voters during the twentieth century than the majoritarian countries. Part of the story is simply that left parties won early and often after the expansion of the franchise and the transition to proportional representation in the early twentieth century in Northern Europe. In countries like Sweden and the Netherlands, workers' parties and their allies spent much of the early postwar period in power. In majoritarian countries, urban parties have spent much of the postwar period in the political wilderness, and when they have emerged victorious, it was often by holding the interests of urban voters at arms' length to achieve success in the relatively conservative suburbs.

Europe's more extensive systems of social insurance and economic redistribution cannot be explained exclusively by victories of left parties, however. Some European welfare states were built or at least maintained by dominant center-right Christian Democratic or Catholic parties, as in Germany, Belgium, and Italy. Proportional electoral systems provided incentives for these parties to cultivate urban voters, and in fact, these parties had strong links to their own urban labor unions. Mainstream parties of the right in the majoritarian countries—for example the American Republicans, the British and Canadian Conservatives, and Australian Liberals—abandoned cities and developed antagonistic relationships with labor unions. The contrast with the labor-friendly outlook of European Christian Democracy is striking.

These long-term differences in policy outcomes are directly related to the key insight of the previous chapter. Political competition in proportional democracies creates incentives to cater to the national median voter, whereas competition in majoritarian democracies focuses on the median district. Recall that when leftists are asymmetrically concentrated in urban districts, the median district is more conservative than the national median voter.[20]

The greater responsiveness of proportional democracies to urban interests has shaped long-term policy differences well beyond the traditional areas of emphasis for labor unions and workers' parties. For instance, European democracies have invested more in urban transportation infrastructure than majoritarian democracies. And the proportional democracies of Northern Europe—above all Sweden, Denmark, Finland, and the Netherlands—have been leaders in facilitating the growth of the urban knowledge economy.[21] In the wealthy societies of Europe, North America, and Australasia, demands for environmental protection have grown throughout the twentieth century, primarily among young urban voters. And scholars have shown that environmental protection is significantly more stringent in countries with proportional electoral systems.[22] Urban voters also tend to have more liberal views on issues related to crime and punishment, and proportional democracies engage in less incarceration. Urban voters are also typically more socially progressive on issues of gender and sexuality, and countries with proportional electoral systems have adopted civil union or gay marriage legislation more rapidly than majoritarian countries.[23] In short, the policy agenda favored by urban voters since World War II has gone further in countries with proportional representation, even as that agenda has expanded from union recognition, pensions, and health insurance to investment in the knowledge economy, environmental protection, and progressive social causes.

ALL OF THESE observations lead to a simple question: If proportional representation is so good for urban voters, why don't parties of the urban left—when they have their occasional moments in the sun in majoritarian democracies—try to change the electoral system? In fact, the *insurgent* parties of the left are among the staunchest supporters of proportional representation. Parties who typically lose out in the coordination game within districts—and suffer the most in the transformation of votes to seats—have much to gain from electoral reform. These include the Canadian NDP, British Liberal Democrats, an assortment of insurgent parties of the left in New Zealand, and Green parties everywhere. But even though the winner-take-all system puts them at a disadvantage, elites in the mainstream parties of the left have incentives to suppress electoral reform, precisely because they fear it will benefit these insurgent challengers.

Moreover, leaders of urban parties of the left are often longstanding incumbents with safe seats. It is easy to understand why they might not want to exchange their power and influence for the uncertainty associated with major reform that might not only invite challenges from parties like the Green Party, but also imperil their own position of leadership within the party.

For the most part, debates about electoral reform in majoritarian countries in the postwar period have been forced by insurgent challengers, like the NDP in Canada or the Liberals, Social Democrats, and now Liberal Democrats in the United Kingdom. These parties have adopted the strategy of running candidates in a large number of districts, hoping to eventually either supplant the mainstream party of the left, or more realistically, force the mainstream party into a coalition, the price of which would be electoral reform. In spite of decades of effort, they have never quite been able to pull this off, and the mainstream parties of the left have flirted with but ultimately resisted calls for reform.

Canada's most recent flirtation with electoral reform was especially illuminating. In the 2011 federal election, the combined vote share of the left—the Liberals, NDP, and Greens—was well above the Conservatives' vote share, but as in the previous two elections, a lack of coordination on the left allowed the Conservatives to win the most seats and form a government. But in 2011, for the first time, the NDP won more votes and seats than the Liberals. It seemed plausible that the NDP was on the cusp of achieving what the British Labour Party achieved in the early twentieth century—the replacement of the Liberals as the dominant party of the left. It was in this context that Justin Trudeau made a campaign pledge in June of 2015 to reform the electoral system, committing that if the Liberals were elected,

2015 would be the last election held under the "first past the post" electoral system. The Canadian Liberals, sensing the possibility that they would be squeezed out, seemed ready to embrace proportional representation if given the chance. Since the Greens, NDP, and Bloc Quebecois all supported electoral reform as well, it appeared to be a serious possibility.

However, the Liberals' fears turned out to be unfounded. Many left voters abandoned the NDP in the 2015 election and coordinated to support the Liberals, who came roaring back and were able to win an outright majority, reclaiming once again their status as the mainstream party of the left. Predictably, their interest in electoral reform suddenly waned. Still, a Special Committee on Electoral Reform was formed with representatives from all of the parties. After extensive testimony, it issued a report recommending a national referendum on proportional representation. It became clear that the only electoral reform that would be acceptable to the Liberals was an Australian-style system of ranked-choice voting. Evidently, their hope was that a system of ranked-choice voting would allow them to resolve their coordination dilemma with the NDP and Greens without losing ground to them, much in the way that the Australian Labor Party has benefited from being the second choice of voters who prefer Greens and other new left parties. In the end, however, Justin Trudeau declared that proportional representation would not be good for Canada. Critics pointed out that it would also not be good for the Liberal Party, which would probably not be able to govern alone again under a system of proportional representation.

The Canadian Liberals behaved as mainstream parties of the left have always behaved in majoritarian systems when they believe they can marginalize their insurgent challengers. Even while suffering in the transformation of votes to seats, labor parties have steadfastly resisted electoral reform in Britain, New Zealand, and Australia.

It is possible, however, to break through that wall of opposition to reform that has typically united mainstream parties of the left and right in majoritarian systems. New Zealand is a fascinating example. The beginning of the story in New Zealand was strikingly similar to that of early twentieth-century Britain. The Liberals were the dominant urban party on the left before the rise of Labour. When Labour was the insurgent in the early twentieth century, it called for proportional representation, while the dominant

Liberals supported the system of winner-take-all districts. But as in Britain, Labour's rise was swift, and the Liberals began to find themselves squeezed out in the urban districts. Once in power, quite predictably, Labour came to support the existing system, and the Liberals embraced PR. They were too late, however, and the Liberals were rather quickly squeezed out of existence.

In the two-party system that emerged in the postwar period, the story of New Zealand's Labour Party was similar to the story told about other labor parties in the other majoritarian countries. Labour's support was highly concentrated in city centers, in industrial-era working-class housing, along railroad tracks, and near docks, warehouses, factories, and universities. This was (and still is) true not only in Auckland, Wellington, and Christchurch, but also in smaller cities like Hamilton, Hastings, Napier, Dunedin, Nelson, and Palmerston North. Each of these cities has a pronounced partisan gradient like those in other cities explored in earlier chapters, with left voters concentrated in city centers and an increase in right voting as one moves through the suburbs and into the rural periphery.

New Zealand Labour faced the same dilemma as its copartisans in Australia and Britain in the early postwar period. The party had overwhelming support in its core urban districts, but struggled to win the pivotal suburban and small town districts. For decades, Labour found it difficult to reconcile its urban purists to the platform moderation that was necessary to win in the suburbs. As a result, for much of the postwar period, it had a highly concentrated cross-district support distribution and suffered in the transformation of votes to seats, spending the vast majority of the period from World War II to the 1980s out of power. In the late 1970s, it faced a center-left insurgent—Social Credit—and as in the days of the Liberals, it once again faced a coordination problem. In fact, a combination of district-level vote splits with Social Credit along with Labour's perennial urban concentration led to a consecutive pair of elections, 1978 and 1981, when Labour won more votes than any other party, but the National Party on the right received a majority of seats.

Subsequently, as in Australia, Labour moved its platform dramatically to the right in the 1980s, and upon returning to power in 1984, implemented neoliberal economic reforms that came to be known as "Rogernomics," named after Minister of Finance Roger Douglas. These reforms were deeply unpopular among urban Labour stalwarts, however, and a left-wing urban splinter faction known as the Alliance rose to challenge the newly centrist Labour. Labour went from fending off a center-left suburban insurgent to fending off an urban insurgent on its left flank.

After winning the popular vote but failing to gain a majority of seats in two consecutive elections, one might have expected Labour to have fully embraced the idea of proportional representation. However, it had the same countervailing concern that gave pause to Justin Trudeau and the Canadian Liberals. Proportional representation would be a gift to the urban insurgents, and it would undermine Labour's ability to form single-party governments going forward.

During the 1984 campaign, after twice winning the popular vote but losing Parliament, Labour promised to appoint a Royal Commission on electoral reform if elected. As with the recent Canadian experience, the Commission recommended proportional representation—in this case, a mixed-member proportional system that maintained single-member districts but added seats that would be elected according to proportional representation—and a national referendum on the topic. But as in Canada, after their return to power, the leaders of the mainstream party of the left had lost interest in reform. In a speech in the 1987 campaign, the Labour leader promised to hold that referendum—but after Labour's success in the election, reneged on his pledge.

The opposition National Party (or National) viewed the broken promise as an opportunity, and in spite of its strong opposition to electoral reform, vowed to carry on with a nonbinding referendum if elected. The National Party won the 1990 election, and did indeed hold a nonbinding referendum. In 1992, when an overwhelming majority of voters supported the transition to the mixed-member proportional (MMP) system recommended by the Royal Commission, the government was forced to hold a binding referendum in 1993. On this occasion, elites from both Labour and National mounted an energetic and expensive campaign against the reform. Nevertheless, it passed easily once again, and the new electoral system came into effect in 1996.

As a result of the reform, the structural bias against urban parties has come to an end. In the eight elections since the reform, four resulted in governments led by National, and four by Labour. This even split is remarkable, given that Labour had won a majority of seats in only five of the seventeen elections held between 1945 and 1996. Labour's fears have been realized, however, in that it is no longer able to form governments without help from flourishing smaller parties of the left and center. And on two occasions, it has been forced to cooperate with the populist anti-immigrant party, New Zealand First. Relatively small new parties have entered the legislature on the left, right, and center. The two major parties are still the focal points for government formation, however, and the right is sufficiently consolidated that the National Party can still hope to form single-party governments.

Some New Zealanders are unhappy with the complexity of the MMP system, the notion of coalition government, the strengthened role of party leaders, and the ability of small parties like New Zealand First to hold the governing coalition hostage to its policy aims. Hoping to capitalize on pockets of discontent and regain its structural geographic advantage, the National Party introduced another referendum on the retention of the MMP electoral system in 2011. The system survived, with 58 percent of the voters favoring its retention. Of those who voted against the MMP system, fewer than half expressed a preference to return to the old first-past-the-post system, while the rest favored other variants of proportional representation. The New Zealand Electoral Commission has released detailed precinct-level results of the referendum, and it is clear that support for the MMP system in the 2011 election was overwhelming in the city centers where left parties are strongest. MMP also received well over 50 percent of the vote in pivotal and right-leaning suburban and exurban areas. "No" votes were concentrated in National's strongholds in the rural periphery.

By no means did the MMP system bring urban-rural polarization in New Zealand to an end. Support for Labour, the Greens, and other small parties of the left is still highly concentrated in urban centers, and National is most successful in exurbs and rural areas. However, by encouraging new parties, it has also facilitated some "unbundling" of issues. For instance, United Future, which has coalesced with both Labour and National, was a Christian Democratic–style party with socially conservative but economically centrist positions. ACT New Zealand is based on classical liberalism, supporting less regulation in both the social and economic realms. Both have received urban and suburban support, and both have been part of coalitions led by National. New Zealand First draws more support from rural areas, combining nationalism, anti-immigrant populism, and advocacy for senior citizens with several left-leaning economic policy positions that it shares with Labour. In coalition negotiations with Labour, New Zealand First has extracted concessions aimed squarely at helping rural voters.

In short, the presence of small parties with more heterodox ideological positions has begun to nudge the large parties to accommodate new geographic constituencies. A common complaint about proportional representation systems is that they force mainstream parties to negotiate with extremists. This is sometimes the case. However, an overlooked benefit of proportional systems is that more often they force the largest parties to negotiate with centrist parties, or more to the point, with parties that have bundled their positions on various issues in different ways, which can create more geographically heterogeneous governing coalitions.

THE KEY CLAIM of this chapter is that the rules of the democratic game are important. They shape the strategies of the players, and they can even help determine who wins and who loses. Winner-take-all districts with only one representative encourage voters to abandon small parties. Electoral competition is whittled down to a small number of competitors. In the extreme case—the United States—there are only two. This has led parties of the left in majoritarian democracies to become catchall urban parties, and parties of the right to become exurban and rural parties. Because of the geography of partisanship and political preferences created by the industrial revolution and the process of suburbanization, this arrangement has been extremely advantageous for both the voters and the political elites representing nonurban areas. Governments in majoritarian democracies in the postwar period have been dominated by parties of the right that receive very little support in cities.

In contrast, proportional systems have followed a different path over the same period. Multiple parties have bundled issues into heterogeneous packages, such that a victory for the right is not necessarily a loss for cities or even a serious setback for labor unions. In the long run, proportional electoral systems favor neither the left nor the right in the formation of governments. However, they have been far more likely than majoritarian democracies to advance the interests of labor and urban voters more generally.

CHAPTER 9

The End of the Dilemma?

T HIS BOOK HAS explored the long legacy of what is known as the second
industrial revolution—an era of large factories and rapid urbanization in the late nineteenth and early twentieth centuries. In countries with
winner-take-all legislative districts, the corresponding growth of cities and
transformation of party systems generated a pattern of political geography
that eventually led to pronounced urban-rural polarization and the underrepresentation of the urban political party. For labor parties in Britain and
the Commonwealth countries, this pattern has been visible for decades. In
the United States—with its history of slavery, regionalism, and denationalized political competition—this pattern has not manifested itself on a national scale until recent decades.

We are currently in the midst of what is being called the third industrial
revolution. The rise of the knowledge economy has led to the concentration
of jobs and prosperity in global cities that attract the most educated workers.
In countries with proportional electoral systems, a variety of parties—some
on the right and some on the left—compete for the votes of educated urban
and suburban professionals in knowledge-economy cities. However, in the
United States, these voters have become closely allied with the Democratic
Party. And more traditional exurban and rural manufacturing and agricultural interests have become firmly aligned with the Republican Party. As a
result, the rise of the knowledge economy has only exacerbated the pattern of
urban-rural polarization that started with the second industrial revolution.

The knowledge-economy revolution may have ushered in something else as well: a nationalist backlash of the rural periphery against globalization, immigration, cosmopolitan values, and free trade. In countries with proportional electoral systems, nationalist parties like Germany's Alternativ für Deutschland (AfD) or the Sweden Democrats have gained vote shares and have high hopes to force their way into governing coalitions. But in the United States, where there are only two parties, a presidential candidate using similar anti-immigration, anti-globalization rhetoric was able to use the unique American system of presidential primaries to take over the entire mainstream party of the right.

It is far too early to judge, but it is possible that this transformation of the Republican Party could have long-term consequences for political geography. Conceivably, the transformation of the Republican Party could undermine its geographic advantage, which stems from its relative appeal in the pivotal suburbs. With a reputation shaped by the interests and aspirations of their urban supporters, the Democrats, like other leftist parties shaped by the second industrial revolution, have struggled to win in pivotal suburban districts. However, it is entirely possible that rural backlash following the third industrial revolution will lead the Republicans and other parties of the right to be overtaken by the interests and aspirations of their rural core supporters on issues like trade and immigration. If so, the tables could turn, and mainstream parties of the right could lose their grip on the pivotal suburban districts.

This chapter speculates about the future of political geography and representation in the era of globalization and the knowledge economy, especially in the United States. This book has described a geographic pattern with deep roots, and a process through which urban-rural polarization has built upon itself in majoritarian democracies over a period of decades. However, it is important to recognize that the world can and does change—sometimes quite dramatically. The second industrial revolution is but one example. In recent decades, coal miners and social conservatives have become Republicans; computer programmers and feminists have become Democrats. Under a range of scenarios, the pattern of political geography and representation described in this book could come undone. For those interested in shaping or at least preparing for the future, it is useful to consider these scenarios.

First, if Republicans lose support in suburban and exurban areas in enough cities, it is plausible that intense urban-rural polarization will remain, but the representation bias against Democrats will evaporate. But it is also possible that what appears to be a major Trump-era realignment of suburbia turns out to be merely a short-term wave of disapproval. In that case, Democrats might receive a bonanza of votes and seats in the suburbs, convincing them that their geography problem is a thing of the past, only to discover a few years later that their success in the pivotal districts was a fleeting mirage.

Alternatively, a longer-lasting electoral wave could bring in a tide of moderate, self-styled Democrats in nonurban districts. This could have the effect of reducing urban-rural polarization—potentially for quite some time. Other conceivable paths to diminished urban-rural polarization include major changes in the platforms and reputations of the parties or the breakup of one of the existing parties.

Another possibility worthy of consideration is that urban-rural polarization will be reduced not by changes in the strategies of the parties or the preferences of voters, but by reforms to electoral institutions or the process of redistricting. After all, radical electoral reform took place in Europe after the second industrial revolution, and more recently in New Zealand. Perhaps like New Zealanders, Americans will eventually have their fill of the two-party system and find their way to reform.

Even if none of these things happen, there are long-term demographic and locational trends afoot in the United States that might ultimately reduce geographic polarization, and hence the legislative underrepresentation of the Democratic Party. Above all, ongoing suburbanization and changing residential patterns mean that the most rapidly growing parts of the United States are becoming more heterogeneous and politically competitive.

Finally, this book concludes by considering the unattractive prospect that urban-rural polarization is here to stay. In that event, the United States might fall back on the coping mechanism it has always used to deal with geographic sectionalism: a strong tradition of federalism and decentralization.

WITHOUT A DOUBT, the nomination of Donald J. Trump changed the Republican Party, and it will likely have a lasting impact on the party's policy reputation. Even before the 2016 election, the Republican Party had been losing support among young voters, especially those with college degrees, and those working in knowledge-economy professions. Suburbs of knowledge-economy hubs like Boston, Seattle, and San Francisco have been strongly Democratic for some time. However, in most other cities, the partisan gradient discussed in this book has been much steeper. As one moves from the overwhelmingly Democratic urban core to the middle- and outer-ring suburbs of nineteenth-century manufacturing cities, the Republican vote share increases rapidly, and Republican candidates typically have the upper hand in suburban congressional and state legislative districts. This leaves the Democrats with massive victories in the urban core but narrower losses elsewhere. To win the pivotal districts and gain control of Congress and state legislatures, they often have to wait for an unpopular war, scandal, or recession that can be blamed on their opponents.

In the 2018 midterm election, reaction to a very unpopular Republican president provided the Democrats with a large national swing in their favor. This swing in vote shares was observable everywhere. Working-class neighborhoods in postindustrial towns that had shifted to the Republicans in 2016 returned to their historical voting patterns and provided majorities for Democratic candidates. Even many rural areas saw gains for Democratic candidates. Perhaps one of the most striking and consequential shifts in 2018 was in suburban areas, where the wave was large enough to provide Democratic congressional candidates with victories in traditionally Republican seats. This was true not only in coastal areas with high rates of employment in knowledge-economy professions, but also in places like Des Moines, Tucson, and Oklahoma City.

A distressing possibility for Republicans is that this is evidence of the beginning of a realignment of the middle- and outer-ring suburbs. It is plausible that by embracing an anti-globalization, anti-immigration agenda that plays well in rural areas, they have damaged the party's reputation in pivotal suburban districts, leaving room for Democrats to reach further from the urban core into the suburbs of typical postmanufacturing cities. This would provide the Democrats with narrow victories in districts where comfortable Republican victories had been the norm. Republicans might even fear that these suburban losses will continue into the future if millennials retain their Democratic affiliation, start voting in larger numbers as they age, and move to the suburbs.[1]

If this happens on a large scale and lasts longer than an electoral cycle or two, the geographic distribution of partisanship described in this book will change. The partisanship of the median district will no longer be more Republican than the cross-district mean. As a result, the Democrats' frustration at not being able to transform votes into seats might come to an end. However, it is very difficult to know the difference between a permanent realignment and a short-term electoral wave until many years later. Consider the experience of "New Labour" in Britain. After the Conservatives suffered from a series of scandals, Tony Blair benefited from an extraordinary wave election in 1997. A 10 percentage-point swing in favor of Labour led to victories in vast swaths of marginal and even reliably Tory suburban, exurban, and small-town constituencies. This led some observers to prematurely conclude that with its new suburban-friendly platform, Labour's geographic concentration problem was a thing of the past. However, this period only lasted for a decade. After Labour lost its majority, it was left once again with only its old urban core constituencies. The party's urban platform and reputation returned, and so did its difficulty in transforming votes to seats. The same thing happened to "New Labour" in New Zealand in the 1980s. For a brief time, it was able to adopt a suburban platform and win suburban victories, but the moment was fleeting, and a few years later, its geography problem was worse than ever.

It is entirely possible that a suburban backlash against Trumpism will turn out to be a temporary phenomenon, much like the decade during which the Tories were discredited in suburban Britain. It is quite possible that the Democrats' urban policy reputation will persist or even strengthen— emboldened by evident success—while the Republicans find a way to restore their edge in the suburbs. Recall the survey data indicating that while cities and suburbs are increasingly aligned when it comes to social issues, voters in the urban core are well to the left of suburban voters on economic issues. As urban socialists experience a resurgence, the age-old battle on the left between urban firebrands and suburban moderates will take center stage once again.

IF THE REPUBLICAN Party's reputation becomes too "rural" for the pivotal suburbs in the era of Trump, it will have given a prodigious, even if temporary, gift to the Democrats. But this gift would do nothing to combat the larger underlying phenomenon of urban-rural polarization. The current level of geographic polarization in the United States is worrisome and costly regardless of one's political persuasion. We have reached a situation where a victory for the Republicans is a devastating loss for cities. With only a handful of exceptions, the Republican delegation in the US House of Representatives contains no representatives of cities. There are a few Republican representatives who might describe themselves as representing places like Cincinnati, Charlotte, or Houston, but a look at district maps reveals that their districts only dip into a small portion of these cities or their suburbs. Moreover, Republican representatives in such districts receive very limited support in the city and inner suburbs; their victories are won in the sprawling exurbs and rural periphery. When Republicans win control of Congress, cities are left largely without representation.

Likewise, a victory for Democrats is viewed as a stinging loss in rural areas throughout much of the United States. Many Republicans believe that a victory for Democrats is a victory for a set of urban interest groups, and the elevation of a set of distasteful secular values associated with San Francisco or New York. In recent years, some voters from each party have come to view a win for the other party as an existential threat to their sense of national identity and way of life. This is quite a contrast with European democracies, where urban voters are an important part of the support coalition for governments of the right, and where parties of the left often include rural representatives in government. In most well-functioning industrialized democracies, elections are not winner-take-all battles between geographic places.

In addition to battles about issues like guns, abortion, and immigration, the two parties have attached themselves to different sectors of the economy, and elections can have very high stakes for investors. The Democrats are unquestionably the party of the knowledge economy, and Republicans are the party of domestic manufacturing and resource extraction. We have now seen that a small number of votes on Election Night in a crucial state can be the difference between heavy government investment in green technology and subsidies for coal, or between free trade and tariffs. This ultimately has costs for the economy. It is difficult for investors to make prudent long-term decisions in an environment of polarization and policy uncertainty.

The stakes are also growing in battles over the interregional flow of resources. Growing regional inequality means that a small number of metropolitan areas with large knowledge-economy sectors produce tax revenues that subsidize the rest of the country. While Hillary Clinton won fewer than 500 counties and Donald Trump won more than 2,500 in 2016, according to Internal Revenue Service (IRS) data, the Democratic-majority counties were responsible for over two-thirds of federal income taxes collected in 2014. The recent Republican tax reform attempted to offset some of the revenue losses from tax cuts by eliminating deductions used by residents of overwhelmingly Democratic metropolitan areas with high state and local taxes and expensive real estate. Future Democratic administrations will likely attempt to shift the tax burdens back onto a different group of wealthy taxpayers in suburbs and exurbs of red states. Again, the policy uncertainty generated by the politics of geographic sectionalism creates distortions and inefficiencies, not to mention strong emotions.

Worse still, the current American geographic sectionalism is undermining trust in democracy. Elections in pivotal districts and states often boil down to turnout battles between urban Democrats and exurban or rural Republicans. When Democrats lose close elections in states with Republican administrations, they often blame their losses on voter suppression efforts such as limited polling hours, early voting practices, strict registration rules, changing polling place locations, voter list purges, and voter identification requirements. The burden of these policies falls primarily upon students and urban voters with unstable residential addresses, while having little impact on middle-aged suburbanites who live for decades at the same address. As a result, the partisan implications of these policies are quite predictable, and aspects of election administration that would be uncontroversial in other countries have become highly partisan battles in the United States.

When Republicans lose close elections, many are easily convinced that the vote differential can be explained not by voter suppression, but by dirty tricks carried out in cities, including votes by noncitizens or dead people, or even ballot-stuffing by corrupt election administrators. In every presidential election, there are a handful of precincts in Philadelphia and other large cities where the Republican candidate records zero votes. Instead of viewing this as an indicator of urban-rural polarization, conspiracy theorists interpret it as evidence of fraud. On both sides, strong partisans can easily become convinced that narrow losses for their party are illegitimate.

The urban-rural divide plays out not only *across* districts, but also *within* districts. Even far away from big cities, Democratic candidates successfully mobilize poor renters, minorities, college professors, unionized schoolteachers, and public employees living near Main Street and around the railroad tracks in small nineteenth-century American cities. Meanwhile, Republican candidates mobilize voters living in sparser single-family developments built in more recent decades on the outskirts of town, near the interstate and big box stores, and in the rural periphery.

All of this started with urban industrial workers over a century ago, and as we've seen, a map of Democratic voting today in much of the country is largely identical to a map of early industrialization. But urban-rural polarization really took off when (1) a new set of urban social issues was bundled together with the old economic issues, and (2) the globalized knowledge economy took off in cities, while traditional manufacturing relocated to the outskirts of cities and the interstate highways of the rural periphery.

As long as there are only two parties, and voters' preferences on most of the salient issues of the day are correlated with population density, it stands to reason that votes for the parties will also be correlated with population density. However, one can imagine scenarios in which the correlation reaches its apogee and begins to descend once again. The extent of urban-rural polarization is exaggerated by the stark choice between one party that bundles affirmative action and economic redistribution with abortion rights and globalization, and another that bundles tax cuts and immigration restrictions with religious values and now tariffs. Many Americans prefer alternative mixtures of policies. Some knowledge-economy professionals, for instance, would prefer a party favoring less government regulation in both the economic and social spheres, but more public investment in education and research. Some Christians might prefer a party that combines traditional social values with an expansion of the government's role in providing social insurance. Such parties have been central players in European elections and governments since World War II.

The surest way to reduce the level of urban-rural polarization is to begin to "unbundle" the urban and rural packages offered by the two parties. This could be achieved if new parties gained prominence, or if existing parties adopted different strategies.

With only two parties in a diverse society, both must try to be many things to many people, and both are stretched to near breaking point under the strain. The entry of third parties in majoritarian democracies is not unthinkable. The Liberals, Social Democrats, and now the Liberal Democrats have found an opening by offering alternative bundles of issues than those offered by the mainstream Labour Party in Britain. The New Democratic Party and Liberal Party in Canada have coexisted for decades now, the former with a stronger base in the urban core and the latter with a base in the suburbs. Years ago, the Catholic-oriented Democratic Labor Party split from the Australian Labor Party, as have the Greens in recent years. Similar splits on the left have happened repeatedly in New Zealand. The French left has fragmented dramatically. A point could come when the battle for the soul of the Democratic Party in the United States leads a frustrated splinter group—either urban purists or suburban pragmatists—to run its own slate of candidates.

Splits on the left have been more common in majoritarian systems than splits on the right because of the ideological distinctiveness of cities. However, it is possible that the anti-globalization backlash and the rise of rural populism will create a similar effect on the right. In fact, this has already happened in Canada, where the Reform Party broke away from the Progressive Conservatives in western Canada in the late 1980s, leading to a decade-long bifurcation of the Canadian right. Former House Speaker John

Boehner has said that the pre-Trump Republican Party, which he characterized as "taking a nap somewhere," might eventually wake up and break free
of what he referred to as the "Trump Party." Alternatively, establishment
suburban Republicans might eventually regain control, spurring an exodus
of rural populists.

Boehner's successor, Paul Ryan, made an astute observation: "We basi-
cally run a coalition government without the efficiency of a parliamentary
system."[2] Ryan was expressing frustration with the fractious nature of the
Republican delegation, but his remark draws attention to the key reason
third parties are less likely to emerge in US congressional elections than in
parliamentary elections. Precisely because Mr. Ryan was not able to wield
the threat of a no-confidence vote to keep his backbenchers in line, Republican candidates who opposed him had no reason to run under alternative
party labels. They could run, and win, as rebellious Republicans, and the
same is true of Democrats who disagree with their leaders.

Another possibility is that the existing parties might begin to "unbundle" these packages of issues on their own, even without electoral reform or
partisan breakup. For instance, it is conceivable that a candidate like Bernie
Sanders could win the Democratic presidential nomination with a platform
of left-wing anti-globalization populism and a moderate reputation on gun
control. It is conceivable that such a shift could lead the Democrats to lose
some support in dense, knowledge-economy corridors and gain some votes
in exurban and rural areas hardest hit by the loss of manufacturing jobs
to China. More generally, future Democratic candidates might experiment
with mixtures of platforms that are more appealing outside of cities. In statewide and presidential elections, Democratic candidates might eventually rediscover paths to victory that involve not only maximizing urban turnout,
but also minimizing the extent of losses in rural areas.

Governors have been experimenting successfully with this sort of unbundling of issues for decades. In the era of urban-rural polarization,
Republican gubernatorial candidates in even the most extremely Democratic states—from Massachusetts to Maryland and even Vermont and
California—have been surprisingly successful by marketing themselves as
fiscally conservative counterweights to Democratic legislatures, while taking

centrist or even left-leaning positions on issues like environmental protection and gay marriage. Likewise, Democrats have been able to distinguish
themselves from the national party and craft winning platforms in gubernatorial elections in red states like Montana and Kansas. This type of local
tailoring is perhaps easier in gubernatorial elections than in Senate or House
elections, because a statewide chief executive is less likely to be pressured by
copartisans to vote for legislation that was crafted by other members of the
national party.

An important challenge identified in this book is that absent a wave
election, by appealing to urban voters to achieve victory in statewide elections, the Democrats tend to position themselves as an urban party that cannot win in the crucial, relatively conservative suburban and mixed districts
needed to control Congress and state legislatures. In many US states, it appears that the Democrats must either take active steps to change the party's
reputation, or they must support self-styled candidates who run as Democrats in suburban and rural districts without fully embracing the party's
platforms. In other words, they must take advantage of Paul Ryan's observation about heterogeneous political parties in presidential systems. This latter
approach—the "blue dog" strategy—has worked for the Democrats in the
past. Self-styled local Democratic candidates swept into office in suburban
and rural districts in a pro-Democratic wave in 1964, and many of them
remained in office for decades. Their presence in office may have helped slow
the rise of urban-rural polarization for a couple of decades. The blue dogs
helped lend ambiguity to the party's reputation so that other ideologically
heterogeneous Democrats could distance themselves from the party's old
core of urban labor supporters and its burgeoning core of social and racial
progressives, so as to run credible campaigns outside of cities. In a sense,
the internal heterogeneity of the Democrats has at times achieved some of
the ideological unbundling of economic and social issues that is typically
found in a multiparty system.

Perhaps the clearest path to reducing urban-rural polarization would be
for the Democrats to return to the era of the blue dogs, allowing suburban
and rural moderates to thrive in a heterogeneous party. Several such Democrats achieved victory in the 2018 midterm election, and will seek to expand

their influence in the years ahead. Likewise, one might imagine a future scenario in which a renegade group of moderate Republicans capitalizes on a future scandal or Democratic failure and makes headway in some urban areas. However, when a party benefits from a national wave election, its elites often feel they are operating from a position of strength, and wanting to consolidate their power, they might draw the inference that they are better off with a strong, unified national platform rather than a heterogeneous set of local platforms.

Moreover, it remains to be seen whether congressional and state legislative races can be as effectively "localized" today as they were in the 1970s. It is more difficult for local candidates to credibly disavow their party leaders in an era where control of the legislature is constantly in play, and where outside money, nationalized media, and ever-present social media are always there to provide a national context for each race. Nevertheless, the recent success of Democratic Senate candidates in settings ranging from rural Minnesota to Montana and West Virginia, and the popularity of Republican governors in the Northeast, suggest that a return to more widespread localized electoral competition is entirely possible.

ANOTHER MORE RADICAL way to pull apart the urban and rural policy bundles offered by the two parties is to follow the path of early twentieth-century Europe or late twentieth-century New Zealand and adopt electoral reform. The multiparty systems facilitated by proportional electoral systems have spawned successful urban parties that coalesce with the right, and rural parties that sometimes join the left. It is difficult to predict the types of parties that might emerge in a proportional system in the United States. As in Europe, a party based on classical liberalism might appeal to a segment of educated voters in and around knowledge-economy cities and college towns. One could imagine such a party coalescing with either the left or right. The same might be true of a socially conservative party that focused on the interests of lower-income voters. A split between a far-left urban party and a center-left party might allow the latter to thrive in suburbia, as in Canada.

Electoral reform in the wake of the second industrial revolution emerged in Europe largely because urban incumbent legislators from the existing parties were fearful that new socialist parties would put an end to their careers. Democratic legislators in the United States face no such threat, and they have shown no interest in electoral reform—even though it would resolve their geography problem. If anything, the populist incursion on the right associated with the third industrial revolution seems to have endangered the careers of traditional suburban Republicans, at least for the moment. If any group of existing political elites stands to gain from proportional representation, it might be, oddly enough, traditional Republicans who are being squeezed out of their party by the populists.

However, the lesson from majoritarian democracies in the postwar period is that electoral reform is quite unlikely to be initiated by elites from the existing parties. Reform is most likely to emerge via constant pressure from citizens' groups, who use initiatives and referenda to circumvent the traditional gatekeepers. This type of movement is most likely to succeed in the United States at the state and local levels, and in Canada at the provincial level.

Voices in favor of the reform of basic electoral institutions are gaining strength, especially at the local level. The case for proportional representation is becoming increasingly clear for those who view the American two-party system as broken beyond repair. But a more active area of reform in the United States is more limited in scope: a coalition of independents, Republicans, and especially Democrats is seeking to change the process through which electoral districts are drawn. The most popular reform proposals involve independent commissions that are instructed to avoid partisan considerations, or politician commissions that are intentionally bipartisan.

There is little reason for optimism that such reforms would have much impact on urban-rural polarization. This basic fact of life in US politics has little to do with the way districts are drawn. We have seen that the polarization shows up whether we use county-level or precinct-level data, and it shows up in US states and in other countries where districts are clearly not manipulated for partisan gain. In fact, because of the concentration of Democrats within city centers, redistricting reform based on compact districts that respect municipal boundaries would likely only generate an *increase* in the correlation across districts between population density and Democratic voting.

In any event, the main goal of reformers is not to reduce urban-rural polarization, but to enhance fairness. As described in previous chapters, the most recent round of redistricting was led by unified Republican state legislatures in a number of pivotal states. And without a doubt, districts drawn by Republican legislators have made things considerably worse for the Democrats in recent years. However, in the past, Democrats like Phil Burton in California have also been leaders in the craft of gerrymandering. To many reformers, the answer seems simple: remove the politicians from the process, forbid them from considering partisanship when drawing districts, or find ways of getting Democrats and Republicans to offset each others' efforts at partisan gain.

A key insight of this book, however, is that Democrats end up inefficiently distributed across districts even when commissions, divided governments, court-appointed special masters, computer algorithms, or even Democrats themselves have drawn the districts. These facts do not obviate the need for redistricting reform, but rather, call for attention to its substance. In many states where districts are currently drawn by Republican operatives, the Democrats would undoubtedly be better off with an independent commission that is told to draw compact districts that respect municipal and county boundaries to the extent possible and ignore partisanship. However, in many states, such districts would likely *still* provide the Republican Party with a substantial edge. In states where the Democrats have an especially poor geographic support distribution—mostly in the postindustrial Midwest and the New South—the Democrats need something beyond a party-blind process if they wish to achieve 50 percent of the seats with 50 percent of the votes. In some cases, they will need a redistricting process that slices up large cities and judiciously combines them with their suburbs. In some cases, they would need a process that carefully travels along nineteenth-century rail lines and pulls together disparate postindustrial and college towns.

In states like Illinois, where Democrats occasionally gain control of the redistricting process, they are able to attempt such maneuvers. If the

Democrats gain control of the redistricting process in some pivotal states, they might relish the opportunity to turn the tables and pursue these and other strategies aimed at combatting the underlying geographic inefficiency of their support. In other words, given that compact, contiguous districts often work against them, the Democrats have much to gain from carefully drawing districts in a way that most would consider a form of gerrymandering. In most states these efforts would not produce a Democratic advantage, but rather neutralize a preexisting disadvantage.

When it comes to regular voters, redistricting reform is broadly popular among Democrats, Republicans, and independents. When it comes to party elites, Democrats have been more enthusiastic about redistricting reform than Republicans, in part because Republicans controlled far more states in the last round of redistricting. If the Democrats come to control the redistricting process in some crucial states, the positions of party elites on redistricting reform might reverse. A party-blind redistricting process might be especially palatable for Republican elites in states where Democrats are most geographically concentrated.

Broadly speaking, there are two approaches to redistricting reform in the United States. One notion of fairness in redistricting focuses merely on process. One might say that a redistricting plan is fair if it was determined by an even-handed process, like the deliberations of an independent commission that ignored partisanship. Alternatively, one might go further and say that a redistricting plan is fair only if it delivers a certain outcome, like the expectation that 50 percent of the votes will correspond to 50 percent of the seats. In many states, Democratic reformers are better off pushing for the latter notion of fairness. If one is willing to tolerate relatively noncompact districts that straddle municipal boundaries, there are workable districting plans in every state that would not favor either party. Such plans could be drawn by hand by commissioners who are explicitly trying to achieve partisan symmetry. Alternatively, a commission could choose an option from among a large number of computer-generated plans that achieves partisan symmetry while satisfying some other basic criteria. Or a commission might work interactively with software designed to facilitate districts with certain agreed characteristics. But in many states, fair redistricting plans would not occur without *explicitly* considering partisan data.

For years, the reform community has focused primarily on a process-oriented notion of fairness. However, reformers have recently turned to more outcome-oriented approaches. For example, in 2018, Michigan voters passed Proposition Two, which specifies that the Independent Citizens' Redistricting Commission must "not give a disproportionate advantage to any political party." This seems to require that the commissioners carefully analyze partisan data and make efforts to break up urban Democratic strongholds, but the details have not yet been worked out. Also in 2018, Missouri voters passed a constitutional amendment that is much more specific, requiring a state-appointed demographer to facilitate partisan fairness by analyzing the efficiency of support for each party across districts. These are important developments, and as redistricting reform catches on in a broader group of states, it will be interesting to see how such provisions are put into practice, and interpreted by state courts, in future rounds of redistricting and the lawsuits that are likely to follow.

EVEN IF THE parties double down on their current strategies and platforms and reform efforts fizzle, there is another path to reduced urban-rural polarization: population movement. It is easy to get the impression that as people pick up their lives and move to new locations in search of prosperity and happiness, the long-term trend is toward ever-increasing geographic polarization. The second industrial revolution turned dispersed rural peasants into concentrated urban socialists. Suburbanization generated high-income, relatively conservative enclaves outside cities. And the third industrial revolution is fostering the concentration of knowledge-economy workers and prosperity in select cities.

But in the United States, there are striking countervailing trends worth consideration. In recent years, Americans are moving less than in the past, and while some older voters are moving to Florida and other retirement destinations, many of those who move across metropolitan areas tend to be younger and more educated. Many do not yet have children or own homes and are thus less constrained by the family and economic considerations that prevent many Americans from moving to areas with higher-paying jobs.

Given the current alignment of the two parties, this means that movers increasingly tend to be Democrats.[3]

Moreover, most of them are not moving to dense city centers. Some cities—especially those that have attracted employers in knowledge-intensive occupations—have slowed the pace of urban population loss or even turned it around. But Americans are continuing to spread themselves out in space, and the United States is becoming increasingly suburban with every passing year. Among those departing from American city centers are African Americans and Hispanics, who are now mimicking the earlier migration of whites to suburbs, making many American suburbs increasingly heterogeneous.

Residential moves might have two types of political implications. First, individuals with specific characteristics select into certain types of environments. And second, upon their arrival, those who move are shaped by their new environments. Social scientists refer to these as "selection" and "treatment" effects. Those who decided to move to cities to take factory jobs in the early twentieth century may well have had different personalities and preferences than their relatives who stayed behind and lived out their lives on the farm. But as with John Updike's fictional Earl Angstrom in his unionized print shop, they were also profoundly influenced by the left-wing organizers who mobilized them upon arrival in the city. Likewise, Earl's son, Harry Angstrom, had personality characteristics that drew him to abandon the city and move to the exurbs. But throughout the Rabbit novels, it seems that his partisanship and political views were shaped less and less by his father, and more by his exurban friends and neighbors.

Social scientists have found it difficult to disentangle these selection and treatment effects. But both academics and journalists have come to suspect that the selection effect is an important part of the mechanism through which geographic polarization has grown over time. For instance, high-income individuals who choose to live in an apartment or condominium in a city center often have different political preferences than individuals of similar income who choose to live in a gated community in the exurbs. In surveys, there is ample evidence that Democrats prefer much denser and more racially diverse residential environments than Republicans.[4] A very popular claim is that Americans are sorting themselves into homogeneous communities that serve as partisan echo chambers.[5] In this account, geographic polarization has emerged because Democrats are congregating in places with high "walkability" and good sushi, while Republicans are seeking neighborhoods with convenient parking and a proliferation of Cracker Barrel restaurants.

There is probably some truth to this narrative among a segment of high-income professionals who have many residential options available to them. For instance, young doctors tend to choose not only residential locations, but also specific practices, with large densities of copartisans.[6] However, there is a growing mound of evidence showing that Americans are not, on the whole, sorting according to partisanship in a way that leads to ever-increasing geographic polarization.

First of all, it is simply not plausible that the phenomenal increase in the correlation between population density and Democratic voting documented in this book can be explained by residential moves of Democrats and Republicans to like-minded locations. A recent empirical study of voter registration records demonstrates that "partisan bias in moving choices is far too small to sustain the current geographic polarization of preferences."[7] Much of the relevant movement was not by people across space, but by party platforms across issues. In the 1970s, rural and exurban social conservatives had no strong reason to prefer Republican candidates. Nor did computer programmers, laboratory scientists, physicians, or other educated professionals have reasons to prefer Democratic candidates. Over time, the parties adopted polarized platforms on new issues, and voters gradually sorted into different parties.

Democrats and Republicans express residential preferences in surveys that would, if put into practice, yield substantial geographic sorting by partisanship. But their actual behavior is another matter. Americans make locational choices based largely on a mix of preferences and constraints related to housing, jobs, and schools. Once these are satisfied, there is not much scope for party-based sorting.[8] Both Democrats and Republicans are moving to neighborhoods that are more *Republican*.[9] And recall that Democrats are also more likely to move in the first place. In the aggregate, Democrats are *not* sorting into neighborhoods with other Democrats, probably because they are seeking the same things as Republicans: a good mix of schools and housing, usually in the suburbs. This is true not only of whites, but also of racial minorities. An important demographic trend in the United States is the slow but sure decline of racial segregation, and the large-scale movement of minorities to suburbs.[10]

All of this points to an overall trend toward partisan mixing rather than segregation. And this is exactly what we are seeing in the fastest-growing parts of the United States. If we look at the thirty-five counties that have seen the largest population increases in recent years,[11] thirty of them experienced an increase in the Democratic vote share from the 2012 to the 2016 presidential election, even though the nationwide electoral swing was in the other direction. Only five of them became more Republican. The prevailing narrative about inexorable sorting suggests that Democratic hipsters and college graduates are moving to Seattle and the Bay Area, only to make Democratic strongholds more Democratic. However, because these cities have not kept up with the demand for housing, young people can no longer afford to move to many of these metro areas. They are instead moving to places like Austin, Durham, and Houston.

Of those thirty-five supergrowth counties, only five were landslide Democratic counties with an Obama vote share over 60 percent in 2012; twenty-three of these counties were in the range of 40 to 60 percent Democratic in 2012, and fourteen were in the range of 45 to 55 percent. Half of these fast-growing counties had been majority Republican in 2008. Several of the landslide Republican counties in this group became competitive, and marginal counties became Democratic.

In fact, moving beyond these counties, there is a linear relationship between the extent of population growth and the extent to which the Democratic vote share is increasing. Counties that are growing at a clip of around ten thousand per decade have seen a very slight increase in the Democratic vote share; those growing at a rate of fifty thousand per decade have seen an increase in Democratic voting of around 2.5 percentage points, and for the group of counties growing at a rate of one hundred thousand or more per decade, the increase in the Democratic vote share is over 4.0 percentage points. Most of these rapidly growing counties are in competitive states, like Texas,

Florida, North Carolina, Georgia, and Nevada. And much of the growth is *not* in city centers, but in sprawling suburbs.

This book has shown that Democrats tend to be *less* clustered in some of America's newest and fastest-growing metropolitan areas than in the declining manufacturing core. Democrats are not as concentrated in city centers of newer cities, like Orlando and Houston, which came of age in the era of the automobile, as they are in old industrial cities. Many growing American metropolitan areas are sprawling, polycentric expanses of low-density housing. While lower-income Democrats are still more dominant in the city center, there are Republican neighborhoods nearby, and pockets of Democrats scattered throughout the suburbs, with large numbers of precincts that are evenly divided between the two parties. The sprawling areas around Tampa Bay, Sarasota, and Orlando, Florida, are filled with precincts that are evenly divided between the parties. The same is true of the suburban fringes around Sacramento, Reno, Las Vegas, and Albuquerque.

Redistricting simulations at the scale of congressional districts reveal that the Democrats' problem with geographic concentration is less severe or missing altogether in the sprawling cities of the Sun Belt. We can also observe change over time in places where Democrats have been spreading out. For instance, pro-Republican bias in Florida has declined over time. As a large number of Puerto Ricans have escaped the island's economic crisis by moving to Florida, many of the sprawling areas along Interstate 4 between Orlando and Tampa have gone from modestly Republican to toss-up or modestly Democratic, so that if districts are drawn without partisan intent, they will now produce majority-Democratic suburban districts where they once produced majority-Republican districts.

Over time, suburban sprawl in the United States might make it look more like Australia. The inefficient geographic concentration of Labor voters occurred mostly in the old working-class, industrial neighborhoods of Sydney and Melbourne. Labor voters are less concentrated, and Labor has suffered less in the transformation of votes to seats, in growing cities like Brisbane. More generally, continued suburban sprawl in all of Australia's cities has reduced urban-rural polarization and improved the geographic distribution of Labor voters over time.

In sum, although suburbanization helped build geographic polarization, its further development could potentially help reduce it. But we should not get carried away. This trend is very slow-moving, and its impact might end up being limited to a handful of areas. Democrats are still very concentrated in rapidly growing states like Georgia, as well as in declining states like Pennsylvania. Moreover, it is entirely possible that even if Democrats are selecting into more mixed areas, the "treatment" effect of suburban life is powerful, and that the next generation of Democrats that moves to sprawling exurbs may eventually gravitate to the Republican Party. In the short and medium terms, it is clear that urban-rural polarization is probably here to stay.

IF URBAN-RURAL POLARIZATION cannot be assuaged, it must be managed. Fortunately, the United States has considerable experience with this, and some coping mechanisms are built into the US Constitution. The United States has a long history of regional sectionalism and urban-rural conflict going back to its founding. Like other large and diverse countries with that type of history—including Canada and Switzerland—the United States has a federal constitution and a robust system of decentralized taxation, expenditure, and regulation by states and local governments. These institutions and practices are put to the test during periods of heightened geographic conflict. By standing up for their aggrieved citizens, emboldened state and local governments sometimes only fan the flames of sectional conflicts. But by providing alternative decision-making arenas for settling controversial issues, they can also help contain the fires.

On the one hand, activist state and even city governments often volunteer as enthusiastic participants in national-level sectional conflicts. In addition to serving as chief state-level law enforcement officers, state attorneys general have taken on a new role as warriors in national-level battles. Republican attorneys general used a stream of lawsuits to challenge the Obama administration's efforts to administer health care reform. Their Democratic counterparts have returned the favor by challenging the Trump administration's efforts in policy areas ranging from immigration enforcement to climate change. Even secretaries of state, as in Kansas, have used their positions as an entry point into high-profile national battles related to voting rights. City officials too have gotten involved in battles over immigration enforcement.

Nevertheless, federalism and decentralization have some potential to ameliorate the problem of geographic sectionalism. As federal politics becomes increasingly mired in gridlock, investigations, and partisan posturing, voters come to rely on state and municipal governments for practical policy solutions to everyday problems. Successful candidates for governor and mayor often run campaigns portraying themselves as nonpartisan problem-solvers, and as suggested above, they often assemble different bundles of policy positions than the national parties to which they belong. By crafting unique local brands, state and local chief executives can bridge partisan divides and focus on results.

Federalism allows for policy heterogeneity. Blue states—where urban progressives have the upper hand—can enact gun control measures and strict environmental protections, while red states can please their suburban and rural majorities by enacting stricter regulation of abortion and looser regulation of the economy and environment. As long as people with strong preferences are clustered conveniently into different jurisdictions, decentralization can, at least in theory, increase the number of people who are satisfied with government policy.

But there are some obvious limitations to this solution. This book has shown that geographic polarization according to population density in the United States is fractal—it sharpens as we zoom in to lower and lower levels of geography. Even the most Democratic and Republican states are internally quite polarized. For the most part, rural Californians are extremely conservative; some rural residents of the inland northern part of the state are so frustrated with the state government that they would like to secede from the more urbanized coastal areas to the south. Many rural Illinois residents chafe under laws that they believe are dictated by Chicago. Likewise, urban residents of blue cities in red states, like Louisville or Nashville, are often as progressive as residents of Chicago or Oakland. To these voters, a more powerful state government is not an attractive solution to the problem of geographic sectionalism.

Moreover, in many policy areas, devolution to the level of cities, counties, and municipalities is impractical. Gun control in Chicago cannot be very effective if residents can simply cross the border and purchase weapons in Gary, Indiana. A rural county cannot very well place limits on abortions that its residents might obtain in neighboring counties. Polluters will simply move to jurisdictions with less stringent regulations.

A broad constraint on decentralization as a way of managing polarization is the fact that local governments must often compete with one another. Many conservatives admire this aspect of decentralization: it can keep government lean by forcing local governments to compete for mobile citizens and corporations. This competitive pressure can place powerful constraints on governments' ability to tax and regulate by making the public sector resemble a competitive market. Wasteful taxes and regulations and poor governance can lead to capital flight, which forces local governments to be prudent. For the left, this has always been a liability, not an asset of decentralization. Strong labor unions and protections for workers were hard to maintain in the North when southern states began competing for investment, and today, intergovernmental competition makes it difficult for blue cities and states to enact generous welfare policies or costly regulations. Fiscally strapped cities and municipalities find it difficult to try policy innovations that require revenue or threaten mobile investors.

However, in the era of the third industrial revolution, the game of competition for investment may be changing, at least for the wealthiest cities and states. First, as described in this book, the benefits of being in certain knowledge-economy hubs might be so valuable to both firms and workers that the threat of capital flight is not very credible. Second, unlike some traditional manufacturing firms, technology firms are not necessarily looking for the lowest taxes, cheapest labor, and weakest environmental protections. While they are undoubtedly fond of tax abatements and subsidies, many are also looking for very skilled labor, and thus might be attracted to cities that provide the right mix of amenities, infrastructure, and housing. Some state and city governments might find that greater investments in human capital and urban infrastructure, even if they require higher taxes, can be beneficial in the game of intergovernmental competition. Thus in at least some blue cities and states with the resources to compete in this game—for instance the cities of Palo Alto and Cambridge, or the states of California and Massachusetts—competition for mobile citizens and firms has not deterred activist government.

But due in part to the self-interest of homeowners who conspire to restrict the housing supply and keep their property values high, some of the most successful cities have become incredibly expensive. Salaries have risen accordingly, which means that geographically concentrated knowledge-economy employees contribute a rapidly growing share of federal taxes. Because they already shoulder a disproportionately large federal tax burden, it can be politically difficult for state and local governments in knowledge-economy areas to increase their own taxes and pursue activist local policies. Perhaps more importantly, as a legacy of deals made with strong public-sector unions in previous decades, Democratic city and state governments, especially in the old manufacturing core, must often send a large share of their revenues to personnel and retirees, leaving little for infrastructure or innovative local policies.

Democratic governments of the wealthiest cities and states will undoubtedly continue to use their powers to achieve locally some of the things they cannot achieve at the federal level. Some of the wealthiest and most Democratic knowledge-economy metros are plagued with deep problems of poverty, inequality, homelessness, and crumbling infrastructure. Cities like San Francisco and states like California vote overwhelmingly for a party that promotes higher levels of taxation and redistribution at all levels of government. But a sizable share of the federal tax revenue raised from Californians is spent in the rest of the federation on policies prioritized by a Congress that dramatically underrepresents them. Californians may eventually come to favor a reduced role for the federal government and lower levels of federal taxation, preferring to pour resources into local investments and in-state redistribution rather than continued subsidies to the rest of the country.

While the discussion of "Calexit" in the wake of the 2016 election may not have been especially serious, it illuminates not only the frustration of many urban Californians with rural populism, but also a tension that lurks within the left. As the party of cities, the Democratic Party represents not only San Francisco, but also Scranton. But at least some segment of the coastal knowledge-economy left evidently feels rather little solidarity with the inland postmanufacturing left.

This same tension exists in Britain, where Labour is the party not only of London, but also of Burnley. The tension between knowledge-economy and postindustrial cities was on vivid display in Britain's "Brexit" vote. While Labour-voting Londoners voted overwhelmingly to stay in the European Union, many postindustrial Labour neighborhoods elsewhere voted to leave. One of the most fascinating legacies of the process of urban-rural polarization described in this book is the fact that currently in Britain and the United States, an important part of the base of the mainstream party of the left is a set of extremely prosperous, geographically concentrated voters who are responsible for providing an outsized share of overall tax revenues. Inevitably, their interests will not always align with residents of poor cities with little tax base. Likewise, the mainstream parties of the right must struggle with battles between elements of their base who benefit from trade and integration, and those who hope to benefit from protectionism. Some of the most consequential battles in the years ahead might take place *within* rather than between the parties.

This book has attempted to grapple with the geographic and political legacy of a massive technological and economic revolution that took place well over a century ago. The potential implications of the current, ongoing technological revolution for economic and political geography are only beginning to take shape. Without a century of hindsight, the best we can do is speculate. But one conjecture seems safe: political and economic geographers will have much to study in the years ahead.

Acknowledgments

THIS BOOK'S GESTATION has been lengthy in large part because every time I present the underlying research to a new audience—from Barcelona to Calgary—I learn something new about urban economic and political geography. Each audience also raises a new set of fascinating questions: How are North American cities different from European or Australian cities? How is Philadelphia different from Phoenix? What is the role of economic versus cultural issues in explaining the concentration of left voters in cities? As I've tried to answer these and other questions, I've drawn on conversations and insights from interlocutors at universities around the world, but especially at MIT, where this book first took shape, and at Stanford, where it came to fruition.

I am grateful to all of the colleagues, students, and seminar participants at these and other institutions who have helped me rethink classic questions about political and economic geography over the years. I benefited from the support and intellectual stimulation provided by the Center for Advanced Study in the Behavioral Sciences, the Institute for Research in the Social Sciences at Stanford, and the Juan March Institute in Madrid. I am grateful to collaborators at the Stanford Spatial Social Science Lab, including Claudia Engel, Karen Jusko, and Clayton Nall, and to the Alfred P. Sloan Foundation for financial support. Some of the analysis in this book emerged from fruitful collaborations with former students, including Jowei Chen, Kyle Dropp, Nick Eubank, Adriane Fresh, Chris Tausanovitch, and

Chris Warshaw, as well as with other coauthors including Ernesto Calvo, Aina Gallego, Nolan McCarty, and Boris Shor. I am in debt to all of them. Thanks to Margaret Levi for hosting a conference that helped me reshape the manuscript, Carles Boix, Ron Johnston, and Jon Fiva for providing valuable feedback, Max Brockman and Brian Distelberg for helping me rewrite the book for a broader audience, and Leah Stecher for useful editorial input.

Above all, I wish to thank my family for their support and encouragement: Ammie, Nathaniel, Anna, Evelyn, all the Wilsons and Wrights, and finally, my parents, John and Judy Rodden, to whom this book is dedicated.

Notes

INTRODUCTION

1. Democrats won majorities of the votes cast in state legislative elections for both chambers in Virginia, Michigan, Wisconsin, and Pennsylvania, while failing to win majorities of seats. In Ohio, in the seventeen state senate seats up for election, Democrats won only six, in spite of winning 53 percent of the votes cast for the two major parties.

2. For each Senate since 1990, excluding special elections, I added up the votes cast for candidates of the two major parties in each of the three general elections that led to the composition of that Senate. In 2016 and 2018, this analysis was undermined by the presence of two Democrats on the ballot in California. So for those two California elections, instead of Senate votes, I use the votes cast for Democratic and Republican candidates in the presidential and gubernatorial elections, respectively.

3. David Dailey, *Ratf**ked: Why Your Vote Doesn't Count* (New York: Liveright, 2016).

CHAPTER 1: GEOGRAPHY AND THE DILEMMA OF THE LEFT

1. Joseph A. Dacus, *Revolution in Pennsylvania: A History of the Railroad Union Strike and the Great Uprising of 1877* (St. Petersburg, FL: Red and Black Publishers, 2011).

2. James Hudson Maurer, *It Can Be Done: The Autobiography of James Hudson Maurer* (New York: Rand School Press, 1938), 85.

3. Maurer, *Autobiography*, 83.

4. See Alfred Marshall, *Principles of Economics* (London: MacMillan, 1920); Paul Krugman, *Geography and Trade* (Cambridge, MA: MIT Press, 1991); Edward Glaeser, *Triumph of the City* (London: MacMillan, 2011).

5. This map, like others throughout the book, was created using ArcGIS® software by Esri. ArcGIS® and ArcMap™ are the intellectual property of Esri and are used herein under license. Copyright © Esri. All rights reserved. For more information about Esri software, see www.esri.com.

6. The railroad map includes all railroads constructed before 1911. The data are from Jeremy Atack, "Historical Geographic Information Systems (GIS) database of U.S.

Railroads" (2016). Rail nodes are from the United States Department of Transportation "Railroad Nodes" database.

7. Ernesto Calvo and Jonathan Rodden, "The Achilles Heel of Plurality Systems: Geography and Representation in Multiparty Democracies," *American Journal of Political Science* 59, no. 4 (October 2015): 789–805.

8. See Adam Przeworski and John Sprague, *Paper Stones: A History of Electoral Socialism* (Chicago: University of Chicago Press, 1986). This classic book points out that urban workers were never, strictly speaking, a majority of the population in any country when workers' parties started competing in elections. As a result, they faced a dilemma: "Given the minority status of workers, leaders of class-based parties must choose between a party homogeneous in its class appeal but sentenced to perpetual electoral defeats or a party that struggles for electoral success at the cost of diluting its class orientation" (p. 3). This dilemma is sharpened by the geography of these parties' support in a system with winner-take-all districts.

9. Henry G. Stetler, *The Socialist Movement in Reading, Pennsylvania, 1896–1936: A Study in Social Change* (Storrs: University of Connecticut, 1943).

10. Karl Marx and Friedrich Engels, *The Communist Manifesto* (Harmondsworth, UK: Penguin, 1967), 147.

11. The Norwegian Labor Party formally forbade its members to make any such agreements.

12. In Scandinavia, they also broke through in some rural areas populated with landless agricultural and forestry workers. Landless agricultural workers also formed a base of support for communists and socialists in the Italian "red belt" around Tuscany and Umbria, and in the Spanish region of Andalusia.

13. In many cases, the underrepresentation of workers' and socialist parties was also driven by the fact that reapportionment had not taken place as urban populations grew. The population of urban German constituencies, for example, was substantially larger than that of rural constituencies.

14. Cited in Josep Colomer, "The Strategy and History of Electoral System Choice," in *The Handbook of Electoral System Choice*, ed. J. Colomer (New York: Palgrave MacMillan), 47.

15. Lucas Leemann and Isabela Mares, "The Adoption of Proportional Representation," *Journal of Politics* 76, no. 2 (April 2014): 461–478; Gary Cox, Jon Fiva, and Daniel Smith, "Parties, Legislators, and the Origins of Proportional Representation," *Comparative Political Studies* (April 2018).

16. Technically, a form of proportional representation was introduced in Belgium in 1899, but that system included small, gerrymandered districts that led to a highly disproportionate transformation of votes to seats, and it retained the old system of plural voting.

17. Josephine Andrews and Robert Jackman, "Strategic Fools: Electoral Rule Choice under Extreme Uncertainty," *Electoral Studies* 24, no. 1 (March 2005): 65–84.

18. Richard Johnston, *The Canadian Party System: An Analytical History* (Vancouver, Canada: UBC Press, 2017).

19. Classic works include Werner Sombart, *Why Is There No Socialism in the United States?* (White Plains, NY: M.E. Sharpe, 1976); Seymour Martin Lipset and Gary Marks, *It Didn't Happen Here: Why Socialism Failed in the United States* (New York: Norton, 2000). Important recent books include Alberto Alesina and Edward Glaeser, *Fighting Poverty in Europe and the United States: A World of Difference* (Oxford: Oxford University Press, 2006);

Robin Archer, *Why Is There No Labor Party in the United States?* (Princeton, NJ: Princeton University Press, 2007); and Karen Jusko, *Who Speaks for the Poor?* (Cambridge: Cambridge University Press, 2017).

20. Seymour Martin Lipset, *Agrarian Socialism: The Cooperative Commonwealth Federation in Saskatchewan* (Berkeley: University of California Press, 1971).

21. Matthew Soberg Shugart and John Carey, *Presidents and Assemblies: Constitutional Design and Electoral Dynamics* (Cambridge: Cambridge University Press, 1992).

CHAPTER 2: THE LONG SHADOW OF THE INDUSTRIAL REVOLUTION

1. Because county-level population density is highly skewed, I present natural logs.

2. These regressions are weighted by county population. Both the dependent variable (Democratic vote share) and the independent variable (population density) are logged.

3. Note that there were some relatively rural counties in the manufacturing core where support for the Democrats was as high as in the urban districts during this period, such as unionized mining communities in places like western Wisconsin and northern Michigan.

4. Ira Katznelson, *Fear Itself: The New Deal and the Origins of Our Time* (New York: Liveright, 2013).

5. This is captured by the differences between the three lines for different regions in Figure 2.2, but it is also useful to explicitly divide the states according to their level of industrialization. From the 1930s to the 1980s, the positive relationship between population density and Democratic voting has been highly contingent on the presence of early manufacturing. Using data on manufacturing employment from the 1920 census, I divided the states into four quartiles according to the level of manufacturing intensity and examined the relationship between population density and Democratic voting for each group of states. The impact of population density on Democratic voting was over twice as high in the most manufacturing-intensive states as in the states in the second quartile. And in most years, there was no discernable relationship in the states falling into the third and fourth (least industrialized) quartiles.

6. Richard Walker and Robert Lewis, "Beyond the Crabgrass Frontier: Industry and the Spread of North American Cities, 1850–1950," *Journal of Historical Geography* 27, no. 1 (January 2001): 3–19.

7. Edward Glaeser and Joseph Gyourko, "Urban Decline and Durable Housing," *Journal of Political Economy* 113, no. 2 (2005): 345–375.

8. John Updike, *Trust Me* (New York: Random House, 1987), 97.

9. To draw this conclusion, I pursued two approaches. First, I regressed the precinct-level 2008 Democratic vote share on precinct-level density, allowing the effects to vary according to the county-level manufacturing share in the 1920 census. I found that the relationship was much stronger in counties with higher historical manufacturing employment. Second, I estimated models in which precinct-level population density was interacted with the proximity to the nineteenth-century rail network (my precinct-level proxy for historical manufacturing). I discovered that population density has a much larger positive impact on Democratic voting in precincts located near rail nodes.

10. To make these observations, I have used geographic information systems (GIS) to combine precinct-level election data, historical rail data, and contemporary census information at the level of census block groups.

11. In precinct-level regressions with county fixed effects and controls for median family income, poverty, race, ethnicity, age, population density, occupation, and home ownership, proximity to a nineteenth-century rail node is still a highly significant predictor of contemporary Democratic voting. The same is true of county-level models with state fixed effects and a similar mix of control variables, where the main independent variable is 1920 manufacturing employment. Similar results can be obtained using 1880 manufacturing employment.

12. In the words of the British geographers Ron Johnston and Charles Pattie, "People who talk together vote together." Ron Johnston and Charles Pattie, *Putting Voters in Their Place: Geography and Elections in Great Britain* (Oxford: Oxford University Press, 2006), 46.

13. Christopher Achen and Larry Bartels, *Democracy for Realists: Why Elections Do Not Produce Responsive Government* (Princeton, NJ: Princeton University Press, 2016).

14. All of the unionization data discussed in this section come from the Current Population Survey, as assembled by Barry Hirsch and David Macpherson and made available at unionstats.com.

15. Vincenzo Spiezia, "Measuring Regional Economies," *OECD Statistics Brief*, no. 6 (October 2003).

16. The raw geographic concentration index is defined as follows: $GC = \sum_{i=1}^{N} |y_i - a_i|$, where y is the number of votes received by the party in county i, and a is the county's area. The maximum value the index can take is defined as $CG^{MAX} = 2(1 - a_{min})$, and the adjusted geographic concentration index is defined as $AGC = GC/GC^{MAX}$.

17. The manufacturing core here is defined as Connecticut, Delaware, Illinois, Indiana, Maine, Maryland, Massachusetts, Michigan, Missouri, New Hampshire, New Jersey, New York, Ohio, Pennsylvania, Rhode Island, Vermont, and Wisconsin. The Great Plains include Colorado, the Dakotas, Iowa, Kansas, Minnesota, Nebraska, and Oklahoma. The South includes Alabama, Arkansas, Florida, Georgia, Kentucky, Louisiana, Mississippi, North Carolina, South Carolina, Tennessee, Texas, Virginia, and West Virginia. The Southwest includes Arizona, New Mexico, and Nevada. The Mountain West includes Alaska, Idaho, Montana, Utah, and Wyoming. The West Coast includes California, Oregon, and Washington.

18. On the nationalization of politics, see Daniel Hopkins, *The Increasingly United States: How and Why American Political Behavior Nationalized* (Chicago: University of Chicago Press, 2018).

CHAPTER 3: FROM WORKERS' PARTIES TO URBAN PARTIES

1. See Seymour Martin Lipset and Stein Rokkan, "Cleavage Structures, Party Systems, and Voter Alignments: An Introduction," in *Party Systems and Voter Alignments: Cross-National Perspectives*, ed. Lipset and Rokkan (New York: Free Press, 1967).

2. Karl Marx and Friedrich Engels, *The German Ideology* (Amherst, NY: Prometheus Books, 1998), 27.

3. An important fault line in Canada has always been between the attempts of the eastern manufacturers to establish themselves as the core of an East-West economic union, and the interests of farmers in buying cheaper finished goods from the United States and beyond while getting the best prices for their agricultural and commodity exports. Likewise, recall

from the previous chapter that this urban-rural cleavage between the Protectionist and Free Trade Parties was dominant in early twentieth-century Australia.

4. Ferdinand Tönnies, *Community and Society* (Mineloa, NY: Dover, 1887); Emile Durkheim, *The Division of Labor in Society* (New York: Free Press, 1984).

5. Ronald Inglehart, *Cultural Shift in Advanced Industrial Society* (Princeton, NJ: Princeton University Press, 1989).

6. Enrico Moretti, *The New Geography of Jobs* (New York: Mariner, 2013).

7. Saskia Sassen, *The Global City: New York, London, Tokyo* (Princeton, NJ: Princeton University Press, 2001).

8. Edward Glaeser and Giacomo Ponzetto, "Did the Death of Distance Hurt Detroit and Help New York?" *National Bureau of Economic Research Working Paper* no. 13710 (December 2007).

9. Moretti, *The New Geography*, 4.

10. I count up knowledge-economy jobs published by the Bureau of Labor Statistics (BLS) by using the North American Industrial Classification System (NAICS). First, I count up jobs considered "high technology" by the BLS, and add additional classifications coded as knowledge-intensive by the Massachusetts Department of Workforce Development. See the Appendix of Timothy Hogan, *An Overview of the Knowledge Economy, with a Focus on Arizona* (Tempe: Arizona State University School of Business, August 2011), https://wpcarey.asu.edu/sites/default/files/knowledgeeconomy8-11.pdf.

11. Each of these graphs presents plots based on local regressions, weighted by county population. Education data for the 2016 plot come from the 2010 census. Likewise, education data for the 1996 plot come from the 1990 census, and the data for the 1976 plot come from the 1970 census.

12. Lily Geismer, *Don't Blame Us: Suburban Liberals and the Transformation of the Democratic Party* (Princeton, NJ: Princeton University Press, 2014).

13. Adam Bonica, "Mapping the Ideological Marketplace," *American Journal of Political Science* 58, no. 2 (April 2014): 367–386.

14. "Europe Is Back: And Rejecting Trumpism," *New York Times,* January 24, 2018.

15. Edward Glaeser, Jed Kolko, and Albert Saiz, "Consumer City," *Journal of Economic Geography* 1, no. 1 (January 2001): 27–50.

16. Eric Schickler, *Racial Realignment: The Transformation of American Liberalism, 1932–1965* (Princeton, NJ: Princeton University Press, 2016).

17. Residential locations are placed into the following categories: urban core of a large city (one of the twelve largest metropolitan statistical areas), suburb of a large city, urban core of a smaller city (one of the metropolitan statistical areas ranked thirteen through one hundred), suburb of a smaller city, a nonmetropolitan county that contains a large town (population ten thousand or more), and a rural county (with no towns of ten thousand or more).

18. Matthew Levendusky, *The Partisan Sort: How Liberals Became Democrats and Conservatives Became Republicans* (Chicago: University of Chicago Press, 2009).

19. We use a support vector machine, which identifies the classifier that best separates individuals, based on their ideological coordinates, into the categories of those who report voting for Democratic presidential candidates, and those who report voting for Republican

presidential candidates. See Aina Gallego and Jonathan Rodden, "Policy-Bundling and Religion: An Experimental Approach," paper presented at Yale University, March 20, 2014.

20. Hopkins, *The Increasingly United States.*

21. On partisanship as a form of social identity, see Lilliana Mason, "A Cross-Cutting Calm: How Social Sorting Drives Affective Polarization," *Public Opinion Quarterly* 80, no. 1 (January 2016): 351–377. For a review of the literature on affective (as opposed to purely preference-based) polarization, see Shanto Iyengar, Yphtach Lelkes, Matthew Levendusky, Neil Malhotra, and Sean Westwood, "The Origins and Consequences of Affective Polarization in the United States," *Annual Review of Political Science* 22 (May 2019).

22. See Katherine Cramer, *The Politics of Resentment: Rural Consciousness in Wisconsin and the Rise of Scott Walker* (Chicago: University of Chicago Press, 2016).

23. Nolan McCarty, Keith Poole, and Howard Rosenthal, *Polarized America: The Dance of Ideology and Unequal Riches* (Cambridge, MA: MIT Press, 2006).

24. I am grateful to Adriane Fresh for providing the data on railroads and coal mines.

25. On increasing geographic polarization in Canada, see R. Alan Walks, "Place of Residence, Party Preferences, and Political Attitudes in Canadian Cities and Suburbs," *Journal of Urban Affairs* 26, no. 3: 269–295. On Britain, see R. Alan Walks, "City-Suburban Electoral Polarization in Great Britain 1950 to 2001," *Transactions of the Institute of British Geographers* 30, no. 4: 500–517.

26. In Australia, I use the "two party preferred" vote share of Labor. In Canada, I use the combined vote share of the NDP, Liberals, and Greens. In the United Kingdom, I use the combined vote of Labour, Liberal Democrats, and Greens. In the United States, I use the Democratic share of the two-party vote in the 2016 presidential election, aggregated to the level of US congressional districts.

27. Moretti, *The New Geography.*

28. Richard Florida, *The Rise of the Creative Class: And How It's Transforming Work, Leisure, Community, and Everyday Life* (New York: Basic Books, 2011).

29. The Canadian graph also displays some interesting outliers, where very rural places provide strong support for the left. Some are native communities, and others are long-term rural strongholds of the NDP.

CHAPTER 4: URBAN FORM AND VOTING

1. John Updike, *Rabbit Is Rich* (New York: Random House, 1996), 29.

2. Friedrich Engels, "The Great Towns," in *The Conditions of the Working Class in England in 1844*, originally published in 1845, in *The City Reader*, ed. Richard LeGates and Frederic Stout (London: Routledge, 1996).

3. Paul Hohenberg, "The Historical Geography of European Cities: An Interpretive Essay," in *Handbook of Regional Economics*, Vol. 4, ed. J. Vernon Henderon and Jacques-François Thisse (London: Elsevier, 2004), 3041.

4. Hohenberg, "Historical Geography," 3040; Anthony Wohl, *The Eternal Slum: Housing and Social Policy in Victorian London* (Montreal: McGill-Queen's University Press, 1977).

5. Wohl, *Eternal Slum*, 17.

6. Wohl, *Eternal Slum*, 18.

7. Engels, "The Great Towns," 57.

8. Engels, "The Great Towns," 62.

9. Peter Mieszkowski and Edwin Mills, "The Causes of Metropolitan Suburbanization," *Journal of Economic Perspectives* 7, no. 3 (Summer 1993): 135–147.

10. In economics parlance, suburbanization emerges when the elasticity of demand for land with respect to income is greater than the elasticity of the value of commuting time with respect to income.

11. Stephan LeRoy and Jon Sonsteile, "Paradise Lost and Regained: Transportation Innovation, Income, and Residential Location," *Journal of Urban Economics* 13 (1983): 67–89; Edward Glaeser, Matthew Kahn, and Jordan Rappaport, "Why Do the Poor Live in Cities? The Role of Transportation," *Journal of Urban Economics* 63, no. 1 (January 2008): 1–24.

12. Clayton Nall, *The Road to Inequality: How the Federal Highway Program Polarized America and Undermined Cities* (Cambridge: Cambridge University Press, 2018).

13. Specifically, the graphs resemble what is known as an exponential decay function in increasing form.

14. Note that the cluster of precincts with exceptionally low turnout in Columbus are those serving dorms and residential areas around Ohio State University.

15. James Campbell. *Cheap Seats: The Democratic Party's Advantage in U.S. House Elections* (Columbus: Ohio State University Press, 1996).

16. Pittsburgh has a large knowledge-economy sector, but the share of the population with a college degree is substantially lower than in Philadelphia's city center and especially in its suburbs and exurbs.

17. Peter Mieszkowski and Barton Smith, "Analyzing Urban Decentralization: The Case of Houston," *Regional Science and Urban Economics* 21, no. 2 (July 1991): 183–199.

18. Outside of Maricopa County, very Democratic and sparsely populated Native American reservations are part of this story.

19. William Cronon, *Nature's Metropolis: Chicago and the Great West* (New York: Norton, 1991).

20. Norman Glickman, *The Growth and Management of the Japanese Urban System* (New York: Academic Press, 1979).

21. Barry Edmonston, Michael Goldberg, and John Mercer, "Urban Form in Canada and the United States: An Examination of Urban Density Gradients," *Urban Studies* 22 (1985): 209–217.

22. On patterns of city-suburban polarization in Canada, see R. Alan Walks, "The Causes of City-Suburban Political Polarization? A Canadian Case Study," *Annals of the Association of American Geographers* 96, no. 2 (2006): 390–414.

23. Data from Canadian polling places also reveal that turnout is negatively correlated with population density, as in the United States, but the differences is far less severe than in the United States, where poverty is often concentrated in city centers.

24. In most industrialized countries, red corresponds to the mainstream party of the left on electoral maps, but the US media has settled on the reverse color scheme.

25. Graeme Davison, "Australia: The First Suburban Nation?" *Journal of Urban History* 22, no.1 (November 1995): 63. The claim that Australia is the "first suburban nation" originates with Donald Horne, *The Lucky Country: Australia in the Sixties* (Glasgow: Ringwood, 1964).

26. National and Liberal candidates typically coordinate at the level of constituencies so as not to split votes on the right. The two parties are known collectively as "The Liberal-National Coalition." In some states, the two parties have formally fused in recent years.

CHAPTER 5: WHAT IS WRONG WITH THE PENNSYLVANIA DEMOCRATS?

1. The Democratic minority leader in the House of Representatives voted in favor of the plan, but the Democratic minority leader in the Senate voted against it, publicly arguing that it was unfair to Democrats.

2. The "nearest neighbor" approach originated with Jowei Chen and Jonathan Rodden, "The Loser's Bonus: Political Geography and Minority Party Representation," paper presented at the annual meeting of the American Political Science Association, Boston, August 2018. It was further developed in Nick Eubank and Jonathan Rodden, "Who Is My Neighbor? The Spatial Efficiency of Partisanship," paper presented at the Statistical and Applied Mathematical Sciences Institute, Durham, NC, October 8, 2018.

3. For details on this technique, see Jowei Chen and Jonathan Rodden, "Unintentional Gerrymandering: Political Geography and Electoral Bias in Legislatures," *Quarterly Journal of Political Science* 8 (2013): 239–269.

4. In order to impute vote shares in uncontested elections, I use a two-step process for years up to 2010. First, if the seat was contested at any point during the relevant redistricting cycle, I use the average vote shares in the district in those contested elections. Second, in a very small number of cases, the seat was never contested during the redistricting cycle, so I use the vote shares in the last contested election—always involving the same individual—during the previous cycle. Uncontested elections throughout an entire redistricting cycle have become more common in recent years, and in some cases, it is not useful to examine the incumbent's vote share in a previous contested election because the district boundaries have changed substantially. In recent years, where this problem arises, I use district-level results of the 2012 and 2016 presidential elections to impute the missing votes for candidates in uncontested seats.

5. Historical data were assembled from a data set kindly provided by James M. Snyder, from the Wilkes University Election Statistics Project, and from Carl Klarner et al., *State Election Returns (1967–2010)*, Inter-university Consortium for Political and Social Research (ICPSR) Study no. 34297, Ann Arbor, MI (2013). More recent data were assembled from the Pennsylvania Department of State.

6. State senate elections are held every two years, but only half of the seats are contested in each election (first the odd-numbered districts, and then the even-numbered districts). Thus I combine the votes for odd- and even-numbered districts over each four-year period, and the data marker corresponds to the year of the first election. Thus, 1938 corresponds to the elections of both 1938 and 1940, and so on.

7. Republicans controlled the state legislature during the 1990s round of redistricting, but the governor, Bob Casey, was a Democrat.

8. This was the case not only because of the inefficient packing of Democrats, but also because of asymmetries in the size of districts before the advent of the "one-person, one vote" principle that emerged in the 1964 Supreme Court decision in *Baker v. Carr*.

CHAPTER 6: POLITICAL GEOGRAPHY AND THE REPRESENTATION OF DEMOCRATS

1. This approach to measuring relative geographic concentration was developed by Jowei Chen. See Chen and Rodden, "The Loser's Bonus."

2. I collected the underlying precinct-level election results and joined them with precinct-level geospatial information as part of a project, in collaboration with Stephen Ansolabehere, which was funded by the Alfred P. Sloan Foundation. The simulations were performed by Jowei Chen and David Cottrell. The simulation results are available as part of the data appendix to Jowei Chen and David Cottrell, "Evaluating Partisan Gains from Congressional Gerrymandering: Using Computer Simulations to Estimate the Effect of Gerrymandering in the U.S. House," *Electoral Studies* 44 (December 2016): 239–340.

3. I use statewide vote shares for Senate and presidential electors because statewide vote shares in legislative elections are potentially less reliable indicators of statewide partisanship. Especially in state legislative elections, a very large number of districts are not contested by one party or the other, and in some states, elections are not even held in uncontested seats. Moreover, even when elections are contested, one of the candidates is often very poorly funded and not a serious contender. In any case, the graphs look very similar if I impute the missing values and use statewide legislative vote shares on the horizontal axis.

4. See Eubank and Rodden, "Who Is My Neighbor?"

5. See Jowei Chen and Jonathan Rodden, "Cutting through the Thicket: Redistricting Simulations and the Detection of Partisan Gerrymanders," *Election Law Journal* 14, no. 4 (December 2015): 331–345; "Brief of Political Geography Scholars as *Amici Curiae* in Support of Appellees," *Gill v. Whitford*, Supreme Court of the United States; Jowei Chen, "The Impact of Political Geography on Wisconsin Redistricting: An Analysis of Wisconsin's Act 43 Assembly Districting Plan," *Election Law Journal* 16, no. 4 (December 2017): 1–23; Wendy Tam Cho and Yan Liu, "Toward a Talismanic Redistricting Tool: A Computational Method for Identifying Extreme Redistricting Plans," *Election Law Journal* 15, no. 4 (2016): 351–366; Marina Chikina, Alan Frieze, and Wesley Pegden, "Assessing Significance in a Markov Chain without Mixing," *Proceedings of the National Academy of Science* 114, no. 11 (March 14, 2017): 2860–2864; Gregory Herschlag, Han Sung Kang, Justin Luo, Christy Graves, Sachet Bangia, Robert Ravier, and Jonathan Mattingly, "Quantifying Gerrymandering in North Carolina," arXiv:1801.03783.

6. Decades are defined to correspond to redistricting periods. Since new districts are drawn after each decennial census, the first election held under new districts is typically the year ending in 2, and the last is in the year ending in 0. For instance, the decade called "2000s" includes the years 2002 to 2010.

7. Results of uncontested elections are imputed using information about vote shares of specific incumbents who have run in contested elections in other years, as well as information about presidential election results in the district, and information about other contested elections held in the district during the same redistricting cycle.

8. Like the mean-median difference, this construct also has its roots in the work of British political geographers. Ron Johnston described "wasted votes" as votes obtained in constituencies that a party loses, while "surplus votes" are additional votes obtained by a party in constituencies it wins beyond the number needed for victory. Johnston calculated wasted and surplus votes for Labour and the Conservatives in postwar British elections, as well as the share of "effective" votes received by each party: that is, votes that were neither "wasted" nor "surplus." The latter is a measure of the relative efficiency of support for the parties across districts, and the gap between them is an indicator of the extent to

which support for the Conservatives has been more efficient than support for Labour (or vice versa). See Ron Johnston, "Manipulating Maps and Winning Elections: Measuring the Impact of Malapportionment and Gerrymandering." *Political Geography* 21 (2012): 1–31. With some changes in terminology, this concept was recently adapted for the US redistricting context. See Nicholas Stephanopoulos and Eric McGhee, "Partisan Gerrymandering and the Efficiency Gap," *University of Chicago Law Review* 82 (2015): 831.

9. Robert Erikson, "The Congressional Incumbency Advantage over 60 Years," in *Governing in a Polarized Age: Elections, Parties, and Political Representation in America,* ed. Alan Gerber and Eric Schickler (Cambridge: Cambridge University Press, 2016).

CHAPTER 7: POLITICAL GEOGRAPHY AND THE BATTLE FOR THE SOUL OF THE LEFT

1. Melvin Hinich and Peter Ordeshook, "The Electoral College: A Spatial Analysis," *Political Methodology* 1, no. 3 (Summer 1974): 1–29.

2. A single survey like the GSS does not have enough respondents to make reliable inferences about the ideology of a specific congressional or state legislative district. However, recent innovations in survey research have allowed political scientists to do just that. First, scholars have developed a technique for knitting together several surveys, thus allowing for the observation of a large number of respondents in each district. See Chris Tausanovitch and Christopher Warshaw, "Measuring Constituent Policy Preferences in Congress, State Legislatures, and Cities," *Journal of Politics* 75, no. 2 (April 2013): 330–342. Second, we can leverage demographic information from the census to improve district-level estimates of preferences. This technique is called multilevel regression and poststratification (MRP). See David Park, Andrew Gelman, and Joseph Bafumi, "Bayesian Multilevel Estimation with Poststratification: State-Level Estimates from National Polls," *Political Analysis* 12, no. 4 (Autumn 2004): 375–385. The estimates presented here rely on a combination of these techniques, and come from Nolan McCarty, Jonathan Rodden, Boris Shor, Christ Tausanovitch, and Christopher Warshaw, "Geography, Uncertainty, and Polarization," *Political Science Research and Methods* (March 2018), https://doi.org/10.1017/psrm.2018.12.

3. Perhaps Democratic presidential candidates in general elections try to tailor their platform not to the national median voters, but to the median voter in pivotal states like Pennsylvania, Michigan, and Florida, but the data suggest that the median voter in those states is actually very similar to the national median voter.

4. The exceptions are Maryland, North Dakota, Vermont, Alaska, and Nevada.

5. The exceptions are Arkansas, Connecticut, Iowa, Utah, Kansas, South Carolina, and Oregon.

6. Lewis Gould, *The Most Exclusive Club: A History of the Modern United States Senate* (New York: Basic Books, 2006).

7. I examine a version of this scale that is designed to facilitate comparison between the Senate and House of Representatives. The "common space" DW-NOMINATE scale is available at voteview.com.

8. "Competitive" is defined as having a statewide presidential vote share that is within 10 percentage points of the national vote share.

9. Figure 7.4 presents weighted averages across states for each decade. The weight is the number of congressional seats apportioned to the state, so that larger states receive more

weight. Southern states are excluded. The graph looks very similar whether southern states are included or not, and whether or not the average is weighted by state size.

10. Woodrow Wilson, *Congressional Government: A Study in American Politics* (Boston and New York: Houghton Mifflin, 1885), 117.

11. For a formal model laying out this logic, see Stephen Ansolabehere, William Leblanc, and James M. Snyder, "When Parties Are Not Teams: Party Positions in Single-Member District and Proportional Representation Systems," *Economic Theory* 49, no. 3 (April 2012): 521–547.

12. For a formal model that develops this logic, see Steven Callander, "Electoral Competition in Heterogeneous Districts," *Journal of Political Economy* 113, no. 5 (October 2005): 1116–1145.

13. See Ronald Johnston, "Manipulating Maps and Winning Elections: Measuring the Impact of Malapportionment and Gerrymandering," *Political Geography* 21, no. 1 (January 2002): 1–31.

14. See Joan Rydon, "The Relation of Votes to Seats in Elections for the Australian House of Representatives 1949–54," *Political Science* 9 (1957): 49–65; Graham Gudgin and Peter J. Taylor, *Seats, Votes, and the Spatial Organisation of Elections* (London: Pion, 1979); Simon Jackman, "Measuring Electoral Bias, Australia 1949–1993," *British Journal of Political Science* 24, no. 3 (July 1994): 319–357.

15. The dotted line corresponds to the Liberal Party prior to the formation of the Liberal Democrats in 1988, and to the Liberal Democrats thereafter.

16. Ernesto Calvo and Jonathan Rodden, "The Achilles Heel of Plurality Systems: Geography and Representation in Multiparty Democracies," *American Journal of Political Science* 59, no. 4 (October 2015): 789–805.

17. The NDP and its predecessor, the CCF, are treated as the same party in this graph.

18. As with the Democrats in parts of the rural West with large Native American populations, the NDP is able to win a handful of poor rural districts with long traditions of NDP support.

19. Richard Johnston, *The Canadian Party System: An Analytic History* (Vancouver, Canada: UBC Press, 2017).

20. In constructing this graph, parties of the right are defined as the Conservative Party, the Progressive Conservatives, Reform, the Canadian Alliance, and Social Credit. Parties of the left include the Liberal Party, the NDP, the Greens, and the Bloc Quebecois.

21. In the United Kingdom, the fractionalization on the left goes beyond the Liberal Democrats. The Scottish National Party has replaced Labour as the mainstream party of the left in many Scottish constituencies, and Plaid Cymru has done the same in some Welsh constituencies.

CHAPTER 8: PROPORTIONAL REPRESENTATION AND THE ROAD NOT TAKEN

1. In some proportional systems, like Portugal's, districts are drawn with large asymmetries in size, such that districts with many representatives encompass cities, and smaller districts are drawn in rural areas. This asymmetry in district magnitude can lead to the underrepresentation of urban parties even under PR. See Burt Monroe and Amanda Rose, "Electoral Systems and Unimagined Consequences: Partisan Effects of Districted

Proportional Representation," *American Journal of Political Science* 46, no. 1 (January 2002): 67–89.

2. André Blais and Peter Loewen, "Electoral Systems and Evaluations of Democracy," in *Democratic Reform in New Brunswick*, ed. W. Cross (Toronto: Canadian Scholars Press, 2007), 39–57.

3. Konstantinos Matakos, Orestis Troumpounis, and Dimitrios Xefteris, "Electoral Rule Disproportionality and Platform Polarization," *American Journal of Political Science* 60, no. 4 (December 2015): 1026–1043.

4. Jonathan Rodden, "Keeping Your Enemies Close: Electoral Rules and Partisan Polarization," in *Anxieties of Democracy*, ed. Frances Rosenbluth and Margaret Weir (Cambridge: Cambridge University Press, forthcoming).

5. The data source for these expert surveys is Holger Döring and Philip Manow, *Parliaments and Governments Database (ParlGov): Information on Parties, Elections and Cabinets in Modern Democracies*. www.parlgov.org.

6. This assessment is based on using the overall median as the cut point between right and left.

7. I do not include graphs here to save space, but for detailed analysis with the same conclusion, see Holger Döring and Philip Manow, "Is Proportional Representation More Favourable to the Left? Electoral Rules and Their Impact on Elections, Parliaments and the Formation of Cabinets," *British Journal of Political Science* 47, no. 1 (January 2017): 149–164.

8. I follow the classification scheme of Nils-Christian Bormann and Matt Golder, which does not include Ireland among majoritarian democracies. France is technically a semipresidential regime. Figure 8.1 excludes the years during which proportional representation was in effect in France and New Zealand. See Nils-Christian Bormann and Matt Golder, "Democratic Electoral Systems around the World," *Electoral Studies* 32 (2013): 360–369.

9. Torben Iversen and David Soskice, "Electoral Institutions and the Politics of Coalitions: Why Some Democracies Redistribute More Than Others," *American Political Science Review* 100, no. 2 (May 2006): 165–181.

10. Döring and Manow, "Is Proportional Representation More Favourable?"

11. In New Zealand, this is driven by the fact that, for reasons explored below, the New Zealand Labour Party was classified as right of center for a period of time.

12. Instead of relying on subjective expert assessments of party positions, an alternative approach is to rely on a massive effort by a group of political scientists to collect and code written party platforms according to objective criteria. These data are also available from Döring and Manow, *Parliaments and Governments Database (ParlGov)*. This approach leads to all of the same conclusions. On average, PR systems favor neither the right nor the left, and there is no significant difference between the average composition of voters, parliaments, and cabinets. In majoritarian democracies, however, over the entirety of the postwar period, if anything, voters have supported parties with platforms that are to the *left* of those in proportional systems. However, parliaments and governments are substantially to the *right* of the voters, and on average, to the right of legislatures and governments in proportional systems. Again, for similar conclusions, see Döring and Manow, "Is Proportional Representation More Favourable?"

13. Torsten Persson and Guido Tabellini, *The Economic Effects of Constitutions* (Cambridge, MA: MIT Press, 2003).

14. Iversen and Soskice, "Electoral Institutions and the Politics of Coalitions"; Noam Lupu and Jonas Pontusson, "Income Inequality, Electoral Rules and the Politics of Redistribution," paper presented at the annual conference of the Council of European Studies, Chicago, March 2008.

15. *OECD Employment Outlook 2017* (Paris: OECD, 2017); Torben Iversen, *Contested Economic Institutions: The Politics of Macroeconomics and Wage Bargaining in Advanced Democracies.* (Cambridge: Cambridge University Press, 1999).

16. An economic historian, Peter Lindert, has assembled comparable data on social transfers in fifteen industrialized countries from the nineteenth century to 1980, and I have added data from the OECD that continues the series to the current day.

17. Assar Lindbeck, "The Welfare State: Background, Achievements, Problems," Research Institute of Industrial Economics, Working Paper no. 662 (2006).

18. Anthony Atkinson, "Social Insurance: The Fifteenth Annual Lecture of the Geneva Association," *Geneva Papers on Risk and Insurance Theory* 16, no 2 (1991): 113–131.

19. Michael Jetter and Christopher Parmeter, "Does Urbanization Mean Bigger Governments?" *Scandinavian Journal of Economics* (August 2017).

20. Scholars have also offered other explanations for the differences in economic policy between majoritarian and proportional democracies. Torben Iversen and David Soskice make an argument about how economic classes might form different types of coalitions in these two types of democracies. See Iversen and Soskice, "Electoral Institutions and the Politics of Coalitions." Torsten Persson and Guido Tabellini make an argument about incentives created by electoral institutions for politicians to provide general collective goods versus targeted transfers. See Persson and Tabellini, *The Economic Effects of Constitutions.* Karen Jusko provides an argument about the geography of income and the incentives of politicians to represent poor people. See Karen L. Jusko, *Who Speaks for the Poor? Electoral Geography, Party Entry, and Representation* (Cambridge: Cambridge University Press, 2017).

21. World Bank Institute, *Measuring Knowledge in the World's Economies* (Washington, DC: World Bank, 2008).

22. Per Fredriksson and Daniel Millimet, "Electoral Rules and Environmental Policy," *Economics Letters* 84, no. 2 (August 2004): 237–244; Arend Lijphart, *Patterns of Democracy: Government Forms and Performance in 36 Countries* (New Haven, CT: Yale University Press, 2012); Salomon Orellana, *Electoral Systems and Governance: How Diversity Can Improve Policy Making* (New York: Routledge Press, 2014).

23. Orellana, *Electoral Systems and Governance.* The United States has long had relatively liberal abortion policies, and recently moved to legalize gay marriage. Note, however, that these policies cannot be traced to actions of Congress, but to policies enacted by legislatures in the most urbanized, progressive states and to sweeping decisions of federal courts.

CHAPTER 9: THE END OF THE DILEMMA?

1. See Adam Bonica, "What's Good for Democracy Is Also Good for Democrats," *New York Times*, July 26, 2018.

2. Tim Alberta, "John Boehner Unchained," *Politico Magazine*, October 27, 2017.

3. See Wendy Tam Cho, James Gimpel, and Iris Hui, "Voter Migration and the Geographic Sorting of the American Electorate," *Annals of the Association of American Geographers* 103, no. 4 (2013): 7. In a recent study of registered voters in several states, the authors show that those who move to a new address, both within and across metro areas and states, are far more likely to be Democrats.

4. Jonathan Mummolo and Clayton Nall, "Why Partisans Do Not Sort: The Constraints on Political Segregation," *Journal of Politics* 79, no. 1 (2016): 45–59.

5. Bill Bishop and Robert Cushing, *The Big Sort: Why the Clustering of Like-Minded America Is Tearing Us Apart* (Boston: Houghton Mifflin, 2008).

6. Adam Bonica, Howard Rosenthal, Kristy Blackwood, and David Rothman, "Ideological Sorting of Professionals: Evidence from the Geographic and Career Decisions of Physicians," working paper, Stanford University (2018).

7. Gregory Martin and Steven Webster, "Does Residential Sorting Explain Geographic Polarization?" *Political Science Research and Methods* (2019): 1–17, doi:10.1017/psrm.2018.44.

8. Mummolo and Nall, "Why Partisans Do Not Sort"; Martin and Webster, "Does Residential Sorting Explain Geographic Polarization?"

9. Mummolo and Nall, "Why Partisans Do Not Sort"; Cho, Gimpel, and Hui, "Voter Migration."

10. David Cutler, Edward Glaeser, and Jacob Vigdor, "The Rise and Decline of the American Ghetto," *Journal of Political Economy* 107, no. 3: 455–506.

11. Here I consider the counties that gained at least one hundred thousand residents between the 2000 and 2010 census. Other definitions yield similar insights.

Index

Credit: Jackie Sargent

JONATHAN A. RODDEN is professor of political science and a senior fellow at the Hoover Institution at Stanford University and founder and director of the Stanford Spatial Social Science Lab. The author of the prizewinning *Hamilton's Paradox*, he lives in Stanford, California.